Research Methodology and Quantitative Methods

Research Methodology and Quantitative Methods

G. NAGESWARA RAO
Ph.D.
Associate Dean (Rtd.)
College of Agriculture
Acharya N.G. Ranga Agricultural University
Rajendranagar, Hyderabad-500 030

BSP **BS Publications**
A unit of **BSP Books Pvt. Ltd.**
4-4-309/316, Giriraj Lane, Sultan Bazar,
Hyderabad - 500 095
Phone: 040 - 23445605, 23445688

Published by :

BSP BS Publications
A unit of **BSP Books Pvt. Ltd.**

4-4-309/316, Giriraj Lane, Sultan Bazar,
Hyderabad - 500 095
Phone : 040 - 23445605, 23445688
e-mail : info@bspbooks.net

ISBN : 978-93-85433-33-7 (HB)

Dedicated to

My Parents

Late Smt. G. Venkata Ramanamma

and

Late Shri. G.V. Krishna Rao

Preface

I guided good number of M.Sc. and Ph.D. students of Agriculture, Veterinary and Home Science students in their thesis work with respect to statistical analysis as a minor advisor in Acharya N.G. Ranga Agricutural University, Hyderabad. I also offered course on 'Data Analysis for Managers' for several batches of 'Master in Agri Business Management' (MABM) students in Acharya N.G. Ranga Agricultural University, Hyderabad. Further I have been offering courses on 'Quantitative Methods I and II' and 'Planning Analysis and Techniques' to B. Tech (Planning) and M. Tech (Planning) students in School of Planning and Architecture, Jawaharlal Nehru Architecture and Fine Arts University, Hyderabad to several batches.

In view of the above experience, I felt there is an urgent need of a text book on 'Research Methodology and Quantitative Methods'. This book is of immence help to students who are undergoing the courses on Quantitative Methods and also for students of final year in B. Tech and M. Tech programmes for preparation of project reports.

I feel this book is also very useful to students at Ph.D. level in Social, Biological and Agricultural Sciences for data analysis and presentation of research work. This book is also intended to meet the requirements of MBA, MABM students for their course work, conducting research projects, analysis and presentation. This book is written in lucid manner and understandable to non-mathematical students. Illustrations using statistical tools are given in the areas of production, industry and other applied fields.

I am thankful to M/s Nikhil Shah and Anil Shah of BS Publications, Hyderabad for taking initiative in bringing this book.

G. NAGESWARA RAO

Contents

Chapter 4

Sampling Methods

Chapter 5

Scale Construction Methods

Chapter 6

Elementary Decision Theory

Chapter 9

Measures of Central Tendency and Dispersion

Chapter 12

Correlation and Regression

Chapter 13

Analysis of Variance

Chapter 14

Time Series and Index Numbers

Chapter 15

Non-Parametric Tests

Chapter 16

Elementary Queuing Theory

CHAPTER 1

Introduction

1.1 Research

It can be said that anything we think about deeply about its consequences in future can be called as research. In other words, if we increase the knowledge or refine or redefine the existing knowledge on the subject, can be termed as research. Invention of new method, new object, new variety of crop, new medicine for health improvement, new engineering equipment, new method of imparting of knowledge to students, new method of preparing food, new breed of animal etc., can be considered as products of research.

Similarly new laws on the theorems developed in mathematics, physics and chemistry etc., are the outcomes of research investigation.

1.2 Basic Research

The research conducted to know the laws of nature which may not be of immediate applicability and it enhances the existing knowledge in mathematics, physics, chemistry etc., are viewed as basic research. Basic research is like a foundation on which the applied research can be built. It is so important that it provides breakthrough in the existing knowledge system which have major consequences in the development of society. For example, invention of gene, G.N.A, light and sound and their properties, electronics and communication etc. Basic research is being conducted in Tata Institute of Fundamental Research in Mumbai. Many major universities in India and abroad which are funded by Govt. of India through University Grants Commission (UGC), Council of Scientific and Industrial Research (CSIR) etc., in India. Sometimes basic research is being conducted for enhancement of knowledge with sheer interest and enthusiasm of the scientist.

1.3 Applied Research

If research is conducted for a particular purpose of achieving something or solving major or minor problem facing the society is termed as applied research. For example by applying genetic theory in evolving new high yielding varieties of a crop or crops, new breeds of high milk yielding animals, new poultry breeds, new techniques of controlling diseases in human beings, animals and crops, new modes of fuel saving transport vehicles, new powerful computer systems with high storage facility, new mobile communication system, space technology, new machines in industry are the products of applied research. Applied research takes intensive help of basic research directly or indirectly. CSIR laboratories, ICMR laboratories, ICAR research institutions etc., are some of the organizations in India conducting applied research.

1.4 Basic Research Vs Applied Research

There is no class or adversity between basic research and applied research. In fact one is complementary to other. Basic research is being conducted to enhance the knowledge and which may create major changes in the knowledge world. Further it may benefit mankind in a big way sometimes. Applied research is being conducted to achieve a specific objective for immediate benefit. In doing so it takes major or minor use of basic research.

1.5 Disciplines of Research

Research can be conducted in any area of education which include (i) Sciences (ii) Social sciences (iii) Engineering (iv) Medicine (v) Agriculture, veterinary and food science (vi) Humanities like English and any other language literature, philosophy etc.

1.5.1 Research in Science

When research is conducted in subjects or disciplines like mathematics, Statistics, Physics, Chemistry, Botany, Genetics, etc., is known as research conducted in Science.

1.5.2 Research in Social Sciences

If research is conducted in disciplines like, Socialogy, Economics, Psychology, Planning, Education etc., is called research in social sciences.

1.5.3 Research in Engineering

If research is conducted in engineering subjects like (i) Civil engineering (ii) Electrical engineering (iii) Mechanical engineering (iv) Computer science engineering (v) Information technology etc., is known as research in engineering.

1.5.4 Research in Medicine

When research is conducted in disciplines of medicine such as (i) Medicine (ii) Anatomy (iii) Surgery (iv) Pathology (v) Pharmacology (vi) Dermatology (vii) Radiantology (viii) Physiology etc., can be considered as research in medicine.

1.5.5 Research in Agriculture, Veterinary and Food Sciences

If research is conducted in disciplines of agriculture such as (i) Agronomy (ii) Plant breeding (iii) Soil science and agricultural chemistry (iv) Entomology (v) Pathology (vi) Plant physiology (vii) Horticulture etc., can be called as Research in agriculture science.

Similarly research is done in veterinary subjects like (i) Medicine (ii) Anatomy (iii) Surgery (iv) Pathology (v) Parasitology (vi) Pharmacology (vii) Animal science (viii) Dairy science (ix) Poultry science etc., is known as research in veterinary science.

Also if research is conducted in discipline like (i) Food nutrition (ii) Food preparation etc., is termed as research in food science.

1.5.6 Research in Humanities

If research is conducted in language literatures of English, Hindi, Telugu etc., with respect to styles, grammer, subject etc., and also in subjects like philosophy is called research in humanities.

1.6 Types of Research

Research can be classified as (i) Descriptive and (ii) Analytical.

If the research work of any aspect of a problem is presented in a descriptive manner without giving much data and their analysis then it is called descriptive research. The investigations carried out in social sciences and business are termed as 'Ex post facto research'. The opinion studies, preference to purchase of certain commodities, i.e. market research, exit polls in elections etc., are known as descriptive research. The presentation of percentages and averages without analyzing using statistical techniques is considered as descriptive research. If the research presentation is done by applying statistical techniques to data obtained in an investigation then it is known as analytical research.

1.7 Scientific Research

The analytical research is sometimes called scientific research where logical reasoning, interrelationships and their relationship to existing body of knowledge is studied.

1.8 Experimental Research

Experiment is conducted either in laboratory or agricultural experimental field to bring out new information or to test the existing facts. Most of these experiments are conducted under controlled conditions by the experimenter. Most of the experiments conducted for medical research, Industrial research, laboratory research in agriculture, veterinary, home science, engineering, psychology, biological sciences belong to experimental research. The agricultural field experiments though they are not conducted in laboratory still come under the category of experimental research because the treatments, crops, seed, water etc., are predetermined and the designs such as completely randomized, randomized block, Latin square, split plot etc., are prefixed. Also the experiments conducted under glass houses for crops, animal experiments etc., fall under the category of experimental research.

1.9 Survey Research

The investigations carried out through survey is called survey research. The survey research is generally followed in social sciences including psychology and planning. The survey usually is conducted to know the actual facts from the respondents. The surveys are carried out for doing research in economics, sociology, psychology, town planning, education etc.

1.10 Significance of Research

Research is very important for every nation or country for its progress in terms of protection or defence, health, economy, education etc. In other words, for constant development and progress of any country, continued research is essential to take stock of the present situation and to plan for the future growth in every indicator of economy for well being of human society. In view of the above, after attaining independence, our country had undertaken several steps to establish research laboratories in industry, medicine, defence, agriculture, engineering, veterinary etc., for carrying out investigations for finding solutions to the problems faced by our country and bring out solutions suitable to our environment and people in general.

Further, research work is carried out by individuals for getting M.Phil and Ph.D degrees for enhancing their academic qualifications. Also research projects are undertaken by investigators in different universities on specific problems which are funded by different funding agencies such as World Bank, Foreign countries, Govt. of India, U.G.C, ICAR, ICMR, CSIR etc., depending upon the urgency and importance of the problem at that point of time.

It is well known fact that 'Noble prizes' were instituted by a family in Norway for awarding cash prize of worth about 10 lakh dollars for the best research work done in different areas of sciences, medicine, biology, economics etc., for enhancing the existing knowledge and for improving the living standards of human society. Similarly in our country 'Shanti Swaroop Bhatnagar' awards are presented to research scientists in different areas of 'Science and technology'.

Also Jawaharlal Nehru awards are given every year to best thesis submitted by Ph.D. scholars in different disciplines of agriculture. Young scientists awards are being given to young scientists by different scientific societies at annual conferences for the best research work done in the concerned discipline. These steps indicate to promote creative activity in the young minds towards better future for the society and country in general.

CHAPTER 2

Research Process

The research process consists of several steps to conduct research. It can be said that research can be done without going these steps systematically also. For example Prof. Ramanujam a great mathematician from India did extraordinary research work in Mathematics without going through several steps of Research process. Whatever he used to think and then put on paper and used to solve the equations. The solutions were accepted as outstanding research. But this is an exceptional example. However to cultivate habit of doing research and presenting the results and conclusions of research, research process was introduced and practiced. The following are some of the steps involved in research process.

2.1 Research Problem

Research problem usually selected and approved by either guide or higher authorities based on the necessity, importance and depth of the problem for acquiring M. Phil and Ph.D degrees or for completing the specified project undertaken in Laboratory of University or Research laboratory. For example research problem will be thought of finding new variety of crop which will be significantly giving high yield by crossing high yielding varieties of the same crop. Sometimes a problem may be thought of finding high yielding variety with short height of smaller duration then varieties of same characters will be crossed. Similarly a drug has to be invented to prevent or cure the disease in less time and with less cost. Also a problem can be thought in municipal administration to invent a new tool to clean the roads mechanically in less time when traffic is not there.

In statistics, a problem can be thought of new design which can detect the best treatment with least experimental material like experimental field. In Entomology, a new method of pest management can be thought for crops like rice to increase the yield of crop. In business a new method of marketing can be thought for increasing the sale of the product. In sociology, a problem can be thought of preventing AIDS problem in certain areas or in certain pockets of cities. In town and urban planning a problem can be thought of how parks can be utilized successfully or usefully.

In general, if a research student wants to do research for submitting to get Ph.D. degree, he will be working in the area in which his guide is specialist. Further guide usually gives his student to choose his own problem. The problem arises to student after going through literature extensively. Now-a-days, NETWORK using computer is ready reckoner wherein he gets most of the literature on the subject or specialized area of interest. He can find gaps in the research work done so far and then discusses with guide for suitability or otherwise for submitting to get Ph.D. degree or not. Further a committee of major and minor guides will accept or reject the problem looking to the capability of student, facilities including financial and time involved in completing the work etc.

In basic or fundamental research, the selection of problem is much more difficult. The involvement of guide or minor guides is very much less. Whatever student gets ideas and solutions will be sent as a research paper to a standard journal. If the paper is accepted then the student and guide will have an idea that the problem is worth pursuing and deserves further probe. Sometimes, a number of such research papers will form a major content of the thesis.

In view of the above, it can be said that a research problem can be developed either by one's own creative capability or by studying extensive literature or for looking to the necessity for society. Usually to research problem will be the title of the thesis for submitting to get Ph.D. degree or title of the research project sponsored by funding agencies like UGC, CSIR, ICAR, world Bank etc. For example, if the research work was done on some gaps of research then the title of the thesis would be "Some contributions to such research, work area". In agricultural economics, the research problem could be 'Economics of particular high yielding variety just released and adopted by local farmers'.

2.2 Objectives of Research

Having chosen the research problem, the researcher has to list out the objectives of the research work to be undertaken in order to systematically accomplish the envisaged research work problem. If the research work has to be completed for the purpose of achieving a Ph.D. degree, it will be undertaken in different steps or parts. For example, a new experimental design has to be developed in the field of 'statistics' then the design has to be developed for different field conditions, for different treatments and replications looking to the availability of seed etc., and for different climatic conditions. Further, statistical analysis has to be developed for analyzing the experimental data obtained after using this new design. These aspects are to be listed out as objectives of research problem. Similarly, in a continuous research project, the objectives will be listed out and submitted in a format required by the funding agency for sanctioning financial assistance. Also any research project to be undertaken with financial assistance from UGC, CSIR, ICAR, ICMR, world Bank, any foreign country, the research problem particulars including 'objectives of the research work' has to be submitted in a specified format. For example, Reddy (1992) submitted thesis for partial fulfillment of M.Sc. (Ag) degree on research problem 'Uniformity trial on groundnut' with objectives as (i) to study the nature of soil heterogeneity, (ii) to determine optimum plot size in groundnut by conducting a uniformity trial and by applying Fair field smith's variance law for determining optimum plot size n groundnut, (iii) to make general recommendations regarding optimum block size for conducting field experiments on groundnut, and (iv) to obtain direct and indirect effects of plant characters viz. (a) number of branches per plant (X_1), (b) number of leaves per plant (X_2) and height of the plant (X_3) on pod weight (Y) of groundnut with the help of path analysis.

Balaji Thiagarajan (1989) submitted a thesis on ‘Statistical Analysis of changes in Agricultural land use for a part of Andhra Pradesh using satellite remote sensing data’ in partial fulfillment for the award of M.Sc. (Ag) degree with the objectives as (i) to see the feasibility and usefulness of satellite remote sensing data in generating land use statistics in two study areas in Prakasam district of Andhra Pradesh, (ii) Statistical evaluation of classification accuracy of different classification algorithms, and (iii) Use of multi-temporal data from LANDSAT and IRS satellites to detect change in land use over a period of time.

Rao (1993) submitted a thesis on a problem entitled “Contributions to construction and analysis of non-orthogonal designs” in partial fulfillment of the award of Ph.D. degree in statistics with the objectives as (i) to develop different approach for the analysis of non-orthogonal lay-outs (ii) Mathematic proof for the known construction method of Agarwal, (iii) solutions to different series of two-way elimination of heterogeneity designs, (iv) a solution for the construction of $(t - 1)$ mutually orthogonal F-squares of the type $F(n; m^t)$ where ‘t’ is a prime or prime power and $m \geq 1$, a positive integer and is less than or equal to square root of t and (v) introduction of multistage generalized two-way elimination of heterogeneity designs. As it could be seen that this thesis problem is based on theoretical aspects of research work where as earlier two researcher problems were on applied aspects.

If the research problem is on ‘Examination system’ the objectives of the research could be (i) the difficulties and drawbacks of the present system of admission; (ii) the type of conducting examination and type of setting paper and weightage system; (iii) the improvement and refinement required in conducting examination and setting question paper; (iv) the relevance of marks of the qualifying examination in the admission of the present degree program; and (v) the variation in percentage of admission from rural and urban areas and between English and local language medium students.

If the research problem is undertaken in business with regard to ‘Introduction of new product in the market’; the possible objectives could be (i) the performance with respect to net profits from the existing product and competitive products in the market; (ii) The opinion survey with regard to present product or products among the consumers with regard to quality and economic viability among middle class etc.,; (iii) the requirement and necessity of new product and expected customers within the country and abroad; and (iv) the estimate of profits accrued by introducing new product in the market.

If the research problem is on 'regional and urban planning with regard to improvement of town planning of say Pilgrim city, the objectives of the research problem could be (i) the present status of the infrastructure facilities like transportation, roads, sanitation, water, electricity etc., for the existing flow of pilgrims; (ii) the opinion of the residents in widening roads and other dislocation of existing facilities; (iii) the requirement of infrastructure facilities to meet the demand of future inflow of pilgrims; (iv) the preparation of master plan with respect to facilities like roads, accommodation, transport, water, electricity, sanitation and health etc.

2.3 Review of Literature

This is an important area for initiating a research work or project. The research problem cannot be chosen instantaneously without knowing the background and coverage of it by several research workers or institutions at present or earlier. It is possible that several research workers might have attempted this problem or related problem elsewhere in the world. The research problem should not be chosen just to repeat the same method or process or same direction. As far as possible the research problem should be new one, new method, new area or location, new theory, new solution etc. In order to verify whether it is new research problem, the scanning of literature extensively is essential. Otherwise it appears that research is probing in darkness and later it may come out be duplication and futile exercise wasting financial resources and valuable time. Therefore quality research is always based on extensive survey of literature and discussion in seminars and symposia where several experts participate in the specified field.

2.3.1 Internet

Now-a-days with the advent of computer internet is the most valuable and readily available gadget for scanning on any subject of interest. This gadget can be explored thoroughly for review of literature on any research problem or for any research project. The references of literature can be downloaded from the internet and studied thoroughly before formulating research problem and objectives of research problem. Since internet gives world coverage, there will be less chance for missing related literature on the subject of internet.

2.3.2 Theses of other Authors

Sometimes, the literature of interest can be obtained from the 'Bibliography' of theses submitted by other authors who worked on the subject. This procedure is handy to the students who are submitting for award of Ph.D. degree.

2.3.3. Research Journals

Research journals provide extensive coverage of literature details in the related research fields. In going through these journals, sometimes, one may get new idea or approach to a unsolved problem in theoretical research. Therefore it is advantageous not only getting literature for review in the thesis but also for developing new problem for present or future research. It is always advisable to go through research journals for every research scientist.

2.3.4 Seminars and Symposia

Seminars or symposia provide a useful platform for providing relevant research literature. Also they give us an opportunity to test our research tools and methodology among top level scientists. The scientific papers submitted by us would be discussed thoroughly with respect to positive and negative aspects of our research work. In this way mid term course correction can be attempted in our research project.

2.3.5 Latest References

Latest references have to be included in the thesis submitted by student for a degree. In doing so that out attempt on research problem has taken care of latest work in that area. Further, latest research methods, technology also are reviewed and incorporated in out work. In this way new knowledge is created.

2.3.6 Old Literature

Sometimes the old literature might be available in ancient languages such as Sanskrit, Latin etc. For example a research problem is attempted on “Vasthu Sastra’ one need to go through Sanskrit literature in original though English translations might be available. In such situations one has to depend upon the experts of that area who are also able to understand Sanskrit scripts. Without going through original scripts of literature our review of literature is incomplete and inadequate.

2.4 Preparation of Undertaking Research Problem

As mentioned in chapter 1, there are two types of research problems (i) theoretical research and (ii) applied research.

2.4.1 Theoretical Problem

For undertaking theoretical problem, the points to be considered as (i) the guide who will provide guidance in undertaking research problem as he or she should be expert in that area for selecting the problem. Sometimes minor guides can also be included depending upon the problem selected; (ii) the capacity and skill of research scholar in the field of research problem; (iii) the time required for completing the research problem as per objectives; (iv) finanacial resources and support from the funding agency; (v) the facilities available with regard to laboratory, library and computer system.

2.4.2 Applied Problem in Sciences

For preparation of undertaking applied research problem in sciences, the points to be considered as (i) the guide and his expertise in that area of specialization; (ii) the capacity of research worker, his knowledge and enthusiasm in the area of specialization; (iii) the laboratory and or experimental field or experimental animals available for conducting research; (iv) the duration of period of research; and (v) the financial resources or funding agency for supporting research financially.

2.4.3 Research Problem in Social Sciences

For preparation of undertaking research work in social sciences, one need to conduct survey either small scale or large scale depending upon the problem. The points to be considered for conducting research in social sciences are (i) the guide and minor guides in the area of specialization; (ii) the capacity, knowledge and skill of the research investigator; (iii) the facilities like human resources for conducting survey; (iv) the time required for conducting survey and its analysis and completion of report; and (v) the financial resources or funding agency for funding the research survey work.

In psychological research problem, the preparation for conducting research is usually the same as applied research conducted on human beings by developing structured instrument like questionnaire. Similarly the preparation work for conducting research work in Engineering is done with machines, tools and equipment in controlled conditions.

CHAPTER 3

Methods and Materials

3.1 Materials in Conducting Research

The materials used in conducting research are different with respect to field of research. In biological sciences, the materials to be used may be plants, animals, soils, insects, birds, fruits, vegetables, grain, chemicals etc. In sciences and Engineering, the materials to be used can be instruments, machines, equipment, chemicals, etc. In medical research the materials used can be small animals, patients, chemicals, drugs etc.

In social science, research the materials or subjects used can be human beings, areas under crops, areas under forests, water bodies, parks, roads and buildings. Similarly the materials used in psychology research are human beings such as children, patients, adults etc.

In theoretical and fundamental research, the materials used can be both chemicals, animals, instruments etc. However, in mathematics research, no material is needed for conducting research except pen and paper.

3.2 Methods in Conducting Research

The methods used in conducting research vary from discipline to discipline. In applied research, for example, in agriculture research experimental designs like completely randomized design, randomized block design, Latin square design, split plot design, strip plot design, confounding experiment, factorial experiment etc are being used as field experiments. Further, analysis of variance: one-way, two-way, three-way, etc., factorial experiments are being used in laboratory and glass house experiments. In all these designs, Null hypothesis and Alternate hypothesis are framed and tested with the help of data obtained from experiments. The conclusions drawn from these experiments are taken as research findings. Sometimes, these experiments are conducted as pot culture experiments initially and later repeated in field in a specific experimental design layout since the findings are to be adopted in farmers field conditions. In all these designs 'analysis of variance' is used as a technique for testing the different sources of variation with the help of statistical test called F-test.

3.3 Analysis of Variance

Before going to describe the method of analysis of variance technique some concepts involved in this technique are listed here.

3.3.1 Variable

The characteristic which varies is called variable. For example height, yield, income, production etc., are variables.

3.3.2 Data

The numbers or figures given to measurements of variable are called "data". The production figures, area figures, height figures are examples of "data". Also number of persons, number of fields, number of parks are also called as "data".

3.3.3 Quantitative Variable

The variable which can be measured with a standard scale is called quantitative variable. Area under parks, area under water bodies, age, income, production are some of the examples of quantitative variable.

3.3.4 Qualitative Variable

The variable which cannot be measured with a standard scale is called qualitative variable. Short person, red flower, intelligent person, quality product, progressive person are some of the examples of "qualitative variable".

3.3.5 Random Variable

The variable occurs by chance or without any prediction is called "random variable". Temperature, relative humidity, sunshine, wind velocity, adult height at maturity cannot be predicted in advance and therefore they are called as random variables.

3.3.6 Discrete Variable

A variable which can take only fixed number of values called "discrete variable". In other words, there will be definite gap between any two values. Number of parks, number of successes, number of factories, number of chairs etc., are examples of discrete variable.

3.3.7 Continuous Variable

A variable which can assume any value between any two fixed limits is known as continuous variable. Area under crops, area under parks, daily cement production of a factory etc., are examples of continuous variable.

3.3.8 Population

A large group of values of a variable is called population or statistical population. Areas of parks in city, heights of students in an university, body temperatures in Fahrenheit of all patients in hospital, dialy production of a factory in a year are examples of statistical population.

3.3.9 Sample

A part of a statistical population is called sample. Production figures of cement for few days from the large data is called sample.

3.3.10 Treatment

An object of testing in laboratory or experimental field is called treatment. For example, fertilizer dose, psychological test, factory, machine, variety of a crop etc., are treatments.

3.3.11 Experimental unit

The basic unit on which treatment is applied is known as experimental unit. The area of a plot, say 4 m × 4 m in an experimental field, experimental animal, patient in an hospital are examples of experimental unit.

3.3.12 Randomization

If the treatments are allotted randomly to the experimental units then it is known as randomization. The allotment of treatments to experimental units can be done with the help of random number tables which are given in many text books on "Statistics". Also this allotment of treatments can be done by "Lottery Method" also. Randomization ensures the validity of applying statistical tests like F-test and t-test in analysis of variance.

3.3.13 Replication

Repeated application of treatments on experimental units is known as replication. Replication of treatment reduces experimental error in the experiment and also provides experimental error and which is essential for carrying out statistical test such as F-test in analysis of variance.

3.3.14 Local Control

Grouping of experimental units based on a specific characteristic is known as local control. Grouping of factories according to number of years of production, grouping of cities according to age of establishment, grouping of plots based on fertilizer gradient as blocks in agricultural experimental field, grouping of experimental animals according to their initial body weight, grouping of children according to their age in psychological tests are some examples of where local control concept is applied.

3.3.15 Control or Control Treatment

If research investigator does not interfere with the experimental unit with the treatment which he wants to test is known as control or control treatment. For example, in an experiment of testing new machines imported from abroad with respect to their performance, an old machine which is existing in the factory can be taken as control or control treatment. Another example which can be given here as Government wanted to improve the tank irrigation system by repairing or replacing the sluice gates, surplus weirs, canal lining etc., by investing money. The impact of this improvement can be compared with a tank where no improvement steps are undertaken. This tank where no improvement steps are effected is called 'control' or 'control tank'.

3.3.16 Analysis of Variance

If more than two treatments are to be tested simultaneously with respect to their performance then "Analysis of Variance" technique is used. In this method, the total variation in the data is analyzed according to different sources of variation. The variation due to different sources are compared with experimental variation. If the variation occurred due to different sources introduced by experimenter is significantly larger than experimental error variation then it can be concluded that then there is significant difference between different sources of variations. For example, new machines installed in a factory produce significantly higher variations than experimental variations then it can be concluded that there is significant difference between new machines with respect to their performance.

3.3.17 Completely Randomized Design

Design is generally referred to layout plan on the experimental field. This design is generally used when the experimental material such as soil is of uniform nature. In this layout experimental field is divided into plots of equal size and shape such as rectangular or square in shape and 5×6, 6×4 sq. meters with irrigation channels on boarders. This design can also be used in pot culture experiments as well as laboratory experiments, since the analysis of this experiment is same as one-way analysis of variance technique. Each treatment is allotted to the plot in the layout randomly with the help of random number tables. If a particular random number comes in selection then the first treatment is allotted to the plot having serial number equal to the random number selected. For example, random number 14 comes first then treatment is allotted to the plot with serial number 14. In this design concepts of randomization and replication are used. If the treatment mean square is significantly higher than error mean square then it can be concluded that treatment effects are significantly different from each other.

3.3.18 Randomized Block Design

This design is also called randomized complete block design. In this design, whole experimental field is divided into homogeneous blocks based on soil fertility etc. Then plots of equal size and shape are formed within each block. The blocks are formed in such a way that there will be more homogeneity within the blocks and more heterogeneity between the blocks. This is one-way elimination of soil heterogeneity in the experimental field. Since the neighboring plots are expected to have uniform fertility gradient, blocks are formed in such a way that if the fertility gradient is in the direction of North to South then blocks are formed perpendicular to the fertility gradient i.e., East to West and vice-versa. However, in medical experiments, the grouping can be done based on age group of patients. In animal experiments the grouping of animals can be done based on initial body weights, age, litter, sex etc.

The analysis used for the data obtained from this design is two-way analysis of variance. Here the two sources of variation are treatments and blocks. The treatment and block mean squares are compared with error means square separately. If they found significantly higher than error mean square then it can be concluded that there is significant difference between treatment effects and also block effects. For example, in medical experiments, the age effects and treatment effects are compared. In this design, the concepts of randomization, replication and local control are used. The blocks in this design are also complete replications. Sometimes, this design is also known as "randomized replications design".

3.3.19 Latin Square Design

If the heterogeneity of soil is present in two directions in experimental field, this design is adopted. This design, therefore, is known as two-way elimination of heterogeneity design. The blocks are formed from North to South and East to West in this design as columns and rows respectively.

The Latin letters such as A, B, C etc., which are used as treatments are allotted randomly to the plots or experimental units such that each letter occurs once and only once in each row and each column. Each row and each column will be complete replication. Since Latin letters like A, B, C etc., are used in this design layout and which is a square therefore it is known as Latin design. The layout of this design with 5 treatments is given in Fig. 3.1.

N

	B	E	A	D	C	
	C	A	B	E	D	
W	D	B	C	A	E	E
	E	C	D	B	A	
	A	D	E	C	B	

S

Fig. 3.1

In this design, the significant difference between rows, columns and treatments can be tested with the help of statistical test F-test and later on with t-test. Though this design is quite useful in medical and animal experiments but also useful in psychological and other experiments. In laboratory experiments this is known as three-way classification of analysis of variance. For example, this design can be used in industry when equal number of testers are testing the quality of product at equal number of locations and at equal number of timings. The quality of teaching can be tested with equal number of teaching methods, equal number of sections or classes and equal number of schools. In animal experiments, the rations, initial body weights and ages could be considered as three characteristics while using this design. The efficiency of this design is superior to randomized block design. In general Latin squares of size 4×4 to 12×12 are being used in practice.

3.3.20 Factorial Experiments

Factorial experiments are not having separate layout. In other words they are not having separate design. It is only a method of analysis where in different factors are tested at different levels. These factors along with levels will become treatments and they are tested in layouts such as completely randomized design, randomized block design, Latin square design, split plot design etc. In this experiment the difficult factors and their interactions are tested simultaneously without using each factor separately in separate layout.

3.3.20.1 2^2 Factorial Experiment

If there are two factors each at two levels then there would be 4 treatments in all and is denoted as 2^2 experiment where the index indicate the number of factors and the number of levels by base. For example there are two teaching methods which are implemented at two levels at primary and secondary levels of schools and replicated 4 times. The means of marks obtained are presented in the following Table 3.1

Table 3.1 Teaching Method

Level	A	B	Response to Method
(Primary) P	38	64	26 (64 – 38)
(secondary) S	46	78	32 (78 – 46)
Response to Level	(46 – 38) 8	(78 – 64) 14	

From Table 3.1 it can be noted that the values given in marginal totals such as 26 and 32 are called the simple effects of teaching methods. Similarly 8 and 14 are the simple effects of levels of schooling. The average of simple effects $\frac{26+32}{2} = 29$ and $\frac{8+14}{2} = 11$ are called main effects of teaching methods and levels of schooling respectively. Also $\frac{32-26}{2} = 3$ and $\frac{14-8}{2} = 3$ are known as "interaction effect" of teaching method with level of schooling. The simple effects of teaching methods are shown in Fig. 3.2 and Fig. 3.3 respectively.

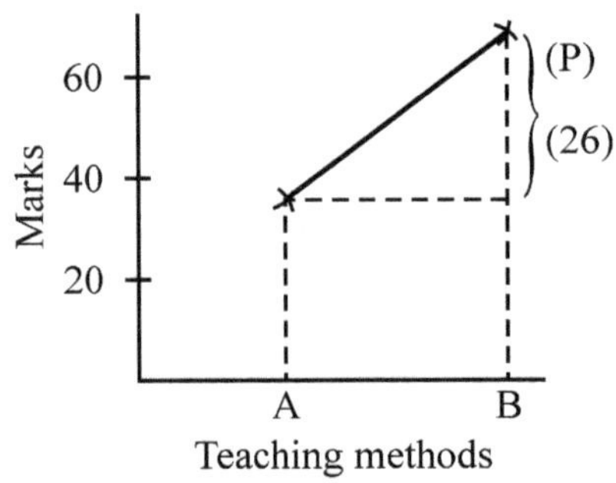

Fig. 3.2

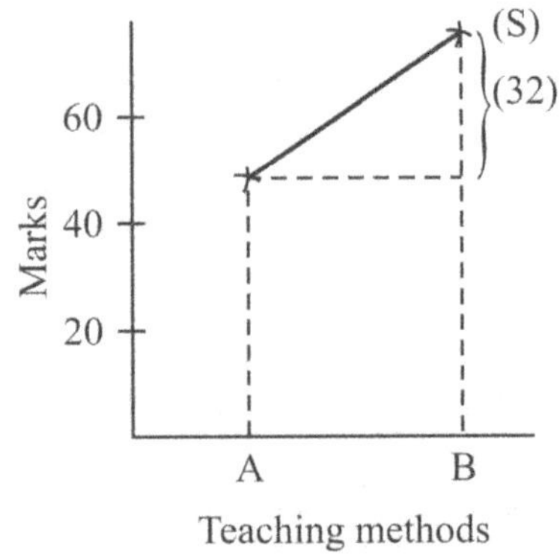

Fig. 3.3

Similarly simple effects of levels of schooling can be displayed on graphs.

The interaction effect of teaching methods with levels of schooling is displayed is Fig. 3.4.

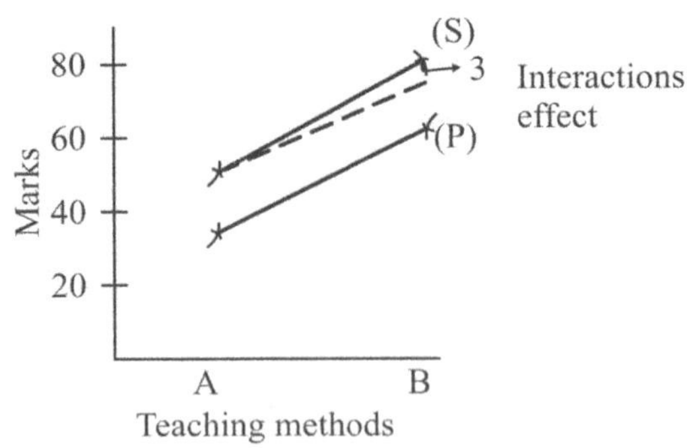

Fig. 3.4

The analysis of variance table for this experiment with 4 treatments and 5 replications is presented in Table 3.2.

Table 3.2

Source	d.f.	S.S.	M.S.	F_w	F_{tab} (d.f.)
Replications	5 – 1 = 4	R.S.S	R.M.S	$\frac{R.M.S}{EMS}$	4, 12
Treatments	4 – 1 = 3	Tr.S.S	Tr.M.S	$\frac{Tr.M.S}{EMS}$	3, 12
Methods	2 – 1 = 1	M.S.S	M.M.S	...	1, 12
Levels	2 – 1 = 1	L.S.S	L.M.S	...	1, 12
Method × Levels	1 × 1 = 1	ML.S.S	ML.M.S	$\frac{ML.M.S}{EMS}$	1, 12
Error	19 – 7 = 12	E.S.S	E.M.S		
Total	20 – 1 = 19				

The computation of sums of squares, mean sums of squares are not presented here.

The reader is advised to refer the book, Rao (2007) for further details on the analysis aspect of these experiments.

3.3.20.2 2^3 Factorial Experiment

In an experiment when three factors are used each at 2 levels then that experiment is known as 2^3 factorial experiment. In this experiment there will be 3 main effects, $3C_2$ = 3 two factor interactions and $3C_3$ = 1 three factor interaction can be estimated and tested using two or more replications. The main effects and interaction effects can be obtained by using Yates algorithm. For further details the reader is advised to refer to Rao (2007).

3.3.20.3 Mixed Factorial Experiment

This experiment is also known asymmetric factorial experiment. In this experiment, the number of levels of each factor may not be equal. For example if 3 × 4 experiment is conducted then there will be 2 factors and the first factor will have 3 levels and second factor will have 4 levels. Further there will be one two factor interaction between these two factors. The mixed factorial experiment is widely used in research experiments either in the laboratory and field experiments. Also they are useful in psychology and industrial experiments. For further details and analysis the reader is advised to refer to Rao (2007).

CHAPTER 4

Sampling Methods

4.1 Introduction

In applied research, survey method is being used in social sciences and sometimes in sciences also. Survey method is not a controlled experiment as it is done in experimental field where all methods and materials are decided before hand by experimenter. In survey method whatever data or information is available with respondent or respondents with regard to socio-economic variables will be collected.

4.2 Census

If the information is obtained from all the respondents in the population or in a specified geographical area then it is called census. For example, population census is being conducted for every 10 years conducted by Government of India in our country to know the existing population at that point of time. In this survey, all the households in the country are units of population or universe. In the year 2011, the population census was conducted by Government of India is the latest one. Since the census is to be conducted in the whole country, large number of enumerators are selected and trained in collection of data. In order to collect the reliable data, large number of school teachers are usually recruited as enumerators as part time employees as they are assumed to have more patience in extracting reliable information from households in their locality.

In census if the area to be covered is large then it requires huge amount of money, lot of time and large number of trained manpower. However, the data obtained from census is more accurate, reliable and does not involve any sampling errors. Census method of survey is useful irrespective of whether the universe is homogeneous or heterogeneous or any other factors effecting the area of a survey. If research is conducted by census method, there is no problem of generalization to whole area and its implications like sampling errors.

4.3 Sample

The sample is a part of a population or universe. If the population is all households in a city then the sample is some households in the same city. If there are 100 factories in a city then selecting 20 factories out of these 100 factories is a sample. In order to know certain information about respondents, sampling method is generally adopted to save money, time and manpower. Sometimes sampling is essential rather than any alternative method of collecting information. In collecting blood samples from patients, testing electric bulbs and explosives, sampling method is a must rather than procedure. In earlier times the housewife is used to check the rice whether it is cooked properly or not by inspecting a few grains from the boiling pot. The implication of these examples is that whenever the population or universe is uniform or homogeneous there is no need of resorting to census. On the other hand sampling gives the same result and conclusion by saving money, time and manpower.

4.4 Sampling Design

The method of selecting a sample is called sampling design. Since we are selecting a part of the population as a sample for estimating the population parameters such as mean, standard error, it is essential to give utmost importance for selection procedure of the sample. If we know rough idea about the units in the population with respect to homogeneity, heterogeneity, availability of data, area to be covered, precision required for the estimates, the objectives of a survey, time and money at disposal, the method of sampling will be chosen.

4.4.1 Probability Sampling Methods

Drawing a sample from population based on probability theory is called probability sampling method. If the sample is selected without using probability theory is known as non-probability sampling method. Some of the probability sampling methods used in research are (i) simple random sampling, (ii) stratified random sampling, (iii) cluster sampling, (iv) systematic sampling, (v) two-stage random sampling etc.

4.4.2 Non-Probability Sampling Methods

Sometimes samples are selected without using probability theory. These methods are generally used in sociological surveys and opinion surveys. These are also known as Non-random sampling methods. Some of these methods are (i) purposive sampling, (ii) convenience sampling, (iii) judgment or quota sampling etc.

4.5 Simple Random Sampling

In this method if a sample of size 'n' is to be drawn from a finite population of size ' N' then every possible sample out of NC_n possible samples will have equal probability of selection as a sample. For example if a sample of size '2' is to be selected out of '6' units in the population then there will be $6C_2$ i.e. 15 possible samples. Everyone of these 15 samples will have equal chance of being selected as a sample. The 15 possible samples of 2 are (1,2), (1,3), (1,4), (1,5), (1,6), (2,3) (2,4), (2,5), (2,6), (3,4), (3,5), (3,6), (4,5), (4,6) and (5,6). These 15 samples are having equal probability of being selected as a sample in simple random sampling.

4.5.1 Selection of a Random Sample

All the units in the population of size 'N' which is assumed to be finite will be listed. This is called sampling frame. Then a sample of 'n' units will be drawn with the help of random number tables which are given in text books, such as Fisher and Yates (1948), Snedecor and Cochran (1968) etc. For example if there are 300 houses in a colony and if 20 houses are to be selected by the method of simple random sampling then select a page of random number tables out of pages of random number tablets available in the text book. Select 3 columns since the population size 300 is a three digit figure. Then go on selecting numbers such that each is less than or equal to 300 till 20 numbers are selected. In this process of choosing numbers if the first three columns are exhausted then next three columns are considered for selection and so on.

4.5.2 Sampling without Replacement

Here every unit is drawn from the available units of sampling frame and noted its number and not replaced back. In this way all the numbers in the samples drawn will be distinct numbers. If there are 10 numbers in all in the sampling frame, 4 numbers are to be drawn without replacement; the first number will have probability 1/10, the second number will have probability 1/9 and so on. However at each stage of selection, the probability of each of the remaining units to be selected is same. If there are 'N' distinct units in the population and 'n' units are to be selected in the sample by this method there will be NC_n distinct samples in all.

4.5.3 Lottery Method of Sampling

In this method, simple random sampling without replacement method is followed. For example if there are 200 houses which are to be allotted to 400 customers then lottery method is followed. All the customers who have applied for allotment of house are listed from 1 to 400. These numbers are painted on metal tokens and put in a metal vessel specially prepared for the purpose. The vessel is rotated manually or mechanically so that all the tokens in the vessel are mixed thoroughly so that no number could get more probability of selection than another number. In other words bias in selection is eliminated. After several rounds of rotation, one token is taken from the vessel without looking inside into the vessel. That number customer will be allotted the first house out of 200 houses. Again vessel is rotated several times and second token is taken from the vessel and that number customer is allotted 2nd house from the available 199 houses. In this way all 200 houses are allotted to 200 customers from among 400 customers. Sometimes public schools admit students by this method when the number of applicants are much larger than number of seats available. Also State Governments follow this method for lotteries to award 1st, 2nd etc., prizes for those winning lottery ticket owners.

4.5.4 Sampling with Replacement

If a number is drawn from the sampling frame and replaced back before drawing a second number and so on till all numbers are drawn as per size of sample then such method of sampling is known as sampling with replacement. If the number is repeated then it will not be considered and again another number is drawn. This process will be continued till all distinctive units are included in the sample. In this method all numbers or units will have equal probability of selection at each stage of drawing numbers or units. Any number of number of samples can be drawn by this method if repeated samples are accepted.

4.5.5 Accuracy

The research work based on survey requires and demands accurate information. If the information or data obtained from survey is not accurate then conclusions drawn from sample cannot be generalized and have no relevance to ground truth. For example if the enumerator or respondent gave false information about landholding, yield of the crops, size of family, income of the family etc., then the estimates computed from such data will give wrong conclusions about population. Even cleaning of data obtained from schedules may not be able to prevent such inaccuracies of data. Proper supervision and cross checking may prevent inaccuracies of data. Now-a-days third party surveys are implemented to ensure accuracy of data in certain large scale surveys conducted with financial assistance provided by World Bank and other agencies.

4.5.6 Accuracy of Measurement

Accuracy of measurement depends upon precision, the tools available for measurement and skill of the investigator undertaking survey. Though absolute or 100 per cent accuracy is not possible in surveys, a reasonable degree of accuracy is needed. For example, monthly income of a person should be rounded to the nearest hundred and age of the person to the nearest year.

4.5.7 Precision

Precision is the product of tabulated value of z or t. statistic and standard error. For example, 95 per cent level is required for estimating the confidence interval in which population mean will lie then z (tabulated) value is taken as 1.96 and which is multiplied by standard error. The confidence interval will increase if the precision is to be increased as z (tabulated) value will increase if the confidence level increases. If 99 per cent is required, z (tabulated) value is 2.58. Similarly in small samples, t (tabulated) value will increase with the increase in confidence level. For example, if the estimate is Rs 200 and the precision desired is ± 4%. Then the true value will be not less than 192 and not more than 208. In other words the true value will lie between the range 192 to 208.

4.5.8 Standard Error

The standard deviation of the sampling distribution of statistic such as mean, standard deviation etc., is termed as standard error of mean, standard error of standard deviation respectively.

If x follows normal distribution with mean as μ and standard deviation, σ then $\bar{x}$ the mean which is based on 'n' observations also follows normal distribution with mean as μ and standard deviation as $\sigma/\sqrt{n}$.. This standard deviation of $\bar{x}$ i.e. $\sigma/\sqrt{n}$ is called standard error of mean. Also $(\bar{x}-\mu)/\sigma/\sqrt{n}$ follows normal distribution with mean as zero and standard deviation as 1.

For example, if $\sigma = 20$ and $n = 16$, the standard error of mean is

$$\frac{\sigma}{\sqrt{n}} = \frac{20}{\sqrt{16}} = \frac{20}{4} = 5$$

The standard error is used in all the sampling methods to estimate the precision of the estimates as well as for estimating the confidence interval of mean and also in tests of hypotheses such as z - test, t – test etc.

4.5.9 Confidence Interval

It is the difference between upper limit and lower limit in which population parameter such as mean will lie. For example the confidence limits of population mean are obtained as $\bar{x} \pm 1.96\frac{\sigma}{\sqrt{n}}$.

where $\bar{x}$ = mean, 1.96 is the tabulated of z at 5 per cent level of significance and $\sigma/\sqrt{n}$ is the standard error of mean when $\bar{x}$ follows normal distribution. $\bar{x} + 1.96\,\sigma/\sqrt{n}$ is the upper limit and $\bar{x} - 1.96\,\sigma/\sqrt{n}$ is the lower limit of population mean, μ and these limits are also known as fiducial limits. The difference between upper and lower limits is called confidence interval

If $\bar{x} = 20$, $\sigma = 2$ and $n = 4$ then the upper confidence limit is

$$20 + 1.96 \times \frac{2}{\sqrt{4}} = 21.96$$

and lower confidence limit is $20 - 1.96 \times \frac{2}{\sqrt{4}} = 18.04$

and confidence interval is $21.96 - 18.04 = 3.92$.

4.5.10 Estimates of Population Mean and Standard Error in Simple Random Sampling

If 'N' is the size of the population and 'n' is the size of the sample which is selected by simple random sampling and $y_1, y_2, \ldots\ldots y_n$ are the variate values in the sample, then the estimate of population mean is given as $\bar{y}_n$ where

$$\bar{y}_n = \text{Mean of } y = \frac{\sum_{i=1}^{n} y_i}{n}$$

The estimate of variance is given as

$$\text{Estmate v}\left(\bar{y}_n\right) = \frac{N-n}{Nn} s^2$$

where $s^2 = \frac{1}{n-1} \sum_{i=1}^{n} \left(y_i - \bar{y}_n\right)^2$ = mean square deviation based on the sample.

The estimate of standard error (S.E.) is given as

$$\text{Estimate S.E.}\left(\bar{y}_n\right) = \sqrt{\text{Est. v}\left(\bar{y}_n\right)}$$

The upper confidence limit is $\bar{y}_n + t_{(n-1)} \times \text{Est. SE}\left(\bar{y}_n\right)$ and

lower confidence limit is $\bar{y}_n - t_{(n-1)} \times \text{Est. S.E.}\left(\bar{y}_n\right)$

where $t_{(n-1)}$ is the tabulated value of t-statistic with $(n - 1)$ degrees of freedom.

4.6 Stratified Random Sampling

In this method of sampling, the population is divided into different homogeneous groups termed as strata and simple random sample is selected from each of the strata. This method is applied when the population is heterogeneous with respect to a particular characteristic related to study variable. By doing so, the estimate of population mean can be estimated more efficiently in comparison to simple random sample. For example in a state, districts can be viewed as strata as they are formed on the basis of geographical contiguity, administrative convenience, dialect, culture, food habits etc. Similarly in a district, talukas or mandals can be considered as strata as they are formed in the similar criteria as districts. For example, in order to estimate the net profits of a product produced by different factories, the total number of factories can be divided into large, medium and small factories as strata. If we are interested to study the living conditions of employees in cities in a state, the cities can be grouped as A, B^+, B and C-class cities as strata. In large scale sample surveys in research, stratified random sampling is followed very often.

4.6.1 Proportional Allocation of Sample

When the sizes of strata varies considerably in the population then the allotment of sample to different strata is according to the same proportion then it is known as proportional allocation. This type of allocation of sample improves the efficiency of the estimate in comparison to random allocation of sample to different strata. If N_i is the size of the i-th stratum and there are k-strata in the population and $\sum_{i=1}^{k} N_i = N$ is the size of the population. If n is the size of the sample to be selected from N then n_i is the size of the sample to be selected from i-th stratum for I = 1, 2, … k. According to proportional allocation, n_i is obtained as

$$n_i = n \times \frac{N_i}{N} \quad \text{for i =1, 2, . . . , k.}$$

For example if there are 100 houses in the 1st ward, 150 houses in the 2nd ward and 200 houses in the 3rd ward of a locality in a city and a total of

45 houses are to be allotted according to proportional allocation then the allocation of sample is given as follows

$$1^{st} \text{ ward} = 45 \times \frac{100}{450} = 10$$

$$2^{nd} \text{ ward} = 45 \times \frac{150}{450} = 15$$

$$3^{rd} \text{ ward} = 45 \times \frac{200}{450} = 20$$

Total sample = 10 + 15 + 20 = 45.

4.6.2 Neyman's Allocation or Optimum Allocation

In this method, total sample is allocated to different strata based on not only size of the strata but also mean square deviation of that strata assuming that mean square deviation values are available either from previous survey or obtained as secondary data from any source. If n_i is the size of the sample to be selected from i-th stratum

where

$$n_i = n \times \frac{N_i \; S_i}{\Sigma N_i \; S_i}$$

where $$S_i^2 = \frac{1}{N_i - 1} \sum_j \left(y_{ij} - \bar{y}_{Ni}\right)^2$$

where $\bar{y}_{Ni}$ is the mean of i-th stratum in the population and N_i is the size of the i-th stratum for I = 1, 2, ….., k.

For example, if there are 100 houses in the 1st ward, 150 houses in 2nd ward and 200 houses in 3rd ward with $S_1 = 4$, $S_2 = 5$ and $S_3 = 6$ for 1st, 2nd and 3rd wards respectively, A sample of 36 houses are to be selected by optimum allocation is as follows.

Table 4.1

Ward	**N_i**	**S_i**	**$N_i S_i$**	**n_i**
1	100	5	500	6
2	150	6	900	11
3	200	8	1600	19
			3000	**36**

4.6.3 Selection of a Sample with Probability Proportional to Size

In research surveys, often it is proposed to select a sample based on proportional to size. In industrial survey, factories are selected in the sample based on their capacity of production. For example if there are 20 factories and 5 factories are to be selected from them with probability proportional to size then the procedure is given as follows.

Table 4.2

Factory (1)	Daily Production (tons) (2)	Cumulative Total (3)	Factory (1)	Daily Production (tons) (2)	Cumulative Total (3)
1	18	18	11	62	467
2	25	43	12	65	532
3	30	73	13	71	603
4	36	109	14	78	681
5	42	151	15	82	763
6	44	195	16	86	849
7	48	243	17	92	941
8	51	294	18	99	1040
9	54	348	19	101	1141
10	57	405	20	105	1246

The factories are arranged in ascending order of magnitude based on daily production and these figures are presented in column (2) of Table 4.1.

The cumulative totals of figures are presented in column (3). Select a random number out of 1246 and if it falls between 1 and 18 then 1st factory is selected in the sample. If the random number is say 182 then it lies between 151 and 195 in col. (3) then factory with serial number 6 is selected. In this way all the 5 factories can be selected with probability proportional to capacity of production.

4.6.4 Estimates of Population Mean and Standard Error

If N_i is the size of the i-th stratum for i = 1, 2, … , k and N= $\sum_{i=1}^{k} N_i$ is the total size of the population and n_i is the size of the i-th stratum in the sample and n = $\sum_{i=1}^{k} n_i$ is the total size of the sample, y_i is the i-th variate value in the sample, then

$$\bar{y}_{n_i} = \frac{1}{n_i} \cdot \sum_{i=1}^{n_i} y_i$$

Estimate of population mean is $\bar{y}_{st} = \sum_{i=1}^{k} \frac{N_i}{N} \bar{y}_{ni}$

Estimate of variance, Est. $V\left(\bar{y}_{st}\right) = \sum_{i=1}^{k} \frac{N_i^2}{N^2} \frac{(N_i - n_i)\, s_i^2}{N_i n_i}$

where $s_i^2 = \frac{1}{n_i - 1} \sum_{j=1}^{n_i} \left(y_{ij} - \bar{y}_{ni}\right)^2$ is the mean square deviation of i-th stratum.

Est. S.E. $\left(\bar{y}_{st}\right) = \sqrt{\text{Est. V}\left(\bar{y}_{st}\right)}$ = Estimate of the standard error.

Confidence limits of Population Mean

Upper limit = $\bar{y}_{st} + t_{(n-1)} \times$ Est. S.E. $\left(\bar{y}_{st}\right)$

Lower limit = $\bar{y}_{st} - t_{(n-1)} \times$ Est. S.E. $\left(\bar{y}_{st}\right)$

where $t_{(n-1)}$ is the tabulated value of t-statistic with (n – 1) degrees of freedom.

4.6.5 Merits and Demerits of Stratified Random Sampling

4.6.5.1 Merits

(i) The method ensures representation from each group of the population. Therefore the estimate based on this sampling method is better representative of population mean with respect to characteristic under consideration and

(ii) The estimate based on stratified random sampling method is more efficient than simple random sampling method.

4.6.5.2 Demerits

If the stratification of population is not done based on important characteristic related to study variable then the estimate based on this method may not be efficient one compared to simple random sampling method.

4.7 Cluster Sampling Method

In this method, the population is divided into sub groups called clusters. A sample of clusters is selected at random and the units in the selected clusters will be studied for the estimating the population mean, standard error and confidence limits.

For example, if the district is considered as a population of villages then mandals or talukas are considered as clusters. These mandals are considered as clusters because they are the groups consisting of villages. The villagewise statistical data will be available in the official data collected by Directorate of Economics and Statistics rather than household data. In order to estimate the area irrigated per village in a district, it is convenient to use cluster sampling method. Further, the cost of conducting survey can be reduced since the survey of villages within mandals will be less expensive than between mandals. Similarly in surveys where consumption pattern of milk etc., is to be estimated, families or house holds can be considered as clusters consisting of members of family as units within each cluster.

4.7.1 Estimates of Population Mean and Standard Error

Let y_{ij} be the variate value of j-th unit in the i-th cluster in the sample for $j = 1, 2, \ldots M$ and $i = 1, 2, \ldots, n$.

Let 'n' clusters be selected at random from 'N' clusters and each cluster consists of 'M' units.

The mean of the i-th cluster $\bar{y}_{iM} = \frac{1}{M} \sum_{j=1}^{M} y_{ij}$

The estimate of population mean is

$$\bar{y}_{cl} = \frac{1}{n} \sum_{j=1}^{M} y_{iM}$$

The estimate of variance is

$$\text{Est. } v\left(\bar{y}_{cl}\right) = \frac{N-n}{Nn}\, s_b^2$$

where
$$s_b^2 = \frac{1}{n-1} \sum_{i=1}^{n} \left(\bar{y}_{im} - \bar{y}_{cl}\right)^2$$

is the mean square deviation between cluster means.

$$\text{Est. S.E. } \left(\bar{y}_{cl}\right) = \sqrt{\text{Est. } v\left(\bar{y}_{cl}\right)} = \text{estimate of standard error.}$$

Confidence limits of Population Mean

The upper limit is $\bar{y}_{cl} + t_{(n-1)} \times \text{Est. S.E.} \left(\bar{y}_{cl}\right)$

The lower limit is $\bar{y}_{cl} - t_{(n-1)} \times \text{Est. S.E.} \left(\bar{y}_{cl}\right)$

where $t_{(n-1)}$ is the tabulated value of t-statistic with (n–1) degrees of freedom.

4.8 Systematic Sampling

In this method of sampling if one unit is selected at random then the other units of the sample will be selected automatically. For example if there are 100 houses in the residential colony with 10 streets and each street consists of 10 houses. Suppose 4th house is selected randomly from the 1st 10 houses of 1st street then 14th house in the 2nd street, 24th house in the 3rd street and so on and 94th house in 10th street will be automatically selected in the sample without going to randomizations from each street separately.

In general if 'N' be the size of the population and 'n' be the size of the sample such that N = nk where k is a positive integer or sampling interval. In other words N is a multiple of 'n'. If one unit is selected at random from 1st 'k' units and the remaining (n – 1) units in the sample will be chosen automatically at equi-spaced intervals of k. If 5th unit is selected by random sampling method from the 1st k units then the remaining units in the sample are k + 5, 2k + 5, …. , (n – 1) k + 5. This could be illustrated from the Table 4.3.

Table 4.3

1	2	3	4	.....	k
k + 1	k + 2	k + 3	k + 4	.....	2k
2k + 1	2k + 2	2k + 3	2k + 4	.....	3k
⋮	⋮	⋮	⋮	⋮	
(n – 1) k + 1	(n – 1) k + 2	(n – 1) k + 3	(n – 1) k + 4	.....	nk

From Table 4.3 each column will form one sample.

4.8.1 Estimates of Population Mean and Standard Error

Let y_{ij} be the value of the variable under study for the j-th unit of i-th cluster (sample) bearing the serial number i + (j – 1)k for i = 1, 2, …. , k; j = 1, 2, … , n.

The estimate of population mean is $\bar{y}_{sy} = \frac{1}{n} \sum_{j=1}^{n} Y_{ij}$

The estimate of variance is

$$\text{Est. V}\left(\bar{y}_{sy}\right) = \left(\frac{1}{n} - \frac{1}{nk}\right) s_w^2$$

where $s_w^2 = \frac{1}{n-1} \sum_{j=1}^{n} \left(y_{ij} - \bar{y}_{sy}\right)^2$ is the mean square deviation between units within the selected systematic sample. It can be noted that this estimate of variance is an approximate one available.

$\text{Est. S.E.}\left(\bar{y}_{sy}\right) = \sqrt{\text{Est. V}\left(\bar{y}_{sy}\right)}$ is the estimate of standard error.

Confidence limits

The upper limit is $\bar{y}_{sy} + t_{(n-1)} \times \text{Est. S.E.}\left(\bar{y}_{sy}\right)$

The lower limit is $\bar{y}_{sy} - t_{(n-1)} \times \text{Est. S.E.}\left(\bar{y}_{sy}\right)$

where $t_{(n-1)}$ is the tabulated value of t-statistic with (n – 1) degrees of freedom.

4.8.2 Merits and Demerits of Systematic Sampling

4.8.2.1 Merits

(i) The method of drawing sample is relatively easy and convenient since only one unit is drawn at random.

(ii) This method is applicable in forest surveys for estimation of forest products such as volume of timber, tamarind, honey, lack etc., as the forest region is inaccessible terrain. This method is also useful in estimation of marine and inland fish population. This method is also useful in estimation of prevalence of diseases in crops, human-beings etc. This method can also be useful in opinion surveys for exit polls in elections.

4.8.2.2 Demerits

(i) Sometimes the total population size may not be multiple of sample size i.e., $N \neq nk$. In such case some units may be added to population or some units may be deleted from population.

(ii) The estimate of standard error may be biased one sometimes.

4.9 Two-Stage Sampling

In this method, the sampling is effected in two-stages. For example in a district, mandals or talukas are selected at random at first stage and villages are selected at random from each selected mandal or taluka at second stage then it is known as two-stage sampling and is also called as sub-sampling. This method of sampling is adopted generally in large scale surveys to minimize the cost involved in collection of data. Sometimes it may be uneconomical as well as less efficient to enumerate complete mandal when the villages in mandal are homogenous due to geographical continuity or due to several other factors. Therefore few villages can be selected for enumeration. Further it is known that the larger the size of the mandal the lesser the precision of the estimate. The units in the first stage sampling are called first stage units or primary units. The units selected at second stage sampling are known as second stage units or secondary units. If the procedure is extended to three or more stages of sampling then it is termed as multi-stage sampling.

4.9.1 Estimates of Population Mean and Standard Error

Let y_{ij} be the value of the variable under study for the j-th second stage unit of the i-th first stage unit for i = 1, 2, …. , N; j = 1, 2, …. , M where N be the sign of the first stage units and each consist of M second stage units. Let n be the size of the first stage units and m be the size of second stage units selected in the sample.

The mean of i-th first stage unit is $\bar{y}_{im} = \frac{1}{m} \sum_{j=1}^{m} y_{ij}$

The estimate of population mean is

$$\bar{y}_{ts} = \frac{1}{n} \sum_{i=1}^{n} \bar{y}_{im} = \frac{1}{nm} \sum_{i=1}^{n} \sum_{j=1}^{n} y_{ij}$$

The estimate of variance is

$$\text{Est. v}\left(\bar{y}_{ts}\right) = \left(\frac{1}{n} - \frac{1}{N}\right) s_b^2 + \frac{1}{N}\left(\frac{1}{m} - \frac{1}{M}\right) \bar{s}_w^2$$

where $$s_b^2 = \frac{1}{(n-1)} \sum_{i=1}^{n} \left(\bar{y}_{im} - \bar{y}_{ts}\right)^2$$

is the mean square deviation between first stage unit means

$$\bar{s}_w^2 = \frac{1}{n(m-1)} \sum_{i=1}^{n} (m-1)\, s_i^2$$

is the mean square deviation within first stage units.

where $$s_i^2 = \frac{1}{(m-1)} \sum_{j=1}^{m} \left(y_y - \bar{y}_{im}\right)^2$$

$$\text{Est. S.E.}\left(\bar{y}_{ts}\right) = \sqrt{\text{Est. v}\left(\bar{y}_{ts}\right)}$$

is the estimate of standard error.

Confidence limits:

The upper limit is $\bar{y}_{ts} + t_{(nm-1)} \times \text{Est. S.E.}\left(\bar{y}_{ts}\right)$

The lower limit is $\bar{y}_{ts} - t_{(nm-1)} \times \text{Est. S.E.}\left(\bar{y}_{ts}\right)$

4.9.2 Merits and Demerits of Two-stage Random Sampling Method

4.9.2.1 Merits

It is very useful method and widely applicable in socio-economic surveys. In large scale sample surveys conducted by Government of India, the multi-stage random sampling is adopted. For example, in crop cutting experiments for estimating the average yield of a crop, villages are selected at first stage, farmer's fields are selected at second stage and plots in farmers fields are selected at third stage of sampling. This method of sampling saves expenditure and time and provide unbiased estimates of population mean and standard error.

4.9.2.2 Demerits

When the sizes of second stage units are unequal then the formula for estimating standard error will become complicated. In multi-stage sampling, the formula for estimate of standard error will be more complicated when the sizes of second stage, third stage etc., units are unequal and which is possible in natural situation.

4.10 Non-Probability Sampling Methods

If the sample is selected based on non-probability theory then they are termed as non-probability sampling methods. Some of them are described in this section.

4.10.1 Purposive Sampling

In this method, the selection of units in the sample is not based on random sampling. The selection of units is based on the judgment of the investigator. Therefore this method is also known as judgment sampling. The investigator selects units assuming that they represent the population. However the efficiency of this method depends upon the experience and expertise of the investigator. Case studies are conducted using this procedure for highlighting the success or failure stories of a method, procedure or person so that people can take advantage of this story. The success story of entrepreneur in industry can be viewed as case study. The success story of farmers achieving higher standard of living through farming in Ankapur village, Nizamabad district of Andhra Pradesh can be studied as purposive sampling so that other farmers an emulate from them.

4.10.1.1 Merits

(i) The method of drawing sample is easy

(ii) The representative units can be selected to highlight the objective of the study in research

(iii) The analysis of the data will be easy and simple and

(iv) The investigation can be completed with limited budget and time.

4.10.1.2 Demerits

(i) The selection of sample units is based on the judgment of the investigator and hence may not always be representative as the investigators bias may interfere with selection of units.

(ii) It is not possible to generalize this sample results to population and

(iii) The sampling error can not be assessed

4.10.2 Convenience Sampling

In this method, the investigator selects units in the sample based on his convenience with respect to conducting study. For example, the investigator wants to investigate the problem of drinking water contains fluoride, he selects road side villages having this problem so that he can have transport and other facilities to complete his work in time. This method provides the estimate but it may be biased one. However the method of collection of data is easy and convenient and can be completed within time.

4.10.3 Quota Sampling

In this method, the size of the sample is fixed before hand irrespective of the size of the population. For example, in order to study the problems in industry, the number of factories to be selected is fixed for the categories big, medium, small and cottage industries. Similarly in order to study the nature of town planning, fixed number of different categories of cities such as very old, old, recent, very recent will be selected. Also on any issue of public interest, public opinion will be collected from the fixed number of people such as employees, farmers, students, housewives, elders etc. This method can be adopted in exit polls in election of public representatives in democracy.

4.11 Sampling Errors

The errors occurring through adoption of sampling method instead of census for estimating the population characteristic are known as sampling errors. In other words the difference between the estimate based on sample and the estimate based on population is termed as sampling error. Suppose samples of equal size are drawn at random from the population and their means are computed. These means are different from among themselves and they are different from the population mean unless all the units in the population are exactly equal. The standard deviation of the sampling distribution of these means is called standard error and which is also known as sampling error. These errors occur even when the sample estimate is 'unbiased'.

The sampling error can be reduced by increasing the size of the sample. However, it is not always possible to increase the size of sample as it is directly related to expenditure of survey and also time involved in completing the survey. In census survey, these errors will not occur as all units in the population are studied.

4.12 Non-Sampling Errors

The errors occurring in surveys other than due to sampling are called as non-sampling errors. These may occur through:

(i) observational errors and

(ii) Incomplete samples.

4.12.1 Observational Errors

The enumerator may wrongly report or record the observations in the schedule due to:

(i) Personal bias

(ii) Improper understanding of the questions in the schedule

(iii) Improper understanding of the response of the questions from respondent and

(iv) Improper recording of the observations supplied by third person.

4.12.2 Incomplete Samples

Incomplete filling of schedules by enumerators will be also known as non-sampling errors. The estimates based on incomplete sample data is biased. Further, the cost of the survey will increase if the information has to be collected again and again from the incomplete sample units. In such situations a sub sample is taken for collecting the information from the non-response samples.

4.13 Choice of Sampling Methods

The choice of sampling method depends upon many factors such as:

(i) Objectives of research survey

(ii) Time and money at the disposal for conducting survey

(iii) Area or population to be covered

(iv) Nature of population such as homogenous or heterogeneous

(v) Administrative and supporting staff available

(vi) Human resources required for carrying out the survey and most important is availability of sampling frame

(vii) If the population is homogeneous with respect to characteristic under study then simple random sampling is recommended. If the population is heterogeneous with respect to characteristic under study then stratified random sampling method is appropriate. If the sampling frame is available only for clusters but not for units then cluster sampling method is advised. If the units in the population are in a systematic order and are large in number then systematic sampling may be more suitable. If the area or the population is large and heterogeneous then stratified two-stage random sampling is generally adopted. However, whatever sampling method is adopted if the sample size increases the precision of the estimate increases.

4.14 Size of the Sample

Though it is said that as the sample size increases the precision of the estimate increases, however, it is not possible nor necessary in certain situations like blood sample, testing of electric bulbs and explosives where the population is either homogeneous or testing more units in the sample will become more expensive. If the population is large and heterogeneous then large sample such as 5 to 10 percent of the population size is recommended for sample. In general the decision with respect to size of sample involves:

(i) Aims and objectives of survey

(ii) Area to be covered

(iii) Time and expenditure involved
(iv) Continuous or one-time survey
(v) Availability of skilled and semi-skilled personnel
(vi) Precision required for the estimate etc.

4.15 Determination of Sample Size

The sample size can be determined with the following procedure using one sample standard normal deviate (SND) test

$$Z = \frac{|\bar{x} - \mu|}{\frac{\sigma}{\sqrt{n}}}$$

where $\bar{x}$ = sample mean, μ = population mean, σ = standard deviation of population, n = size of the sample and Z = standard normal deviate statistic.

$$Z \cdot \frac{\sigma}{\sqrt{n}} = |\bar{x} - \mu|$$

$$\sqrt{n} = \frac{Z\sigma}{|\bar{x} - \mu|}$$

$$n = \frac{Z^2 \sigma^2}{(\bar{x} - \mu)^2}$$

Here Z (tabulated) value at 5 percent level of significance is 1.96 and at 1 percent level of significance is 2.58. $(\bar{x} - \mu)$ is to be assumed as 10 or 15 or a value which is given to become significantly different. Usually 'σ' value can be taken from the previous survey or from secondary data which is available from the records of Directorate of Economics Statistics of the State Government.

This method of determining sample size is generally followed for large scale surveys sponsored by Government of India, World Bank and other outside funding agencies, State Governments where statistics has to be collected on large number of variables. In general if the population is small, then 10 percent of the population is taken as sample size. If the population size increases the percent sampling decreases as 8 percent, 5 percent and so on depending upon the time and financial resources.

4.16 Longitudinal Survey

A survey is conducted for several years on the same experimental units or sample units is called longitudinal survey. For example, if a nutritional intervention is implemented for tribal children in certain area of the state or district then the impact of intervention can be assessed through longitudinal survey for the same children for several years.

CHAPTER 5

Scale Construction Methods

In this chapter different scaling methods are described which are used in social, psychological and educational research. Before going to describe the scaling techniques, the levels of measurement is discussed here.

5.1 Measurement

Measurement may be defined as assigning numerical value to objects or events such that numerical values follow certain mathematical laws in physical and biological sciences. However, it is not always possible to assign numerical values which follow certain mathematical for qualitative characters such as intelligence, colour, shape etc., in behavioral sciences.

The levels of measurement are categorized into four levels as (i) Nominal (ii) Ordinal (iii) Interval and (iv) Ratio.

5.1.1 Nominal Scale

This is the lowest level of measurement. When nomenclature is used to identify the groups to which various subjects belong then measurement is said to be done at nominal scale.

For example, the number plates on cars and other vehicles indicate the state, registration office etc. These numbers of cars only identify the cars but a particular number of car say 5857 is not superior to car number 5856. Similarly if numbers are allotted to players in a cricket team, it is only to identify the player. If 10th number is given to one player and 9th number is given to another player then it does not mean that 10th number player is superior to 9th number player. Further average of the numbers of one team has no meaning and cannot be compared with average of numbers of another team. No parametric tests like t-test, z-test, Analysis of variance can be applied for analysing the data based on nominal scale. However, chi-square test and other non-parametric tests can be applied to the data measured on nominal scale. In sample surveys, where measurable data is not possible, nominal scale of measurement is being used for collecting information from respondents. In nominal scale, the only relation involved is equivalence. The equivalence relation is reflexive, symmetrical and transitive.

5.1.2 Ordinal Scale

In nominal scaling, the objects in a group are not much different from each other but they can be ranked according to certain criterion then they are said to be measured on ordinal scale. If the objects are classified as more preferred, more difficult, more intelligent, more mature etc., then they are said to be measured on ordinal scale. For example, the students in a class are classed as above average, average, below average and poor then they are measured on ordinal scale. In a cricket team if the players are ranked as per their skill and quality in playing as A player is greater than B player and so on, then they are said to measured on ordinal scale. The ordinal scale incorporates not only relation of 'equivalence' but also the relation 'greater than'. The 'greater than' relation is urreflexive, asymmetrical and transitive.

5.1.3 Interval Scale

If the distance between any two numbers are known in ordinal scale then it can be said that the measurement is achieved at interval scale. For example, temperature is measured on interval scale. Here two different scales such as centigrade and Fahrenheit are commonly used. The unit of measurement and zero point are different for these two different scales. However, both contain same amount and kind of information. In this measurement, the ratio of any two intervals is independent of measurement and of the zero point. The interval scale measurement not only be able to specify equivalence relation, greater than relation but also be able to specify the ratio of any two intervals. If the data is amenable to interval scale it means that it is a measurement data unlike 'Nominal' and 'Ordinal' scales data.

5.1.4 Ratio Scale

An interval scale with true zero point is called ratio scale. In ratio scale, the ratio of any two scale points is independent of unit of measurement. The scales of height, weight, volume have true zero point. The ratio of any two weights whether they are measured in kgs or pounds they are equal. In physical sciences, ratio scale is used for measurement. Ratio scale satisfies (i) equivalence relation (ii) greater than relation (iii) known ratio of any two intervals and (iv) known ratio of any two scale values.

5.2 Scaling

It is a measurement or number given to abstract thing such as attitude of an individual. Mostly scaling has been used in psychology and behavioural sciences.

5.2.1 Attitude

Attitude of a person is different from his behaviour. A man acts contrary to the way in which he felt because of various reasons. For example, a student joins a particular professional course not necessarily he likes the course but may be the degree fetches quick employment or his parents want him to admit him in that course or his close friend is joining in that course or fees structure, duration and location of the institution is congenial for him and so on. Therefore it is not necessary that there is one to one correspondence between behaviour and attitude. In opinion surveys, attitude of an individual is more important than his behaviour.

In order to extract the attitude of individuals, attitude statements are prepared and presented to them for their response as 'favourable' or 'Not favourable'. These statements are called items. These items are carefully edited and selected in accordance with some criteria. These items are given to large number of individuals for their response as favourable or not favourable. Based on the responses the attititude scale can be developed. As a first step in developing attitude scale is to eliminate all statements in the list which are 'factual' and also which are 'ambiguous'.

5.3 Method of Paired Comparisons

This method is used for developing attitude scale. The ordering of objects based on weights or heights is called 'physical continuum'. Similarly the arrangement or ordering of objects based on judgement of individuals is called 'psychological continuum'. Let S_i be the reaction of an individual when confronted with stimulus 'i' and when he was asked to make a judgement of attribute. It is assumed that S_i's follow normal distribution with mean $\overline{S}_i$ which is termed as 'scale value' of stimulus 'i'. The standard deviation of the distribution of S_i's is denoted as σ_i. Similarly the response of jth stimulus is S_j and its sale value is taken as $\overline{S_j}$ with a standard deviation of σ_j.

For example, 'i' and 'j' are two statements about some opinion on certain object. A large number of individuals will be asked to make comparative judgements whether 'i' statement is more favourable than 'j' or vice-versa then if 0.5 proportion of individuals say 'i' statement is more favourable than 'j' then it can be concluded that 'i' and 'j' statements are exactly equal with respect to attribute under study. The development of attitude scale is illustrated with example given in 5.3.1.

Example

A corporate sector company wants to know the opinion of its share-holders whether two companies A and B in their ownership can be merged for better administration and better profits. In this connection, the corporate office framed 5 statements to elicit the opinion of shareholders. The statements are as follows:

1. The companies A and B can be merged for better administration and better profits.
2. Since company A is not doing well therefore it can be merged with company B since company B is doing well.
3. Merging of companies A and B is the only solution of survival of the corporate company.
4. There is no alternate solution to improve the financial viability of company A except to merge with company B.
5. Merging of companies A and B is going to effect the employees by way of retrenchment and thus reduce the financial burden of the owner.

These five statements were presented in all possible pairs to all the 80 share-holders so that each individual can make 5(5 – 1)/2 = 10 comparative judgements.

Table 5.1 gives the frequency matrix (F-matrix) with which each column statement was judged more favourable than the row statement.

Table 5.1 (F-matrix).

Statements	1	2	3	4	5
1	–	48	69	59	48
2	32	–	15	40	45
3	11	65	–	25	55
4	21	40	55	–	16
5	32	35	25	64	–

The F-matrix is converted into proportions matrix (P-matrix) by dividing each entry in F-matrix by total number of shareholders i.e., 80 or multiply by 1/80 = 0.0125.

Thus P-matrix is given in Table 5.2.

Table 5.2 (P-matrix).

Statements	1	2	3	4	5
1	–	0.600	0.863	0.738	0.600
2	0.400	–	0.188	0.500	0.563
3	0.138	0.813	–	0.313	0.688
4	0.263	0.500	0.688	–	0.200
5	0.400	0.438	0.313	0.800	–
Total	**1.201**	**2.351**	**2.052**	**2.351**	**2.051**

The P-matrix is transformed to Z-matrix where the entries in the Z-matrix are the standard Normal deviate values of the corresponding proportions in the P-matrix. The entries in the Z-matrix are obtained from the table of standard normal deviate vales given in Table of Appendix.

Table 5.3 (Z-matrix).

Statements	1	2	3	4	5
1	–	0.253	1.094	0.637	0.253
2	– 0.253	–	– 0.885	0.000	0.159
3	– 1.089	0.889	–	– 0.487	0.490
4	– 0.634	0.000	0.490	–	– 0.842
5	– 0.253	– 0.156	– 0.487	0.842	–
Total	**– 2.229**	**0.986**	**0.212**	**0.992**	**0.060**
Mean	**– 0.446**	**0.197**	**0.042**	**0.198**	**0.012**
Mean + 0.448	**0.000**	**0.643**	**0.488**	**0.644**	**0.458**

Let Z_{ij} be the entry of (i, j)th cell in Z-matrix and

$$Z_{ij} = \overline{S_i} - \overline{S_j} \qquad \text{for i, j} = 1, 2, \ldots 5.$$

$$\sum_{j=1}^{n} Z_{ij} = n\,\overline{S_i} - \sum_{j=1}^{n} \overline{S_j}$$

$$\frac{1}{n}\sum_{j=1}^{n} Z_{ij} = \overline{S_i} - \frac{1}{n}\sum_{j=1}^{n} \overline{S_j}$$

$$\overline{Z_i} = \overline{S_i} - \overline{S}$$

where $\overline{Z_i}$ = Arithmetic mean of the entries in the i-th column of Z-matrix

$\overline{S_i}$ = Scale value if i-th statement

$\overline{S}$ = Arithemetic mean of scale values

From Table 5.3 it can be observed that the value in column (1) i.e., – 0.448 is the scale value of 1st statement in terms of its deviation from overall mean. Similarly, the entry in column (2) i.e., 0.253 is the scale value of 2nd statement in terms of deviation from overall mean and so on.

Statements with negative scale values are less favourable in comparison to statements with positive scale values in that order. The higher the positive scale is higher the favourable statement. The entire exercise is done to convert ordinal scale measurement of aptitude of share-holders to interval scale measurement. The advantage of interval scale measurement is that it is amenable to statistical analysis for drawing conclusions.

5.4 Consistency

In order to verify whether the scale values obtained for statements in example given in section 5.3.1 are consistent or not, a consistency check is adopted. In other words how far the expected frequencies obtained through scale values are in agreement or closer to observed frequencies or not is tested. The differences between scale values are computed and furnished in Z'-matrix given in Table 5.4.

Table 5.4 (Z' -matrix).

Statements	**$**	**1**	**2**	**3**	**4**	**5**
	Scale values	**0.000**	**0.643**	**0.488**	**0.644**	**0.458**
1	0.000					
2	0.643	– 0.643				
3	0.488	– 0.488	0.155			
4	0.644	– 0.644	– 0001	– 0.156		
5	0.488	– 0.458	0.185	0.030	0.186	–

Here
$$Z'_{12} = \overline{S_1} - \overline{S_2} = 0.000 - 0.643 = -0.643$$
$$Z'_{13} = \overline{S_1} - \overline{S_3} = 0.000 - 0.488 = -0.488$$
$$Z'_{23} = \overline{S_2} - \overline{S_3} = 0.643 - 0.488 = 0.155$$
$$Z'_{24} = \overline{S_2} - \overline{S_4} = 0.643 - 0.644 = -0.001$$

and so on. All the entries in the Z'-matrix are obtained in a similar way.

From Z'-matrix, P'-matrix can be obtained by entering into table of standard normal variate values given in Appendix 1.

The p'_{ij}-values of P'-matrix can be obtained by looking to the body of the table for Z'_{ij}-values. The P'-matrix is given in Table 5.5

Table 5.5 (P'-matrix).

Statements	1	2	3	4	5
1	–				
2	0.260	–			
3	0.313	0.561	–		
4	0.260	0.499	0.438	–	
5	0.324	0.573	0.512	0.574	–

The entries in P'-matrix are obtained as $P'_{12} = 0.260$ and which is the column value corresponding to $Z'_{12} = -0.643$ from the body of the appendix table. Similarly, $P'_{13} = 0.313$ which is the column value corresponding value of $Z'_{13} = 0.488$ from the body of the appendix table.

The differences between p_{ij} and p'_{ij} values are computed and furnished in (P – P') matrix given in Table 5.6.

Table 5.6 (P – P') matrix.

Statements	1	2	3	4	5
1	–				
2	0.140	–			
3	– 0.175	0.252	–		
4	0.003	0.001	0.250	–	
5	0.076	– 0.135	– 0.199	0.226	–
Total	**0.394**	**0.388**	**0.449**	**0.226**	**1.457**

In Table 5.6, the entries are obtained by subtracting p'_{ij} values in Table 5.5 from the corresponding entries of p'_y values in Table 5.2. For example, $p_{12} - p'_{12} = 0.400 - 0.260 = 0.140$, $p_{13} - p'_{13} = 0.138 - 0.313 = -0.175$ and so on.

The absolute average discrepancy (AD) is given as

$$AD = \frac{\sum |p_{ij} - p'_{ij}|}{\frac{n(n-1)}{2}}$$

where n = number of statements

$$AD = \frac{1.457}{\frac{5(5-1)}{2}} = \frac{1.457}{10} = 0.1457$$

The absolute average discrepancy for 5 statements is 0.1457 which appears to be larger than usually reported when statements are measured by paired comparison methods. As the number of statements is increased then the average discrepancy may be decreased.

5.5 Incomplete Data

When p_{ij} values are higher such as 1.00 or 0.99 then these values are deleted for finding the scale values of the statements. The reason for deleting the values is the Z_{ij} values differ largely for the extreme values compared to middle values of p_{ij} such as 0.51, 0.52, 0.48 etc. For example, if p_{ij} values are 0.98 and 0.99 the corresponding Z_{ij} values are 2.054 and 2.326 respectively, where as, if p_{ij} values are 0.50 and 0.51 the Z_{ij} values are 0.000 and 0.025 respectively. In other words for the difference of 0.01 from 0.98 to 0.99 in p_{ij} values, the difference in Z_{ij} values is 0.272 where as for difference of 0.01 from 0.50 to 0.51 of p_{ij} values, the difference in Z_{ij} values is 0.025. If the number of judges are more say more than 200 then even higher value of p_{ij} such as 0.98, 0.99 and 1.00 and lower values such as 0.02, 0.01 and 0.00 may be included for computing scale values of statements or stimuli.

For example, the P-matrix for 7 statements based on 90 judges is given in Table 5.7.

Table 5.7 P-matrix.

Statements	1	2	3	4	5	6	7
1	0.500	0.942	0.958	0.986	0.991	1.000	0.987
2	0.058	0.500	0.584	0.814	0.862	0.926	0.956
3	0.042	0.416	0.500	0.752	0.904	0.910	0.941
4	0.014	0.186	0.248	0.500	0.768	0.865	0.927
5	0.009	0.138	0.096	0.232	0.500	0.742	0.843
6	0.000	0.074	0.090	0.135	0.258	0.500	0.836
7	0.013	0.044	0.059	0.073	0.157	0.164	0.500
Total	**0.636**	**2.300**	**2.535**	**3.492**	**4.440**	**5.107**	**5.990**

From Table 5.7, it can be observed that the comparison between statement 1 and statements 4, 5, 6, and 7 are having higher p_{ij} values which are more than 0.98 and having lower p_{ij} values which are less than 0.02. when statement 1 was compared with statements 4, 5, 6, 7. The p_{ij} values which are greater than 0.98 and also values which are lower than 0.02 are deleted for finding Z-matrix as these values are considered extreme. The Z-matrix after deleting these values are given in Table 5.8

Table 5.8 Z-matrix

Statements	1	2	3	4	5	6	7
1	0.000	1.572	1.728				
2	– 1.572	0.000	0.212	0.893	1.089	1.447	1.706
3	– 1.728	– 0.212	0.000	0.681	1.305	1.341	1.563
4		– 0.893	– 0.681	0.000	0.732	1.103	1.454
5		– 1.089	– 1.305	– 0.732	0.000	0.650	1.007
6		– 1.447	– 1.341	– 1.103	– 0.650	0.000	0.978
7		– 1.706	– 1.563	– 1.454	– 1.007	– 0.978	0.000

Here $Z_{21} - Z_{11} = (\bar{S}_2 - \bar{S}_1) - (\bar{S}_1 - \bar{S}_1) = \bar{S}_2 - \bar{S}_1$

$$Z_{22} - Z_{12} = (\bar{S}_2 - \bar{S}_2) - (\bar{S}_1 - \bar{S}_2) = \bar{S}_2 - \bar{S}_1$$

$$Z_{23} - Z_{13} = (\bar{S}_2 - \bar{S}_3) - (\bar{S}_1 - \bar{S}_3) = \bar{S}_2 - \bar{S}_1$$

$$Z_{2j} - Z_{1j} = (\bar{S}_2 - \bar{S}_j) - (\bar{S}_1 - \bar{S}_j) = \bar{S}_2 - \bar{S}_1$$

If we take the summation of above expressions

$$\sum_j (Z_{2j} - Z_{1j}) = n\bar{S}_2 - n\bar{S}_1$$

$$\frac{1}{n}\sum (Z_{2j} - Z_{1j}) = \bar{S}_2 - \bar{S}_1 = D_{21} \quad \text{(say)}$$

Similarly, we can write

$$D_{32} = \bar{S}_3 - \bar{S}_2$$

$$D_{43} = \bar{S}_4 - \bar{S}_3$$

In general

$$D_{i,\ i-1} = \bar{S}_i - \bar{S}_{i-1}$$

If $\bar{S}_1$ is taken as origin i.e. O then

$$D_{21} = \bar{S}_2 - \bar{S}_1 = \bar{S}_2 - 0 = \bar{S}_2$$

$$D_{32} = \bar{S}_3 - \bar{S}_2$$

$$D_{32} + \bar{S}_2 = \bar{S}_3$$

$$D_{32} + D_{21} = \bar{S}_3$$

Similarly, we have $D_{43} + D_{32} + D_{21} = \bar{S}_4$

The differences in columns of Z-matrix in Table 5.8 were computed and presented in Table 5.9. The differences are obtained only whenever the values are present in both the columns, otherwise they are left blank. The D_{ij} matrix is given in Table 5.9.

Table 5.9 (D- matrix)

Statements	D_{21}	D_{32}	D_{43}	D_{54}	D_{65}	D_{76}
	(2-1)	(3-2)	(4-3)	(5-4)	(6-5)	(7-6)
1	1.572	0.156				
2	1.572	0.212	0.681	0.196	0.358	0.259
3	1.516	0.212	0.681	0.624	0.036	0.222
4		0.212	0.681	0.732	0.371	0.351
5		– 0.216	0.573	0.732	0.650	0.357
6		0.106	0.238	0.453	0.650	0.978
7		0.143	0.109	0.447	0.029	0.978
Total	**3**	**7**	**6**	**6**	**6**	**6**
n	**4.600**	**0.825**	**2.963**	**3.184**	**2.094**	**3.145**
Mean	**1.553**	**0.118**	**0.494**	**0.531**	**0.349**	**0.524**

The scale values of different statements are obtained by using the relationship given above i.e. $D_{32} + D_{21} = \bar{S}_3$, $D_{43} + D_{32} + D_{21} = \bar{S}_4$, $\bar{S}_1 = 0$ and $D_{21} = \bar{S}_2$. The scale values are presented in Table 5.10.

Table 5.10 (Scale Values)

Statements	1 $\bar{S}_1$	2 $\bar{S}_2$	3 $\bar{S}_3$	4 $\bar{S}_4$	5 $\bar{S}_5$	6 $\bar{S}_6$	7 $\bar{S}_7$
Scale values	0.000	1.553	1.671	2.165	2.696	3.045	3.569

From Table 5.10, it can be observed that the scale values are obtained by taking $\bar{S}_1 = 0.000$, $\bar{S}_2 = 0.000 + 1.553$, $\bar{S}_3 = 0.000 + 1.553 + 0.118$ and so on. In other words the values of D_{21}, D_{32}, D_{43} etc., are added cumulatively to obtain scale values.

The method used for developing scale values in this section can be used for the complete Z-matrix also and we can obtain same scale values except that the present method gives the scale differences of adjacent statements whereas earlier method gives scale values as deviations of mean of all the scale values. In both cases $\bar{S}_1$ is taken as '0' on psychological continuum and $\bar{S}_1$ is the scale value of the statement with lowest scale value.

In both methods, the ordinal scale measurement has been converted into interval scale.

5.6 Test of Significance

Test of significance is applied in order to test whether the difference between observed proportions i.e. p_{ij}s and theoretical or expected proportions obtained through normal approximation i.e. p_{ij}s are significant statistically or it is merely due to sampling variation. In other words the scale values obtained for different statements are valid or not can be tested. The chi-square test is used in testing the null hypothesis that there is no significant difference between p_{ij} and p'_{ij} values. The alternate hypothesis is that there is significant difference between p_{ij} and p'_{ij} values. In using the chi-square (χ^2) test Arc sin or angular transformation is used for p_{ij} and p_{ij}^1 values. If the original p_{ij} values follow Binomial distribution where mean is related with variance then variance will change from one statement to another statement. In such case Angular transformation of $\sin^{-1}\sqrt{p_{ij}}$ will be used instead of 'p_{ij}' so that transformed data follow approximately normal distribution with variance equal to

$$\sigma_\theta^2 = \frac{821}{N}$$

Where $\theta_{ij} = \sin^{-1}\sqrt{p_{ij}}$ and N is the total number of judges upon which p_{ij} values are based. The angular values corresponding to p_{ij} values are presented in Table of Appendix. The angular values for the p_{ij} values given in Table 5.2 are given in Table 5.11. Here the angular values are taken for converting p_{ij} values into percentages.

Table 5.11 (θ_{ij}-Values)

Statements	**1**	**2**	**3**	**4**	**5**
1					
2	39.23				
3	21.81	64.38			
4	30.85	45.00	56.04		
5	39.23	41.44	34.02	63.44	

Similarly angular values θ'_{ij} are obtained by converting p'_{ij} values given in Table 5.5 into percentages by entering Table in Appendix. The θ'_{ij} values are given in Table 5.12.

Table 5.12 (θ'_{ij} Values)

Statements	**1**	**2**	**3**	**4**	**5**
1					
2	30.66				
3	34.02	48.50			
4	30.66	44.94	41.44		
5	34.70	49.20	45.69	49.26	

The χ^2 formula is given as

$$\chi^2 = \sum_{i=1}^{5}\sum_{j=1}^{5} \frac{(\theta_{ij} - \theta'_{ij})^2}{821/N}$$

With (n – 1) (n – 2)/2 d.f.

Where θ_{ij} is the angular value for (i, j)-th cell in Table of θ_{ij} values. Similarly θ'_{ij} is the angular value of (i, j)-th cell in Table of θ'_{ij} values where i, j = 1, 2, . . . 5. The values of differences ($\theta_{ij} - \theta_{ij}'$) are presented in Table 5.13.

Table 5.13 $\left[\left(\theta_{ij} - \theta'_{ij}\right)\text{Values}\right]$

Statements	1	2	3	4	5
1					
2	8.57				
3	–12.21	15.88			
4	0.19	0.06	14.60		
5	4.53	7.76	11.67	14.18	

$$\sum\sum\left(\theta_{ij} - \theta'_{ij}\right)^2 = (8.57)^2 + (-12.21)^2 + \ldots + (14.18)^2$$

$$= 1105.9029$$

$$\chi^2 = \frac{1105.9025}{821/80} = 107.76$$

Conclusion

Here χ^2 (calculated) value i.e. 107.76 is greater than χ^2 (tabulated) value i.e. 18.307 with 5(5 – 1)/2 = 10 d.f. at 5 per cent level of significance. Therefore the null hypothesis is rejected. Hence it can be concluded that there is significant difference between p_{ij} and p'_{Ij} values. The scale values obtained may not be valid and some more statements have to be framed for obtaining scale values in this example.

It may be noted that the angular values are given for off diagonal elements in Table 5.11 and 5.12. However, the values for other off diagonal will be the values after subtracting from 90^0. For example, θ_{12} = 39.23 then θ_{21} = 90 – 39.23 = 50.77 in Table 5.11. Therefore the differences of $\theta_{ij} - \theta_{ij}'$ for other off diagonal will remain same. Hence there is no need to calculate the differences $\theta_{ij} - \theta_{ij}'$ of other off diagonal.

5.7 Discriminal Dispersion

Sometimes it may be necessary to know the discriminal variation of each statement framed after finding scale value. In other words the standard deviations of $\bar{S}_i$ values can be found out for each statement or stimuli. Thurstone (1932) developed the formula of standard deviation of i-th stimuli or statement as

$$\sigma_i = a\left(\frac{1}{Vi}\right) - 1$$

where $$a = \frac{2n}{\sum_{i=1}^{n}\left(\frac{1}{V_i}\right)}$$

and n = number of statements

$$Vi = \sqrt{\frac{1}{n}\sum_{j=1}^{n}\left(Z_{ij} - \overline{Z}_i\right)^2} = \sqrt{\frac{1}{n}\left[\sum Z_{ij}^2 - \frac{\left(\sum Z_{ij}\right)^2}{n}\right]}$$

Where Z_{ij} is the normal deviate value of p_{ij} for (i, j) –th entry in the P matrix.

$$\overline{Z}_i. = \frac{1}{n}\sum_{j=1}^{n} Z_{ij} = \text{ mean of i-th column in Z - matrix.}$$

The computation of standard deviation of $\overline{S_i}$ values is illustrated here with the example given in Section 5.3.1. The Z-matrix given in Table 5.3 is presented here in Table 5.14.

Table 5.14 (Z-matrix)

Statements	**1**	**2**	**3**	**4**	**5**
1	0.000	0.253	1.094	0.637	0.253
2	–0.253	0.000	–0.885	0.000	0.159
3	–1.089	0.889	0.000	–0.487	0.490
4	–0.634	0.000	0.490	0.000	–0.842
5	–0.253	–0.156	–0.487	0.842	0.000
(1) $\sum_j Z_{ij}^2$	1.716	0.879	2.457	1.32	1.038
(2) $\sum_j Z_{ij}$	–2.229	0.986	0.212	0.992	0.060
(3) $\frac{\left(\sum_j Z_{ij}\right)^2}{n}$	0.994	0.194	0.009	0.197	0.0007
(4) $\sum Z_{ij}^2 - \frac{\left(\sum_j Z_{ij}\right)^2}{n}$	0.772	0.685	2.448	1.155	1.037

Table 5.14 *Contd...*

Statements	1	2	3	4	5
(5) V^2	0.154	0.137	0.490	0.231	0.207
(6) V	0.392	0.370	0.700	0.481	0.455
(7) $\frac{1}{V}$	2.551	2.702	1.429	2.079	2.198
(8) σ_i	1.327	1.464	0.303	0.896	1.005

The standard deviations on discriminal dispersions of the five statements are given by the formula.

$$\sigma_i = a\left(\frac{1}{V_i}\right) - 1 \qquad \text{for } i = 1, 2, \ldots, 5$$

The values of σ_i are presented in the last row i.e., 8th in the Table 5.14 . Here

$$a = \frac{2n}{\sum_{i=1}^{n}\left(\frac{1}{V_i}\right)} = \frac{2 \times 5}{10.959} = 0.912$$

As a check $\sum_{i=1}^{n} \sigma_i = n$. In other words the sum of the standard deviations of scale values or statements stimuli should be equal to the number of statements. Here

$\sum \sigma_i$ = 4.995 and which is equal to number of statements i.e., 5.

It may be noted that all standard deviations of the scale values of the statements are almost equal except for the statement 3 and which is considerably low.

5.8 Equal-Interval Method

The pairwise comparison method can be used effectively for finding the scale values of the statements when the number of statements are less. If the number of statement are 20 then each judge has to make 20 (20–1)/2 = 190 comparative judgments. Similarly if the number of statements are 30 then each judge has to make 30 (30 – 1)/2 = 435 comparative judgments and so on. Therefore it is a tedius and time consuming process and no judge would like to spare so much time and energy. Therefore Equal-intervals method was developed by Thurstone and Chave (1929) when the number of statements is large for finding the scale values of the statements.

In this method each statement has to be classified into 11 categories starting from 'most unfavourable' to most favourable. These categories are marked on cards with letters A to K where A card represents most 'unfavourable' F card represents 'neutral' and K card represents 'most favourable' attitude towards the statements. Judges are asked to keep the statement on any one of the cards from A to K. The difference between each card is assumed to be equal with respect to attitude. For example, the difference between A to B, B to C etc., are assumed to be equal with respect to attitude towards statement. This is illustrated in Fig. 5.1.

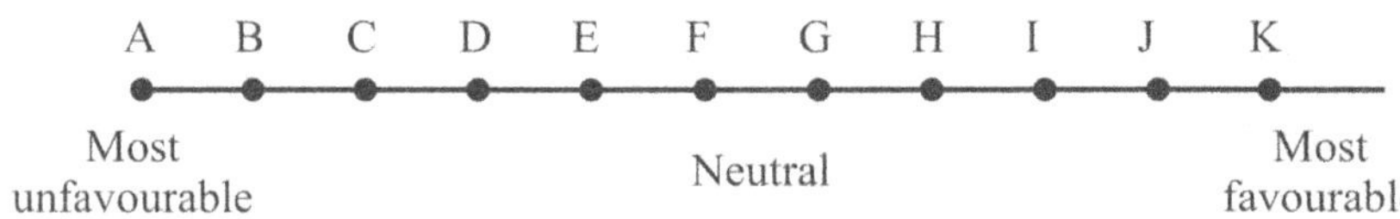

Fig. 5.1 Equal-appearing continuum.

Each card from A to K are then serically numbered from 1 to 11. Here A is given 1, B is given 2 and so on, K is given 11 and F as 6. The number of judges keeping a particular statement on these letter cards is considered as frequency of that letter card. The 'median' value of this frequency distribution is taken as scale value of that statement. Here the computation of scale value of a statement is illustrated by considering 150 judges. The frequency distribution is given in Table 5.15.

Table 5.15 Frequency distribution.

	Category										
Letter	**A**	**B**	**C**	**D**	**E**	**F**	**G**	**H**	**I**	**J**	**K**
Number	1	2	3	4	5	6	7	8	9	10	11
Class	0.5-1.5	1.5-2.5	2.5-3.5	3.5-4.5	4.5-5.5	5.5-6.5	6.5-7.5	7.5-8.5	8.5-9.5	9.5-10.5	10.5-11.5
Frequency	2	3	8	7	10	40	32	25	14	6	3
Cum frequency	2	5	13	20	30	70	102	127	141	147	150

The formula of 'median' is given as

$$M = l + \frac{\left(N/2 - m\right) c}{f}$$

where l = lower limit of the median class, N/2 = median number, m = cumulative frequency just proceeding to the median class, f = frequency of the median class and c = class interval of the median class.

Median class is that class wherein cumulative frequency N/2 exists.

Here N/2 = 150/2 = 75 exists in the class 6.5 – 7.5 and therefore it is a median class. Hence l = 6.5, N/2 = 75, m = 70, f = 32, c = 1

$$M = 6.5 + \frac{(75 - 70)}{32} = 6.7$$

The median value i.e., M = 6.7 is the scale value of the statement considered by 150 judges. Similarly, scale values can be computed for all the statements in the study. However, if a particular judge is placing 30 or more statements on any one of the 11 cards then that judge is not considered in the calculation of scale value of a statement assuming that the said judge is not careful enough in placing the statement.

5.8.1 Inter-Quartile Range

In order to know the dispersion of the scale value obtained by median, inter-quartile range is used. If Q_1 and Q_3 are 1st and 3rd quartiles respectively, then inter quartile range is given as

$$\text{I. Q. R.} = (Q_3 - Q_1)$$

where Q_1 and Q_3 are computed by using the formula as

$$Q_1 = l_1 + \frac{\left(\frac{N}{4} - m_1\right) c_1}{f_1}$$

where l_1 = lower limit of the 1st quartile or Q_1 class, N/4 = Q_1 number, m_1 = cumulative frequency just preceding to the Q_1 class, f_1 = frequency of Q_1 class and c_1 = class interval of Q_1 class where Q_1 class is that class wherein cumulative frequency N/4 exists.

Here $\frac{N}{4} = \frac{150}{4} = 37.5$ which exists in (5.5 to 6.5) class and it is called Q_1 class.

Hence $l_1 = 5.5$, $\frac{N}{4} = 37.5$, $m_1 = 30$, $f_1 = 40$, $c = 1$

$$Q_1 = 5.5 + \frac{(37.5 - 30)}{40} = 5.7$$

Similarly, Q_3 value is obtained by using the formula as

$$Q_3 = l_3 + \frac{\left(\frac{3N}{4} - m_3\right) c_3}{f_3}$$

where l_3 = lower limit of 3rd quartile i.e., Q_3 class, $\frac{3N}{4} = Q_3$ number, m_3 = cumulative frequency just preceding to the Q_3 class, f_3 = frequency of Q_3 class, c_3 class interval of the Q_3 class and Q_3 class is that class wherein cumulative frequency $\frac{3N}{4}$ exists. Here $\frac{3N}{4} = 3 \times \frac{150}{4} = 112.5$ and 112.5 lies in the class interval (7.5 to 8.5).

Hence (7.5 to 8.5) class is called Q_3 class. Hence $l_3 = 7.5$, $\frac{3N}{4} = 112.5$, $m_3 = 102$, $f_3 = 25$, $c = 1$

$$Q_3 = 7.5 + \frac{(112.5 - 102) \times 1}{25} = 7.9$$

The inter quartile range I.Q.R = 7.9 – 5.7 = 2.2. The dispersion measure value of the scale value of the statement under study is 2.2. Similarly, the inter quartile range values can be calculated for all the scale values of concerned statements. If I.Q.R value is large for a particular statement in comparison to I.Q.R. value of another statement then the first statement is considered as more ambiguous in comparison to 2nd statement.

It may be noted that the scale, Q_1 and Q_3 values can also be obtained using graphical method. The graph can be drawn by taking numbers 1 to 11 on X-axis and corresponding cumulative frequencies on Y-axis. If the lines are drawn parallel to X-axis at points N/2, N/4 and 3N/4 on Y-axis to the curve and the corresponding X-coordinate points are scale, Q_1 and

Q_3 values respectively. However, these may be approximate unless the curves are drawn accurately according to scale. For illustration purpose the cumulative frequency curve is shown in Fig. 5.2 for the data given in Table 5.15.

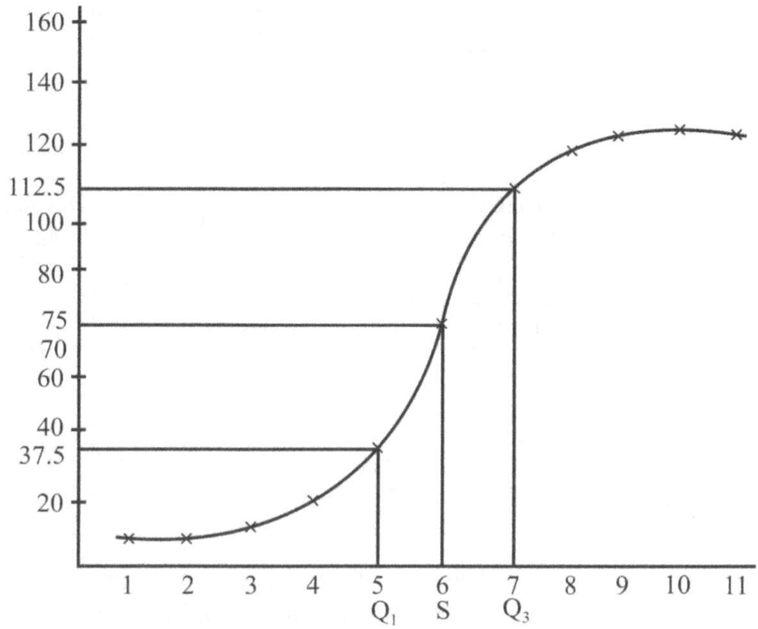

Fig. 5.2 Cumulative frequency curve (less than)

5.9 Summated Ratings

When the number of statements to be judged with respect to favorableness or unfavorableness in comparison to others, the finding of scale values by previous methods is laborious and cumbersome. Here the normal deviate weighting method is described in such situation. It is assumed that the statements can be classified into favorable and un-favorable classes. Here favorable statement is given to a subject or judge to give his or her opinion into say five categories such as strongly agree, agree, undecided, disagree and strongly disagree. In order to analyze the data obtained from such responses, it is required to convert them into numerical values such as 4, 3, 2, 1, 0 respectively in a physical continuum. In other words, the 'ordinal measurement' is converted into interval 'measurement' for amicable to statistical analysis. Normal deviate weighting is adopted for this purpose. This method is illustrated by taking an example.

Example: The favorable statement is given to 150 subjects to express their response in five categories such as strongly disagree, disagree, undecided, agree and strongly agree. The procedure of calculations are presented in Table 5.16 starting from proportions of subjects in row (1) and soon.

Table 5.16

	Strongly Disagree	**Disagree**	**Undecided**	**Agree**	**Strongly agree**
1. p	0.12	0.28	0.22	0.24	0.14
2. cp	0.12	0.40	0.62	0.86	1.00
3. Mid-point cp	0.06	0.26	0.51	0.73	0.93
4. Z	– 1.555	– 0.643	0.025	0.613	1.476
5. Z + 1.555	0	0.912	1.58	2.163	3.031
6. Z rounded	0	1	2	2	3

In row (2) of the above Table 5.16, the cumulative proportions are computed and presented. In row (3) Mid-point cp values are computed as follows.

$$0.12 + \frac{1}{2}(0.28) = 0.26$$

$$0.40 + \frac{1}{2}(0.22) = 0.51$$

and so on.

In row (3), the normal deviate values Z are presented by consulting table of proportions and normal deviate values given in appendix. In row (5) the values of Z are converted into positive values by adding the highest negative value i.e., – 1.555 to all the values in row (4). The Z values are rounded and presented in row (6). The weights obtained nearest to the integer are 0, 1, 2, 2 and 3. These values are close to the values 0, 1, 2, 3 and 4. Likert (1932) found that the weights obtained by normal deviate method weighting and simple numerical values 0, 1, 2, 3 and 4 for the five categories is highly correlated and the correlation coefficient was 0.99. Similarly, the normal deviate weighting method can be used for unfavorable statements with 'strongly agree' category gets 4, agree category 3, undecided 2, disagree 1 and strongly disagree 0.

5.9.1 Selection of Statements

In order to screen the statements whether they are to be included in the set for presenting to the subjects, t-values are calculated. If the t-values of statements are large then they are included in the study according to that order. Otherwise those statements which are having low t-values are not included. The t-values are calculated as described in the following procedure.

The frequency distribution of scores based upon the responses of the subjects is considered. Here 30 percent (say) of the subjects with high scores and 30 percent of the subjects with low scores are considered. Their frequency distributions are presented in Table 5.17.

Table 5.17

	High group				Low group			
Category	**Weight (x_1)**	**f**	**fx_1**	**fx_1^2**	**Weight x_2**	**f**	**fx_2**	**fx_2^2**
Strongly agree	4	12	48	192	4	3	12	48
Agree	3	18	54	162	3	5	15	45
Undecided	2	10	20	40	2	14	28	56
Disagree	1	4	4	4	1	17	17	17
Strongly disagree	0	1	0	0	0	6	0	0
Total		45	126	398		45	72	166

The t-values are computed using the formula as

$$t = \frac{\bar{x}_1 - \bar{x}_2}{\sqrt{\frac{s_1^2}{n_1} + \frac{s_2^2}{n_2}}}$$

where $\bar{x}_1$ = Mean of 1st group i.e., high group here

$\bar{x}_2$ = Mean of 2nd group i.e., low group here.

$$s_1^2 = \frac{1}{(n_1 - 1)} \left[\Sigma\, fx_1^2 - \frac{(\Sigma\, fx_1)^2}{n_1} \right]$$

$$s_2^2 = \frac{1}{(n_2 - 1)} \left[\Sigma\, fx_2^2 - \frac{(\Sigma\, fx_2)^2}{n_2} \right]$$

are the variations of the distributions of responses of 'high' and 'low' groups respectively.

Here $$\bar{x}_1 = \frac{\Sigma\, fx_1}{\Sigma\, f} = \frac{126}{45} = 2.8$$

$$\bar{x}_2 = \frac{\Sigma\, fx_2}{\Sigma\, f} = \frac{72}{45} = 1.5$$

$$s_1^2 = \frac{1}{(45-1)} \left[398 - \frac{(126)^2}{45} \right] = \frac{45.2}{44} = 1.03$$

$$s_2^2 = \frac{1}{(45-1)} \left[166 - \frac{(72)^2}{45} \right] = \frac{50.8}{44} = 1.15$$

$$t = \frac{2.8 - 1.6}{\sqrt{\frac{1.03}{45} + \frac{1.15}{45}}} = \frac{1.2}{0.22} = 5.45$$

In this manner, all the t-values are calculated for all the statements and they are arranged in ascending or descending order. Then 20 to 25 statements are selected with high t-vales. In selecting high t-values, we are using the type of item analysis and the selected statements are useful for opinion study.

5.9.2 Summated Rating

The sum of the scores given by a subject or judge for all the statements is called summated ratings while each score for a statement given by subject is called 'rating'. For example, the scores of 4, 3, 2, 1, 0 given to each statement by a subject is called 'rating' and the total score given by the same subject for all the statements is known as 'summated rating'.

If a subject obtains a score of '0' on a 25 item summated rated scale then he or she is having a unfavorable attitude towards favorable statement and favorable attitude towards unfavorable statement. In other words the subject strongly agree with unfavorable statement and 'strongly disagree' with favorable statement. Similarly, if the score is 100 then the attitude of the subject is favorable to favorable statement and unfavorable to unfavorable statement. However, if the score of the subjects falls between 0 and 100 then it is somewhat difficult to interpret the attitude of the subject more clearly. For comparing subjects with respect to their attitude towards a statement or object, if a score of a particular subject or judge is more than the average scores of all the subjects then it can be interpreted as that subject is having more favorable attitude towards that statement and if that subjects is having less score than the average score of all the subjects then that subject is having un-favorable attitude towards that statement or object.

5.10 Scalogram Analysis

It is a method to examine whether the sets of statements framed for determining the attitudes are accurate or not. Also this method can be used for evaluating the scales already developed or not. This accuracy is measured by 'coefficient of reproducibility'. For example if the coefficient of reproducibility is 0.90 then the proportion of errors in framing the statements is 1 – 0.90 = 0.10 i.e., 10 percent. In other words it can be described as the degree of accuracy with which the responses of statements can be reproduced.

CHAPTER 6

Elementary Decision Theory

In daily life everyone has to take decision with respect to several aspects of life. For example, a student has to take a decision with respect to which type of course of study he or she has to persue after 10 + 2 educational level. Similarly a factory owner has to take a decision which type of product he has to produce to get maximum profit. Also a person has to take a decision which type of job he has to opt, when two or more options are available. A new entrepreneur has to take decision with regard to which type of industry he or she has to establish and where to establish and when to establish etc. Also consumer has to take a decision which brand he or she has to purchase, where to purchase and when to purchase etc. Producer expects maximum profit from the sale of produce and consumer expects quality product with reasonable price.

Decision theory provides some methods which are helpful in taking decisions for producers, consumers, administrators etc. The decisions have to be taken sometimes by 'individuals' or sometimes by group of persons such as governing body, executive committee, cabinet, management committee etc.

The decision making can be done in a situation of certainty where every option is well defined. For example, if there are three brands of cars where the mileage, capacity, durability and sustainability on different road conditions, availability of service points in the country, cost of each brand, driving comfort etc., is known beforehand then decision making is easy and certain. This situation is known as deterministic situation. This situation does not involve any risk or probabilistic criteria.

Linear programming is one of the important techniques used in deterministic situation.

6.1 Linear Programming: Graphical Method

In a linear programming method either two or more activities or candidates are competing for available resources in terms of money or time. In this case graphical method can be used for solving the problem.

For example, a manufacturing company of screws wants to produce two sizes of screws A and B. This is illustrated with the following data presented in Table 6.1.

Table 6.1 Process time by size and department

Section	Size (length)		Available time (hrs)
	A	B	
Cutting	8.0	4.0	2,000
Threading	10.0	14.0	3,500
Packing	2.0	1.0	540
Profit per unit	₹ 20	₹ 30	

From Table 6.1, it can be stated that each unit of product A requires 8.0 units of cutting capacity and each unit of B requires 4 units of cutting capacity and the maximum amount of A and maximum amount of B to be produced should be such that the total demand on the capacity department should not exceed 2000 units. Therefore any specific combination of production of A and B which does not exceed the total allotment of time i.e., 2000 units is a possible solution of this problem. Let *x* and *y* be the number of units to be produced of the products A and B respectively then the inequality for the cutting department is

$$8.0\,x + 4.0\,y \leq 2000 \qquad \text{.....(6.1)}$$

Similarly for the inequalities for threading and packing departments are

$$10.0\,x + 14.0\,y \leq 3{,}500 \qquad \text{.....(6.2)}$$

$$2.0\,x + 1.0\,y \leq 540 \qquad \text{.....(6.3)}$$

The objective in this problem is to obtain one pair of values of x and y resulting in maximum possible level of the function 20x + 30y i.e. maximum possible profit. The inequalities given in eqs. (6.1), (6.2) and (6.3) are presented in graphs as Fig. 6.1, Fig. 6.2 and Fig. 6.3 respectively.

In (6.1) if $x = 0,\ y = \dfrac{2000}{4} = 500$

if $y = 0,\ x = \dfrac{2000}{8.0} = 250$

The two points A(0, 500) and B(250, 0) are represented in graph in Fig. 6.1.

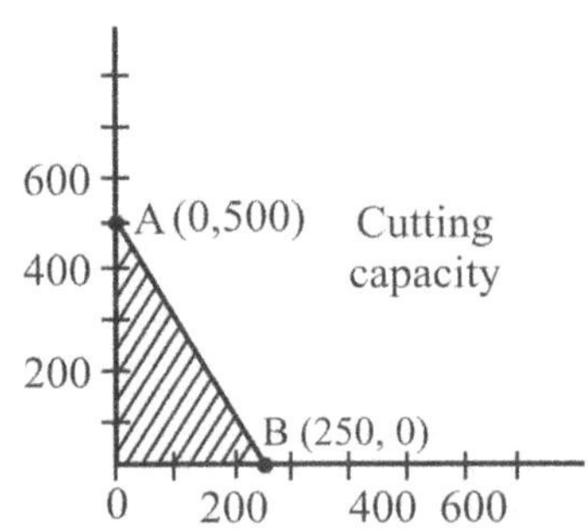

Fig. 6.1

If we exclude negative production i.e. x ≥ 0 and y ≥ 0, the shaded area in Fig. 6.1 gives the possible solutions for cutting department.

Similarly, the two points C(0, 250) and D (350, 0) are represented by graph in Fig. 6.2 for threading department.

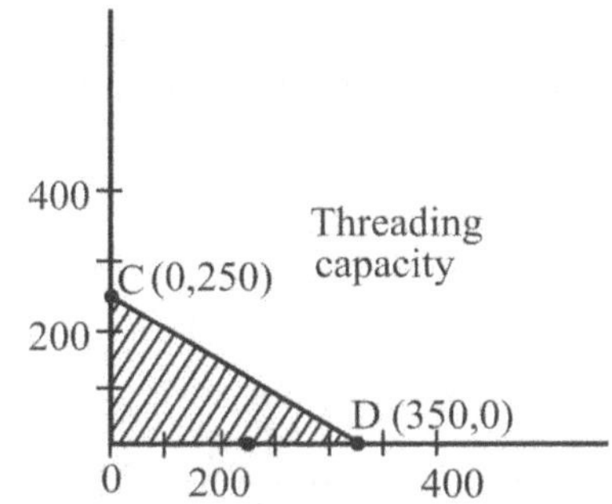

Fig. 6.2

The shaded area in Fig. 6.2 gives the possible solutions for threading capacity.

Also the two points E (0, 540) and F (270, 0) are plotted in graph in Fig. 6.3 for packing capacity.

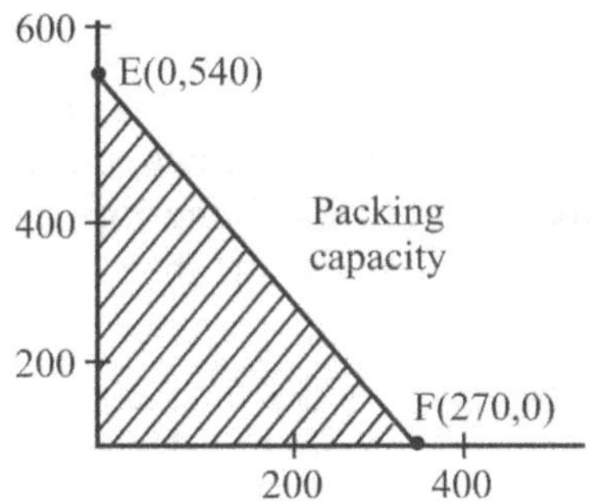

Fig. 6.3

The shaded area in Fig. 6.3 gives the possible non-negative solutions for packing capacity. The figures given in Fig. 6.1, Fig. 6.2 and Fig. 6.3 can be combined and presented in Fig. 6.4.

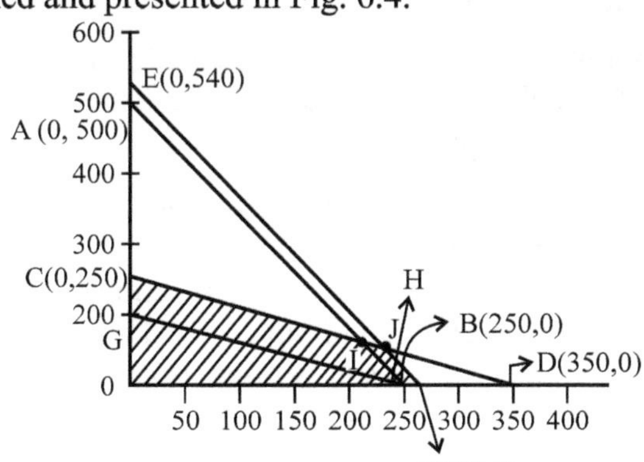

Fig. 6.4

The shaded area in Fig. 6.4 gives the possible non-negative solutions for our problem. Here AB line represents cutting capacity, CD represents threading capacity and EF represents packing capacity and the equations of these lines respectively are:

$$8x + 4y = 2000 \quad .....(6.4)$$

$$10x + 14y = 3500 \quad .....(6.5)$$

$$2x + 1y = 540 \quad .....(6.6)$$

Any point in the shaded area or on the boundary of shaded area of Fig. 6.4 is a possible solution. Therefore it is required to find out at least one point in the shaded area which provides maximum profit to the company.

Suppose we take points G(0, 200) and H(300, 0) in shaded area then the expected profits can be

$$0 \times 20 + 200 \times 30 = ₹\ 6000$$

$$300 \times 20 + 0 \times 30 = ₹\ 6000$$

If the two points G and H are joined then the line GH is called 'Isoprofit' line. These lines can be drawn closer to the boundary of shaded area to get maximum profits. If the line touches corner points of shaded area or one of its boundary points then it is assumed that optimum solution is attained.

In Fig. 6.4, it is found that I is the intersecting point of lines CD and EF. If we solve the equations CD and EF, the point 'I' can be obtained.

$$10x + 14y = 3500$$

$$2x + 1y = 540$$

Solving (6.5) and (6.6) we obtain point 'I' as (222.56, 88.89) and which can be taken as (223, 89).

Hence the optimum solution is to produce 223 units of x and 89 units of y. The profit to be obtained by producing these units is

$$20\ (223) + 30\ (89) = ₹\ 7130$$

Substituting x = 223 and y = 89 in the inequalities (6.1), (6.2) and (6.3), it can be seen that this program fully utilizes cutting, threading and packing departments. However this program requires more capacity for cutting department for getting maximum profit. Therefore the intersection point of AB and CD lines i.e. 'J' can be used as an optimum solution.

$$8x + 4y = 2000$$

$$10x + 14y = 3500$$

The intersecting point for the two lines AB and CD is obtained as (194, 111) and this point fully utilizes all the departments of cutting, threading and packing departments. The profit to be obtained for this optimum solution is

$$20\ (194) + 30\ (111) = ₹\ 7210$$

It can be observed that profit obtained for point 'J' is more than at point 'I'. Therefore 'J' point i.e. (194, 111) is the final optimum solution for this program.

6.1.1 Graphical Method (Three dimensional case)

In two-dimensional case example in Table 6.1, two sizes A and B are considered. In three dimensional case, three sizes A, B and C are considered. This case is presented in Table 6.2.

Table 6.2

Section	Size (length)			Available time (hrs)
	A	B	C	
Cutting	8.0	4.0	3.0	2,000
Threading	10.0	14.0	5.0	3,500
Packing	2.0	1.0	4.0	540
Profit per unit	₹ 20	₹ 30	₹ 40	

The x, y and z can denote the products A, B and C respectively. The data in the Table 6.2 can be expressed as inequalities for each section as

$$8x + 4y + 3z \leq 2000 \qquad .....(6.7)$$

$$10x + 14y + 5z \leq 3{,}500 \qquad .....(6.8)$$

$$2x + 1y + 4z \leq 540 \qquad .....(6.9)$$

where x, y, z ≥ 0.

From equation (6.7), if y, z = 0 then x = 250

if x, z = 0 then y = 500

if x, y = 0 then z = 666.7

The three points give A B C plane in Fig. 6.5

From equation (6.8) if y, z = 0 then x = 350

if x, z = 0 then y = 250

if x, y = 0 then z = 700

The above three points provide D E F plane in Fig. 6.5.

Similarly from equation (6.9) if y, z = 0, x = 270

if x, z = 0, y = 540

if x, y = 0, z = 135

The above three points provide G H I plane in Fig. 6.5.

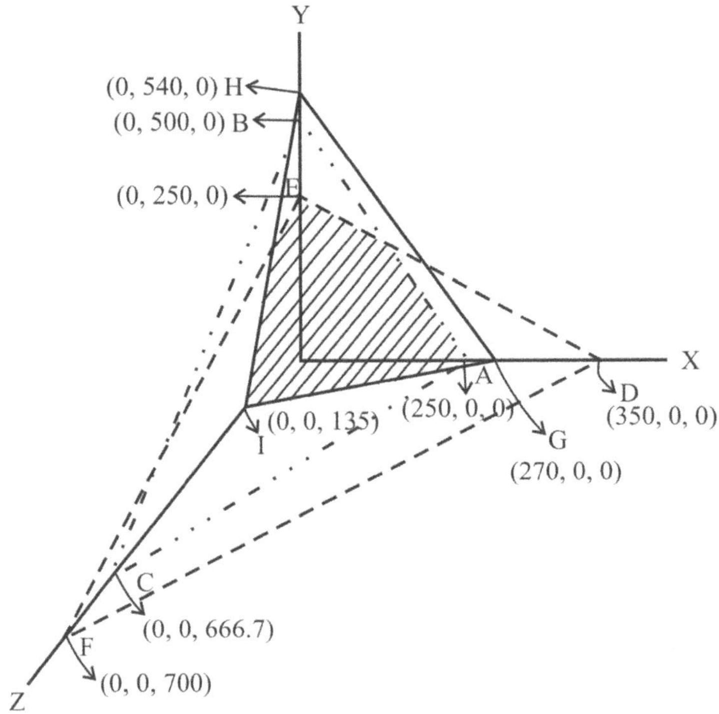

Fig. 6.5

The three planes ABC, DEF and GHI within three axes x, y, z and $x \geq 0$, $y \geq 0$, $z \geq 0$ form a three dimensional solid space containing all possible solutions to the problem.

The feasible optimum solution can be obtained from the surface containing parallel lines away from the origin towards positive quadrant. As we move away from the origin some particular plane touches the outerspace and most remote corners. The space with parallel lines in Fig. 6.5 gives the feasible solutions of the problem. The plane touches the outer corners will give the optimum solution to this problem for providing maximum profit. The coordinates of this point can be obtained by solving the following three equations

$$8x + 4y + 3z = 2000 \quad .....(6.10)$$

$$10x + 14y + 5z = 3,500 \quad .....(6.11)$$

$$2x + 1y + 4z = 540 \quad .....(6.12)$$

By solving equations (6.10), (6.11) and (6.12), the coordinates of the point are obtained as

$$x = 190.7,\ y = 109.4 \text{ and } z = 12.3$$

Substituting these values in (6.6), (6.7) and (6.8), it is seen that this program fully utilizes the capacities of all the sections of the production unit. Further the profit by producing units such as $x = 190.7$, $y = 109.4$ and $z = 12.3$ is given as

$$190.7\,(20) + 109.4\,(30) + 12.3\,(40) = ₹\ 7,588.$$

The amount ₹ 7588 can be considered as maximum profit as the production unit utilizes all the capacities of all sections fully.

6.2 Simplex Method I

It is always possible to find a optimum solution to the problem, if it exists by this method. This method is systematic and easy to obtain optimum solution. This method is illustrated by taking a problem given in section 6.1.1.

Table 6.3

Section	**Size**			**Available time (hrs)**
	A	**B**	**C**	
Cutting	8.0	4.0	3.0	2,000
Threading	10.0	14.0	5.0	3,500
Packing	2.0	1.0	4.0	540
Profit per unit	₹ 20	₹ 30	₹ 40	

The data in Table 6.3 can be written in the form of inequalities as

$$8x + 4y + 3z \leq 2000 \quad .....(6.13)$$

$$10x + 14y + 5z \leq 3500 \quad .....(6.14)$$

$$2x + 1y + 4z \leq 540 \quad .....(6.15)$$

Let us add slack variables s_1, s_2 and s_3 to each of equations (6.13), (6.14) and (6.15) to convert into equalities. The problem can be stated as to maximize the profit.

$$20\,x + 30\,y + 40\,z$$

Subject to conditions

$$8\,x + 4\,y + 3\,z + 1s_1 + 0s_2 + 0s_3 = 2000 \quad .....(6.16)$$

$$10\,x + 14\,y + 5\,z + 0s_1 + 1s_2 + 0s_3 = 3500 \quad .....(6.17)$$

$$2\,x + 1\,y + 4\,z + 0s_1 + 0s_2 + 1s_3 = 540 \quad .....(6.18)$$

where x, y, z ≥ 0 and s_1, s_2, $s_3 \geq 0$.

The above equations can be written in the form of Table 6.4.

Table 6.4

Variables	Coefts	Magnitude	Main body			Identity			
Program	**Profit per unit**	**Qty**	**₹ 20 x**	**₹ 30 y**	**₹ 40 z**	**₹ 20 s_1**	**₹ 30 s_2**	**₹ 40 s_3**	**Net time used per unit**
s_1	0	2000	8	4	3	1	0	0	$\frac{2000}{3} = 666.7$
s_2	0	3500	10	14	5	0	1	0	$\frac{3500}{5} = 700$
s_3	0	540	2	1	4	0	0	1	$\frac{540}{4} = 135$*
Net evaluation row			20	30	40				

From Table 6.4, highest profit column has to be considered first. Here size 'z' which gives highest profit per product i.e. ₹ 40 is chosen. From among the rows, the row which gives lowest value per unit is considered. These are called key column and key rows respectively.

The net evaluation row figures in the bottom of Table 6.4 obtained as follows

$$20 - 0 \times 8 - 0 \times 10 - 0 \times 2 = 20$$

$$30 - 0 \times 4 - 0 \times 14 - 0 \times 1 = 30$$

$$40 - 0 \times 3 - 0 \times 5 - 0 \times 4 = 40$$

The intersection figure of key row and key column is '4'.

Table 6.5

Program	Profit per unit	Qty	₹ 20 x	₹ 30 y	₹ 40 z	s_1	s_2	s_3	Net time used per unit
s_1	0	1595	6.5	3.25	0	1	0	–0.75	$\frac{1595}{3.25}$ = 490.8
s_2	0	2825	7.5	12.75	0	0	1	–1.25	$\frac{2825}{12.75}$ = 221.6
z	40	135	0.5	0.25	1	0	0	0.25	$\frac{40}{0.25}$ = 160*
Net evaluation row			0	20*	0	0	0	–10	

1. The last row in Table 6.5 is obtained by dividing the row values by key number 4. Here s_3 is replaced by 'z' with profit per unit is ₹ 40.
2. The values in the 1st row of Table 6.5 are obtained as follows

$$0-0\times\frac{3}{4} = 0; \quad 2000-540\times\frac{3}{4} = 1595$$

$$8-2\times\frac{3}{4} = 6.5; \quad 4-1\times\frac{3}{4} = 3.25$$

$$3-4\times\frac{3}{4} = 0; \quad 1-0\times\frac{3}{4} = 1$$

$$0-0\times\frac{3}{4} = 0; \quad 0-1\times\frac{3}{4} = -0.75$$

3. The values in the 2nd row of Table 6.5 are obtained as follows

$$3500-540\times\frac{5}{4} = 2825; \quad 10-2\times\frac{5}{4} = 7.5$$

$$14-1\times\frac{5}{4} = 12.75; \quad 5-4\times\frac{5}{4} = 0$$

$$0 - 0 \times \frac{5}{4} = 0; \qquad 1 - 0 \times \frac{5}{4} = 1$$

$$0 - 1 \times \frac{5}{4} = -1.25$$

4. The values in the net evaluation row are obtained as follows

$$20 - 6.5 \times 0 - 7.5 \times 0 - 0.5 \times 40 = 0$$

$$30 - 3.25 \times 0 - 12.75 \times 0 - 0.25 \times 40 = 20$$

$$40 - 0 \times 0 - 0 \times 0 - 1 \times 40 = 0$$

Total profit = 1595 × 0 + 2825 × 0 + 135 × 40 = ₹ 5400/-

Again the key column is to be identified for proceeding to find out the plan which gives more profit than ₹ 5400. The key column is 'y' column since it has maximum net evaluation as 20.

The key row is obtained as s_2 row which is the next lowest after 'z' row in Table 6.5 since 'z' program has been used. The intersection figure of key column and key row is 12.75.

Table 6.6

Program	**Profit per unit**	**Qty**	**₹ 20 x**	**₹ 30 y**	**₹ 40 z**	**0 s_1**	**0 s_2**	**0 s_3**	**Net time used per unit**
s_1	0	874.9	4.59	0	0	1	–0.25	–0.430	
y	30	221.6	0.59	1	0	0	0.08	– 0.098	
z	40	79.6	0.47	0	1	0	–0.02	0.025	
Net evaluation row			–16.5	0	0	0	–1.6	–1.94	

1. The second row in Table 6.6 is obtained by dividing the row values by key number 12.75. Here s_2 is replaced by 'y' with profit per unit is ₹ 30.

2. The values in the 1st row in Table 6.6 are obtained as follows

(i) $0-0\times\frac{3.25}{12.75}=0;$ (ii) $1595\text{-}2825\times\frac{3.25}{12.75}=874.9$

(iii) $6.5-7.5\times\frac{3.25}{12.75}=4.59;$ (iv) $3.25-12.75\times\frac{3.25}{12.75}=0$

(v) $0-0\times\frac{3.25}{12.75}=0;$ (vi) $1-0\times\frac{3.25}{12.75}=1$

(vii) $0-1\times\frac{3.25}{12.75}=-0.25$

3. The values in the 3rd or last row of Table 6.6 are obtained as follows

(i) $40-0\times\frac{0.25}{12.75}=40;$ (ii) $135-2825\times\frac{0.25}{12.75}=79.6$

(iii) $0.5-7.5\times\frac{0.25}{12.75}=0.47;$ (iv) $0.25-12.75\times\frac{0.25}{12.75}=0$

(v) $1-0\times\frac{0.25}{12.75}=1;$ (vi) $0-0\times\frac{0.25}{12.75}=0$

(vii) $0-1\times\frac{0.25}{12.75}=-0.02;$

(viii) $0.25-(-1.25)\times\frac{0.25}{12.75}=0.0245$

Total profit = 874.9 × 0 + 221.6 × 30 + 79.6 × 40 = ₹ 9832

Net evaluation row figures in the bottom of Table 6.6 are obtained as follows

(i) $20-0\times4.59-30\times0.59-40\times0.47=-16.5$

(ii) $30-0\times0-30\times1-40\times0=0$

(iii) $40-0\times0-30\times0-40\times1=0$

(iv) $0-0\times1-30\times0-40\times0=0$

(v) $0-0\times-0.25-30\times0.08-40\times-0.02=-1.6$

(vi) $0-0\times-0.43-30\times0.098-40\times0.025=-1.94$

All the entries in the net evaluation row in Table 6.6 are either zero or negative. This indicates that an optimum solution for this problem has been achieved.

Since the net evaluation value of s_1 at this stage is '0' which means that an introduction of one unit of s_1 will not increase the profit. Further, we are keeping 1 unit of cutting department idle without an increase in profit. Similarly by introducing one unit of s_2 i.e. threading department, the profit will decrease by ₹ 1.6 and for s_3 the profit decrease will be 1.94. The ₹ 1.6 and ₹ 1.94 are called shadow prices of s_2 and s_3 respectively. The value of all the resources is

$$2000 \times 0 + 3500 \times 1.6 + 540 \times 1.94 = ₹\ 6{,}648/-$$

6.3 Simplex Method II

In this method, the minimization of cost of the program is considered. In order to illustrate this method, an illustrative example is taken. Suppose two types of nutrients are required in the feeds of animals which are denoted as feed 1 and feed 2. The hypothetical example is given in Table 6.7.

Table 6.7

Nutrients	Feed		Daily requirement
	F_1	F_2	
N_1	4	8	60
N_2	6	4	40
Cost per unit of feed	₹ 7	₹ 8	

Let x represents the quantity of feed F_1 and y represents the quantity of feed F_2 to be purchased as per the daily requirement such that the total cost of feed for animals to be minimized. This can be stated in inequalities as

Minimize $7x + 8y$ subject to

$$4x + 8y \geq 60 \quad .....(6.19)$$

$$6x + 4y \geq 40 \quad .....(6.20)$$

In order to solve this problem, the above inequalities (6.19) and (6.20) are converted into equalities by introducing slack variables s_1 and s_2 as in earlier method given in section 6.2 as follows

$$4x + 8y - s_1 = 60 \quad .....(6.21)$$

$$6x + 4y - s_2 = 40 \quad .....(6.22)$$

Slack variables can be interpreted as 'free' products with the property that one unit of s_1 contains one unit of nutrient n_1 and one unit of s_2 contains one unit of nutrient n_2. These products come automatically when feeds F_1 and F_2 are purchased.

Now the minimization problem can be modified and stated by introducing slack variables s_1 and s_2 as

Minimize $7x + 8y + 0s_1 + 0s_2$ subject to

$$4x + 8y - s_1 = 60 \quad .....(6.23)$$

$$6x + 4y - s_2 = 40 \quad .....(6.24)$$

where $x, y, s_1, s_2 \geq 0$

The above program can be presented in Table 6.8.

Table 6.8

Program	Cost per unit	Qty	7 x	8 y	0 s_1	0 s_2	C P_1	C P_2
P_1	C	60	4	8	–1	0	1	0
P_2	C	40	6	4	0	–1	0	1
Net evaluation row			7-10C	8-12C	C	C	0	0

Since the introduction of 1 unit of y reduces the cost of feed to be purchased more than 1 unit of x, the y should be brought into the program 1st. therefore y column is a key column.

Here the cost per unit of x and y are calculated as

$$x: \quad 7 - 4c - 6c = 7 - 10c$$

$$y: \quad 8 - 8c - 4c = 8 - 12c$$

These are presented in the net evaluation row. Similarly other entries in the net evaluation row are obtained.

From row P_1, the maximum amount of y that can be brought into the solution is $\frac{60}{8} = 7.5$ units. Similarly from row P_2, the maximum amount that can be brought into the solution is $\frac{40}{4} = 10$ units. Since P_1 value is less than P_2 value, P_1 row is considered as key row. The rest of the procedure for improving this program is exactly the same as that followed in the simplex method of a maximization problem given in earlier section 6.2.

The intersection figure of key row and key columns is '8' and which is called key number. The revised program is presented in Table 6.9.

Table 6.9

Program	Cost per unit	Qty	7 x	8 y	0 s_1	0 s_2	C P_1	C P_2
y	8	7.5	0.5	1	$-\frac{1}{8}$	0	$\frac{1}{8}$	0
P_2	C	10	4	0	$\frac{1}{2}$	–1	$-\frac{1}{2}$	1
Net evaluation row			3 – 4C	0	$1-\frac{1}{2}C$	C	$-1+\frac{3}{2}C$	0

1. The first row 'y' entries are obtained by dividing the entries in first row of Table 6.8 by key number '8'.
2. The 2nd row P_2 entries in Table 6.9 are obtained as follows

(i) $40-60\times\frac{4}{8}=10$ (ii) $6-4\times\frac{4}{8}=4$

(iii) $4-8\times\frac{4}{8}=0$ (iv) $0-(-1)\frac{4}{8}=\frac{1}{2}$

(v) $-1-0\times\frac{4}{8}=-1$ (vi) $0-1\times\frac{4}{8}=-\frac{1}{2}$

(vii) $1-0\times\frac{4}{8}=1$

3. The entries in the net evaluation row of Table 6.9 are obtained as follows

(i) $7-0.5\times 8-4c=3-4c$

(ii) $8-8\times 1-c\times 0=0$

(iii) $0-\left(-\frac{1}{8}\times 8\right)-\frac{1}{2}c=1-\frac{1}{2}c$

(iv) $0-0\times 8-(-1)c=c$

(v) $c-\frac{1}{8}\times 8-\left(-\frac{1}{2}\right)c=-1+\frac{3}{2}c$

(vi) $c-0\times 8-1\times c=0$

4. From Table 6.9 it can be noticed that by introduction of 1 unit of x reduces the cost more than 1 unit of y as 3 – 4 c value is less than '0'. Therefore x column is selected as key column at this stage of program. From row 'y' the maximum amount of x that can be brought into the solution is 7.5/0.5 = 13.0 and from row P_2 is 10/4 = 2.5. Since P_2 row gives less value than y row, P_2 row is considered as key row. Further the intersection figure of P_2 row and x column is '4' and which is a key number. Now the revised program is given in Table 6.10.

Table 6.10

Program	**Cost per unit**	**Qty**	**7** **x**	**8** **y**	**0** s_1	**0** s_2	**C** p_1	**C** P_2
Y	8	6.25	0	1	– 0.1875	0.125	0.1875	– 0.125
x	7	2.50	1	0	0.125	– 0.25	– 0.125	0.25
Net evaluation row			0	0	0.625	0.75	C – 0.625	C – 0.75

1. The entries in the 2nd row or x row in Table 6.10 are obtained by dividing the entries in P_2 row of Table 6.9 by key number '4.
2. The entries in y row of Table 6.10 are obtained as follows

   (i) $7.5 - 10 \times \frac{0.5}{4} = 6.25$ (ii) $0.5 - 4 \times \frac{0.5}{4} = 0$

   (iii) $1 - 0 \times \frac{1}{4} = 1$ (iv) $-\frac{1}{8} - \frac{1}{2} \times \frac{0.5}{4} = -\ 0.1875$

   (v) $0 - (-1) \times \frac{0.5}{4} = 0.125$ (vi) $\frac{1}{8} - \left(-\frac{1}{2}\right) \times \frac{0.5}{4} = 0.1875$

   (vii) $0 - 1 \times \frac{0.5}{4} = -\ 0.125$

3. The net evaluation row entries in Table 6.10 are obtained as follows

   (i) $7 - 0 \times 8 - 1 \times 7 = 0$

   (ii) $8 - 1 \times 8 - 0 \times 7 = 0$

   (iii) $0 - (-0.1875)\ 8 - 0.125 \times 7 = 0.625$

(iv) $0 - 0.125 \times 8 - (-0.25)\, 7 = 0.75$

(v) $c - 0.1875 \times 8 - (-0.125)\, 7 = c - 0.625$

(vi) $c - (-0.125)\, 8 - 0.25 \times 7 = c - 0.75$

It can be see that the entries in net evaluation row of Table 6.10 are either positive or zero. Hence it can be concluded that the optimum solution has been achieved for this problem.

Here the optimum solution obtained as buying 2.5 units of feed F_1 and 6.25 units of feed F_2 daily at a cost of ₹ 67.5 which is obtained as

$$2.5 \times 7 + 6.25 \times 8 = ₹\ 67.5$$

The solution of this problem obviously should meet the daily requirement of nutrients n_1 and n_2 which can be verified as follows

n_1 : $4 \times 2.5 + 8 \times 6.25 = 60$

n_2 : $6 \times 2.5 + 4 \times 6.25 = 40$

6.4 Transportation Model

In linear programming, transportation problem is a major concern for administration. For example, the petroleum products are produced at different 'origins' and they have to be transported to different places called destinations for consumption. The major concern for the administration is to incur minimum cost for transportation. Linear programming helps in providing routes or channels for transportation incurring minimum cost. Though simplex method can be used for transportation problem but there is a separate method with which the problem can be solved easily. However, transportation problem is a special case of linear programming.

6.4.1 Linear Function

Let x_j be the variable representing the j-th candidate or activity competing for the problem and c_j be the corresponding cost variable involved. Then function is given as

$$\phi(x) = c_1 x_1 + c_2 x_2 + \ldots.. + c_n x_n$$

$$= \sum_{j=1}^{n} c_j x_j \qquad \text{for } j = 1, 2, \ldots\ldots, n$$

6.4.2 Linear Function with Constraints

The linear constraints are given as

$$a_{11}x_1 + a_{12}x_2 + ... + a_{1n}x_n \leq p_1$$

$$a_{21}x_1 + a_{22}x_2 + ... + a_{2n}x_n \leq p_2$$

$$..................................$$

$$a_{m1}x_1 + a_{m2}x_2 + ... + a_{mn}x_n \leq p_m$$

These constraints can be written in consize form as

$$\sum_{i=1}^{m} \sum_{j=1}^{m} a_{ij}x_j \leq p_i \qquad \text{for} \quad i = 1, 2, ..., m$$

$$j = 1, 2, ..., n$$

where a_{ij}'s are coefficients and p_is are constraints specified for the problem.

Further $\qquad x_j \geq 0,\ s_i \geq 0$ and $A_i \geq 0$

For j = 1, 2, ……, n; I = 1, 2, ……, n. Where s_i's are slack variables and A_is are artificial slack variables involved in linear programming problem.

6.4.3 Transportation Problem

Let there be three supply origins and the material has to be transported to four destinations. The supply origins are denoted by O_1, O_2, O_3 and O_4; demand destinations are denoted by D_1, D_2, D_3 and D_4. These are presented in the Table 6.11.

Table 6.11

Supply origin	**Demand destination**				**Supply capacity**
	D_1	D_2	D_3	D_4	
O_1	x_{11} (c_{11})	x_{12} (c_{12})	x_{13} (c_{13})	x_{14} (c_{14})	p_1
O_2	x_{21} (c_{21})	x_{22} (c_{22})	x_{23} (c_{23})	x_{24} (c_{24})	p_2
O_3	x_{31} (c_{31})	x_{32} (c_{32})	x_{33} (c_{33})	x_{34} (c_{34})	p_3
O_4	x_{41} (c_{41})	x_{42} (c_{42})	x_{43} (c_{43})	x_{44} (c_{44})	p_4
Demand requirement	d_1	d_2	d_3	d_4	

where x_{ij} is the number units to be transported from i-th origin to j-th destination and c_{ij} is the cost involved in transporting goods from i-th origin to j-th destination. Here it is assumed that

$$\sum_{i=1}^{m} p_i = \sum_{i=1}^{m} d_i \quad \text{where } m = 4 \text{ in this case}$$

The transportation problem can be specified as

Minimize $\quad \phi(x) = \sum_{i=1}^{4} \sum_{j=1}^{4} c_{ij} x_{ij}$

Subject to

$$x_{11} + x_{12} + x_{13} + x_{14} = p_1$$
$$x_{21} + x_{22} + x_{23} + x_{24} = p_2$$
$$x_{31} + x_{32} + x_{33} + x_{34} = p_3$$
$$x_{41} + x_{42} + x_{43} + x_{44} = p_4$$

and

$$x_{11} + x_{21} + x_{31} + x_{41} = d_1$$
$$x_{12} + x_{22} + x_{32} + x_{42} = d_2$$
$$x_{13} + x_{23} + x_{33} + x_{43} = d_3$$
$$x_{14} + x_{24} + x_{34} + x_{44} = d_4$$

Further $\quad x_{ij} > 0$ for $i = 1, 2, \ldots\ldots 4;\ \ j = 1, 2, \ldots\ldots, 4$

This transport problem can be presented in a format for solving by simplex method in Table 6.12.

Table 6.12

Program	**Cost per unit**	**Qty**	C_{12} .. C_{14} x_{12} .. x_{14}	C_{21} ..C_{24} x_{21} .. x_{24}	C_{31} .. C_{34} x_{31} .. x_{34}	C_{41} .. C_{44} x_{41} .. x_{44}	0 .. 0 s_1 .. s_4	0 .. 0 A_1 .. A_4
s_1	0	p_1	1 … 1	0 … 0	0 … 0	0 … 0	1000	0 … 0
s_2	0	p_2	0 … 0	1 … 1	0 … 0	0 … 0	0100	0 … 0
s_3	0	p_3	0 … 0	0 … 0	1 … 1	0 … 0	0010	0 … 0
s_4	0	p_4	0 … 0	0 … 0	0 … 0	1 … 1	0001	0 … 0
A_1	C	d_1	10 … 0	10 … 0	10 … 0	10 … 0	0000	10 … 0
A_2	C	d_2	010…0	010 … 0	01 … 0	010 … 0	0000	010 … 0
⋮		⋮	…	…	…	…	…	…
A_4	C	d_4	00 … 01	00 ... 01	00 … 01	00 … 01	0000	00 … 01

The problem given in format presented in Table 6.12 can be solved by simplex method by specifying the values of p_is and d_is.

6.4.4 North West Corner Method

This method is used as a basic method for solving transportation model. In this method the transportation of goods starts from north west corner of a table when the supply origins and demand destinations are presented in a two-way table as given in Table 6.13.

Table 6.13

N

	Supply origin	**Demand destination**					**Supply capacity**	
		D_1	D_2	D_3	D_4	D_5		
	O_1	35 (10)	25 (6)	10 (7)	(4)	(2)	70	
	O_2	(6)	(2)	35 (12)	5 (10)	(2)	40	
W	O_3	(4)	(5)	(6)	45 (9)	10 (7)	55	E
	O_4	(9)	(5)	(4)	(3)	25 (8)	25	
	Demand requirement	35	25	45	50	35	190	

S

The transportation of goods starts from North west corner of the Table 6.13. The figures in parentheses are the cost of transport. The supply origin has capacity of 70 units and 1st destination D_1 demand is 35 units. Therefore 35 units are transported to D_1 and D_2 requirement is 25 units. Now O_1 has 35 units after 35 units are transported to D_1 out of 70. Therefore 25 units transported to D_2 from O_1 out of 35 units with it. The remaining 10 units are allotted to D_3. From O_2 the requirement of D_2 i.e. 35 units are transported since the total demand requirement for D_3 is 45 units. The remaining 5 units of O_2 are transported to D_4. From O_3 capacity of 55 units, 45 units are transported to D_4 to fulfill the requirement of D_4. The remaining 10 units are transported to D_5. From O_4, the remaining requirement of D_5 are transported. Here the remaining units demand of D_5 and capacity of O_5 are exactly equal. Thus the transported is solved. It can be seen that the number of filled cells are $m + n - 1 = 4 + 5 - 1 = 8$. Further the total cost of transport is obtained as

$$35 \times 10 + 25 \times 6 + 10 \times 7 + 35 \times 12 + 5 \times 10 + 45 \times 9 + 10 \times 7 + 25 \times 8 = ₹\ 1715$$

Since the requirement of D_5 and capacity of O_4 are exactly equal then the solution is said to be not degenerate. This solution is called basic feasible solution.

6.4.5 Stepping Stone Method I

This method is illustrated here by taking two origins of supply and two demand destinations.

Table 6.14

Supply origins	**Demand destinations**		**Total**
	D_1	D_2	
O_1	600 (4)	200 (6)	800
O_2	 (2)	500 (5)	500
Total	600	700	

The figures in parantheses are the costs of transport of one unit from the corresponding cell in the Table 6.14.

In the Table 6.14, the empty cell is 0_2D_1. If cost is reduced by transporting one unit to empty cell O_2D_1 then it is said to be opportunity cost is positive. If the cost is not reduced then the opportunity cost of transporting to that cell is negative. The cost change can be obtained by using the following Table 6.15 with direction arrows.

Table 6.15

	D_1	D_2	
O_1	–1 (4)	+1 (6)	
O_2	+1 (2)	–1 (5)	

The change in cost by shifting 1 unit from $O_2 D_2$ to $O_2 D_1$ is given as

$$-5 + 2 - 4 + 6 = -1$$

Since the shift of 1 unit from $O_2 D_2$ to $O_2 D_1$ reduces ₹ 1 then it is desirable to shift to empty cell. Therefore the opportunity cost of shifting 1 unit from $O_2 D_2$ cell to $O_2 D_1$ cell is positive. The revised program after shifting 1 unit to $O_2 D_1$ cell from $O_2 D_2$ cell is given in Table 6.16.

Table 6.16

	D_1	D_2	
O_1	599 (4)	201 (6)	800
O_2	1 (2)	499 (5)	500
	600	700	

Since the opportunity cost is positive by shifting units from $O_2 D_2$ cell to $O_2 D_1$ cell, it is desirable to shift all the existing in $O_2 D_2$ cell to $O_2 D_1$ cell. It is possible to shift not more than 500 units from $O_2 D_2$ cell to $O_2 D$ $_1$ cell. Suppose all the 500 units are shifted from $O_2 D_2$ cell to $O_1 D_1$ cell then the resulting table is given in Table 6.17.

Table 6.17

	D_1	D_2	
O_1	100 (4)	700 (6)	800
O_2	500 (2)	(5)	500
	600	700	

From Table 16.17 it can be noted that $O_2 D_2$ cell became empty. If one unit is shifted to $O_2 D_2$ cell from $O_1 D_2$ cell the change in cost is obtained as

$$5 - 6 + 4 - 2 = 1 \text{ ₹}$$

In other words in shifting one unit to empty cell $O_2 D_2$ as per arrows given in Table 6.15, the increase in cost is ₹ 1. Therefore the optimum solution for this problem is achieved. The cost involved for the optimum solution is

$$100 \times 4 + 700 \times 6 + 500 \times 2 = \text{₹ } 5600$$

6.4.6 Stepping Stone Method II

In this subsection the basic feasible program given in Table 6.13 is refined using opportunity cost to obtain optimum solution to the problem. Here the changes in costs are calculated for all the empty cells in Table 6.13 and presented in Table 6.18.

Table 6.18

S.No.	Empty Cell	Loop	Change in cost	Opport cost	Action
1.	$O_1 D_4$	$O_1 D_4 - O_2 D_4 + O_2 D_3 - O_1 D_3$	$4 - 10 + 12 - 7 = -1$	1	No
2.	$O_1 D_5$	$O_1 D_5 - O_3 D_5 + O_3 D_4 - O_1 D_4$	$2 - 7 + 9 - 4 = 0$	0	No
3.	$O_2 D_1$	$O_2 D_1 - O_1 D_1 + O_1 D_3 - O_2 D_3$	$6 - 10 + 7 - 12 = -9$	9	No
4.	$O_2 D_2$	$O_2 D_2 - O_1 D_2 + O_1 D_4 - O_2 D_4$	$2 - 6 + 4 - 10 = -10$	10	No
5.	$O_2 D_5$	$O_2 D_5 - O_3 D_5 + O_3 D_4 - O_2 D_4$	$2 - 7 + 9 - 10 = -6$	6	No
6.	$O_3 D_1$	$O_3 D_1 - O_1 D_1 + O_1 D_4 - O_3 D_4$	$4 - 10 + 4 - 9 = -11$	11	No
7.	$O_3 D_2$	$O_3 D_2 - O_1 D_2 + O_1 D_4 - O_3 D_4$	$5 - 6 + 4 - 9 = -6$	6	No
8.	$O_3 D_3$	$O_3 D_3 - O_2 D_3 + O_2 D_4 - O_3 D_4$	$6 - 12 + 10 - 9 = -5$	5	No
9.	$O_4 D_1$	$O_4 D_1 - O_1 D_1 + O_1 D_2 - O_3 D_2$	$9 - 10 + 6 - 5 = 0$	0	No
10.	$O_4 D_2$	$O_4 D_2 - O_1 D_2 + O_1 D_3 - O_4 D_3$	$5 - 6 + 7 - 4 = +2$	–2	Yes
11.	$O_4 D_3$	$O_4 D_3 - O_1 D_3 + O_1 D_2 - O_4 D_2$	$4 - 7 + 6 - 5 = -2$	2	No
12.	$O_4 D_4$	$O_4 D_4 - O_3 D_4 + O_3 D_5 - O_4 D_5$	$3 - 9 + 7 - 8 = -7$	7	No

From Table 6.18, it can be observed that the opportunity cost for empty cell O_4 D_2 is negative which requires inclusion in the next revised program. The revised program is given in Table 6.19.

Table 6.19

	D_1	D_2	D_3	D_4	D_5	Total
O_1	35 (10)	(6)	10 (7)	(4)	25 (2)	70
O_2	(6)	(2)	35 (12)	5 (10)	(2)	40
O_3	(4)	(5)	(6)	45 (9)	10 (7)	55
O_4	(9)	25 (5)	(4)	(3)	(8)	25
Total	35	25	45	45	35	190

From Table 6.19, it can be noted that 25 units are shifted from O_4 D_5 cell to O_4 D_2 cell and consequently 25 units are shifted from O_1 D_2 cell to O_1 D_5 cell keeping the supply and demand requirements constant. The total cost of transportation is thus obtained as

$35 \times 10 + 25 \times 2 + 35 \times 12 + 5 \times 10 + 45 \times 9 + 10 \times 7 + 25 \times 5 =$ ₹ 1470

In comparison to cost involved in basic feasible solution, the revised program cost has been decreased by ₹ 245. Therefore the revised program is the optimum solution to the problem.

6.5 Decision Under Uncertainty

Decision making under uncertainty situation is more difficult than decision making under certainty situation. Most of the business problems come under this category in corporate sector. A corporate company invests huge money in producing a product or products, the company does not know exactly how many customers will be there and how many will be sold in the market competing with similar product and also how much profit the company will be able to secure. In this situation each action will lead to one outcome out of known set of outcomes each is associated with unknown probability. Thus it can be stated as

Events ⟶ acts ⟶ consequences

Consequences consists of profits, losses etc. The decision making under uncertainty situation is illustrated with an example here.

Example

A bakery produces cakes. The cakes are such that they are spoiled unless they are sold on the same day of production. The number of cakes to be prepared depends on number of customers on that day. Here the number of customers is an 'event', the preparation of cakes is 'act' and the 'profit' or 'Loss' obtained is 'consequence'. In this situation the cost of preparation of cake is ₹ 100 and it is sold at ₹ 140 and the profit per cake is ₹ 40. It is known that the customers coming to the bakery are from 50 to 55 on each day. The pay off table is given in Table 6.20 assuming that profit is the difference between value sold and cost of production.

Profit per cake = ₹ 140 – ₹ 100 = ₹ 40.

Table 6.20 Pay off table (₹)

Acts (cakes)

Events (customers)	50	51	52	53	54	55
50	2000	1900	1800	1700	1600	1500
51	2000	2040	1940	1840	1740	1640
52	2000	2040	2080	1980	1880	1780
53	2000	2040	2080	2120	2020	1920
54	2000	2040	2080	2120	2160	2060
55	2000	2040	2080	2120	2160	2200

From Table 6.20, it can be verified that the diagonal element values are the highest in the respective rows indicating that if the number of customers is equal to number of cakes, the profits will be maximum. Therefore the profits are dependent on the capacity of prediction of the number of customers visiting the bakery. Further the opportunity losses are calculated and presented in Table 6.21 for this example.

Table 6.21 Opportunity loss (₹)
Acts (cakes)

(customers) Events	50	51	52	53	54	55
50	0	– 100	– 200	– 300	– 400	– 500
51	– 40	0	– 100	– 200	– 300	– 400
52	– 80	– 40	0	– 100	– 200	– 300
53	– 120	– 80	– 40	0	– 100	– 200
54	– 160	– 120	– 80	– 40	0	– 100
55	– 200	– 160	– 120	– 80	– 40	0

The pay off table in terms of cost is given in Table 6.22.

Table 6.22 Pay off table in terms of cost (₹)
Acts (cakes)

(customers) Events	50	51	52	53	54	55
50	5000	5100	5200	5300	5400	5500
51	5000	5100	5200	5300	5400	5500
52	5000	5100	5200	5300	5400	5500
53	5000	5100	5200	5300	5400	5500
54	5000	5100	5200	5300	5400	5500
55	5000	5100	5200	5300	5400	5500

6.6 Decision making using Baye's Theorem

Sometimes business management will be making a decision with the help of Bayes theorem of probability. For example, if a corporate company owns three or more factories for manufacturing a product. The produce are packed and exported to foreign countries. Since the product is same and owned by same company they are mixed and packed. In order to check the produce to be exported, the management official picks up one piece from the pack for inspection of equality of the piece. In order to know from which factory the piece is manufactured if it is found defective, or not meeting the required standard, the management uses the Baye's theorem of probability for taking corrective steps.

Baye's Theorem

An event a can be described by a set of n exhaustive and mutually exclusive events $B_1, B_2, \ldots B_n$. Given that

(i) a priori probabilities $P(B_1), P(B_2), \ldots, P(B_n)$; $P(B_i) \neq 0$ for $i = 1, 2, \ldots, n$ corresponding to a total absence of a knowledge regarding the occurrence of event A and

(ii) Conditional probabilities $P(A/B_1), P(A/B_2) \ldots P(A/B_n)$

Hence a posteriori probabilities $P(B_i/A)$ are obtained as

$$P(B_i/A) = \frac{P(B_i) \,.\, P(A/B_i)}{\sum_{i=1}^{n} P(B_i) \,.\, P(A/B_i)}$$

The application of this theorem is illustrated with an example here,

Example: A corporate sector company owned three factories A, B, and C which produces screws in the ratio of 2:3:5 respectively. A, B and C factories also produce defective screws 2%, 4% and 5% respectively. The screws are mixed and packed in boxes. A screw was picked up at random and found defective. What is the probability that it was produced from factory C and what is the probability of obtaining a defective screw?

Let P(A), P(B) and P(C) are the probabilities of production of screws by factories A, B and C respectively.

(i) Therefore, $P(A) \simeq \frac{2}{10}$, $P(B) = \frac{3}{10}$, $P(C) = \frac{5}{10}$

Let P (D/A), P (D/B) and P (D/C) are the probabilities of producing defective screws from factories A, B and C respectively.

Here $P(D/A) = \frac{2}{100}$, $P(D/B) = \frac{4}{100}$, $P(D/C) = \frac{5}{100}$

Using Baye's theorem, we have

$$P(C/D) = \frac{P(C) \,.\, P(D/C)}{P(A) \,.\, P(D/A) + P(B) \,.\, P(D/B) + P(C) \,.\, P(D/C)}$$

$$= \frac{\frac{5}{10} \times \frac{5}{100}}{\frac{2}{10} \times \frac{2}{100} + \frac{3}{10} \times \frac{4}{100} + \frac{5}{10} \times \frac{5}{100}}$$

$$= \frac{25}{4 + 12 + 25} = \frac{25}{41} = 0.61$$

(ii) The probability of producing a defective screw from any one of the three factories A, B and C is given as

$$P(A) \,.\, P(D/A) + P(B) \,.\, P(D/B) + P(C) \,.\, P(D/C)$$

$$\frac{2}{10} \times \frac{2}{100} + \frac{3}{10} \times \frac{4}{100} + \frac{5}{10} \times \frac{5}{100} = \frac{4 + 12 + 25}{10 \times 100} = 0.04$$

Using the probability of producing a defective screw which was found to be 0.04, the management of the said corporate company will try to reduce this probability by taking corrective measures. Further, the probability of producing non-defective screw from any factory is $1 - 0.04 = 0.96$.

6.7 Decision Tree Diagram

A decision tree is one which displays number of events, acts and consequences through diagram which resembles like a tree. The acts and events are represented by forks having as many number of branches as the number of acts. The outcome or consequence is depicted at the end position of fork. The decision tree is drawn from left to right without a break. Decision tree is nothing but a network which shows the logical relationship between different stages of decision making using alternative courses of action. The decision tree making is illustrated here by taking an example.

Example 1: A shop owner wants to decide whether to stock commodities A, B and C. If he stocks commodity A and if it is a success he earns ₹ 4,000 and if it is a failure he loses ₹ 6000. If the shop owner stocks commodity B, he earns ₹ 5000 in case of success and losses ₹ 4000 in case of failure. Further the owner stocks commodity C, he earns ₹ 6000 in case of success and ₹ 3000 in case of failure. The probabilities of success of A, B and C commodities are given as 0.6, 0.5 and 0.4 respectively. Draw the acts, events and consequences by a decision tree.

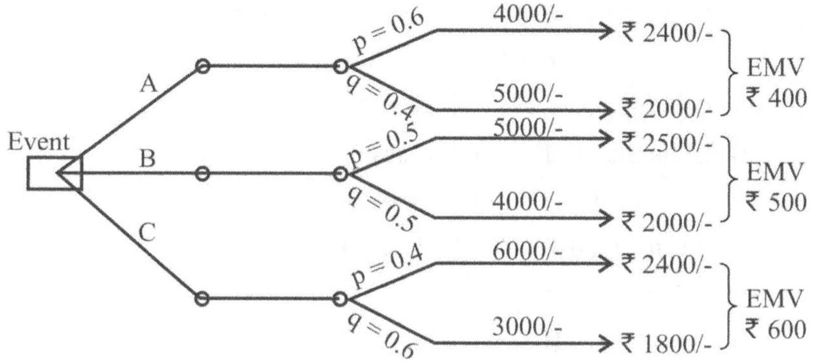

Fig. 6.6

From Fig. 6.6, it can be observed that the effective monetary values (E.M.V) are obtained for commodities A, B and C as

A : $4000 \times 0.6 - 5000 \times 0.4 =$ ₹ 400

B : $5000 \times 0.5 - 4000 \times 0.5 =$ ₹ 500

C : $6000 \times 0.4 - 3000 \times 0.6 =$ ₹ 600

From the E.M.V. Figs. it can be concluded that if the shop owner keeps stocks of commodity 'C' he earns more profit than he keeps commodities A and B.

***Example* 2:** An irrigation dam contractor was given two options. The first option 'A' was that he will be given contract for fixed amount and the second option 'B' was that he will be paid total cost of construction plus 10 percent of the total cost. The dam contractor is not in a position to take a decision since the prices of construction material may go up in case of first option where as the earnings are fixed for the second option. Here the contract for fixed amount is ₹ 200 crores. An amount of ₹ 100 crores is to be spent for construction material and an amount of ₹ 65 crores to be earmarked for labour charges. The prices of construction material are expected to rise by 5 percent, 8 percent and 10 percent with probabilities 0.4, 0.5 and 0.1 respectively.

(i) First option (A)

(a) If the material cost increases by 5 percent

$$100 + 0.05\ (100) + 65 = 170$$

Profit = 200 – 170 = ₹ 30 crores.

(b) If the material cost increases by 8 percent

$$100 + 0.08\ (100) + 65 = 173$$

Profit = 200 – 173 = ₹ 27 crores.

(c) If the material cost increases by 10 percent

$$100 + 0.1\ (100) + 65 = 175$$

Profit = 200 – 175 = ₹ 25 crores.

(ii) Second option (B)

(a) Total cost + 10% on total cost

$$170 + 170 \times 0.1 = 187 \text{ crores}$$

Profit = 187 – 170 = 17 crores.

(b) Total cost + 10% on total cost

$$173 + 173 \times 0.1 = 190.3 \text{ crores}$$

Profit = 190.3 – 173 = 17.3 crores.

(c) Total cost + 10% on total cost

$$173 + 175 \times 0.1 = 192.5$$

Profit = 192.5 – 175 = 17.5 crores.

Table 6.23 Pay off table

Events	Act	
% price rise	Fixed price (₹) (A)	Cost + 10% (₹) (B)
5	30	17
8	27	17.3
10	25	17.5
E.M.V	28	17.2

E.M.V. (A) = $30 \times 0.4 + 27 \times 0.5 + 25 \times 0.1 = 28$ crores

E.M.V. (B) = $17 \times 0.4 + 17.3 \times 0.5 + 17.5 \times 0.1 = 17.2$ crores

From Table 6.23, it can be seen that the effective monetary value (EMV) of option A is more than effective monetary value (EMV) of option B. Therefore the irrigation contractor would opt per option A i.e., fixed price. The above results are presented in a tree diagram given in Fig. 6.7.

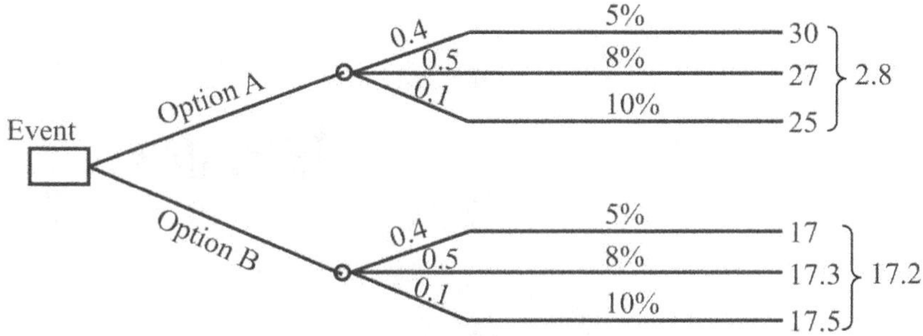

Fig. 6.7

CHAPTER 7

Collection of Data

7.1 Introduction

In any research work, collection of data is the first step to be followed whether it is survey or experiment. The data collected to meet the objectives of survey or experiment for the first time is called as primary data. The data collected from already available records or internet is known as secondary data. The primary data is collected for survey by the methods such as:

(i) By investigator himself or herself (direct observation)

(ii) By questionnaire method

(iii) By schedule method

(iv) By telephone method and

(v) By video conference method

7.2 By Investigator Method

In this method the investigator directly records the observation. The investigator will not take the assistance of any staff. For example, the data collected for research work to be submitted for securing Ph.D. degree in Economics, Sociology, Planning etc., will be considered under this category. Similarly, the data collected during the course of experiment in the science laboratory will also come under this category. Further, if a correspondent collects information directly from public for his newspaper or news channel will also be under this method of collection of data.

7.3 Questionnaire Method

In this method, several number of questions are prepared in a sequential order in relation to the objectives of the survey. These questions should be simple, easy to understand, logical in sequence, objective type such as yes or no type or multiple choice or fill up the blanks etc. Personal type questions should not be included. Some extra questions may be included to extract the true information from respondents. The language of questions should be simple and easy to understand and preferably in local or regional language. The number of pages in the questionnaire should be limited to 5 to 6 pages as the respondent should not take more time to fill up. These questionnaires are sent by post or by E-mail and the filled answers are obtained by post or E-mail.

The units such as cms, kgs etc., should be mentioned in the questionnaire.

7.3.1 Merits

(i) It is simple and easy to adopt.

(ii) It takes less time and involves less money to conduct.

(iii) It requires less trained human resource.

(iv) Easy to approach even remote areas for collecting information.

(v) Easy for respondents to fill up the questionnaire as all the questions are of objective type.

(vi) opinion surveys can be conducted.

7.3.2 Demerits

(i) Respondents may not feel responsible in sending back filled questionnaires in time.

(ii) Respondents sometimes may not send back filled questionnaires.

(iii) Respondents should be educated at least in regional language.

(iv) Sometimes filled questionnaires may not be received in time due to postal delay.

(v) Incomplete questionnaires may be received back.

(vi) Questionnaires may be filled by a person other than respondent.

(vii) Detailed information can not be collected as the respondent may not be in a position to fill up the lengthy questionnaire due to lack of available time or lack of interest or lack of both.

7.3.3 Applications

(i) This method can be successfully used for collecting information from prospective customers before starting construction of new colony.

(ii) Before starting a new factory, the questionnaire method can be used to elicit opinion of customers with respect to their choice with regard to quality, price, competing product as a sort of market survey research.

(iii) This method can be adopted for improving the facilities such as transport, water, electricity, drainage, health etc., for pilgrims in old pilgrim cities like Tirupati, Banaras etc., to collect opinion of residents in the city.

(iv) Government organizations such as CSIT, ICAR, ICMR etc., are using this method for knowing the status of scientific personnel working in their organizations.

7.4 Schedule Method

Schedule is an improved version of questionnaire where in detailed information is collected. Space is provided for answering the questions. Open ended questions are also included in the schedule. The schedule may be up to 10 to 12 pages. The information is collected by interview method. The enumerator will interview the respondent and fill the schedule or respondent may fill up the schedule with or without the help of enumerator. Large scale or small scale surveys are being conducted by this method. Skilled and semi-skilled persons are employed for conducting the survey. NSSO of Government of India conducts large scale and small scale surveys with the help of schedule on different aspects of economy such as industries, irrigation, health, education, defense, information technology, railways, agriculture etc. Population census is being conducted for every 10 years using this method. Usually in schedule, basic information with regard to name, address, educational status of whole family, income of individual members of whole family, family size, land holding, property, details of sources of income, nativity, land under irrigation, crops grown etc are asked. For this type of survey, large number of staff are required which include chief investigator, statistician, middle level supervisory staff, enumerators etc. All the staff are well trained for conducting the survey. As in the case of questionnaire, schedule is presented in regional language to facilitate enumerators to collect exact and truthful information from respondents. The units of measurement should be uniform for all the respondents answers.

7.4.1 Merits

(i) Detailed and exact information can be collected directly from respondents.

(ii) Large area can be covered giving more strength to the estimates calculated from the information collected.

(iii) Number of errors and number of incomplete filled schedules can be avoided.

(iv) This method is popular for Government and Non-Government organizations.

7.4.2 Demerits

(i) This method involves lot of time and money.

(ii) By the time the survey is completed and conclusions are drawn, the results may be vitiated due to passage of sufficient time and conclusions may be obsolete.

(iii) Large number of trained human resource is required.

(iv) Coding and processing of data requires lot of skill.

(v) The preparation of schedule requires lot of inputs from experts from different areas to meet the requirements of objectives of the investigation.

7.4.3 Applications

There are several organizations which are using this method.

(i) Community based tank management project (CBTMP) assisted by world Bank is using this method for collecting information using schedules such as:

(a) Household schedule (b) Water user Association (WUA) schedule

(c) Tank system schedule (d) Landless people schedule

(ii) Horticulture mission at State Government level is using this schedule method for collecting information from the beneficiaries of assistance by third party.

(iii) Surveys conducted by NSSO for specific purpose such as AIDS, virus diseases such as malaria, dengu, chicken gunea etc., information technology, status of industrial labour force used schedule method.

7.5 Telephone Method

The information collected through telephone is called telephone method. Several schemes are introduced by communication companies such as group telephone wherein charge is not levied if the conversation takes place between persons within group who are owning the SIM cards of mobiles of that company. This way, the information can be collected quickly and at very nominal or no price at all directly from the respondent. If the network coverage is available at nook and corners of country and abroad, the information can be collected very fast. By this method, the processing, analysis and conclusions can be arrived at without much loss of time. Government and private organizations are using this method successfully without much expenditure. However in this method the number of questions to be asked should be less and the information required should not involve much time and calculations.

7.5.1 Merits

(i) It involves very less time and expenditure

(ii) The survey can cover large area and countries

(iii) The information can be collected directly from respondents without involvement of any third person

(iv) This method is an improved version of questionnaire method.

7.5.2 Demerits

(i) The coverage of network may not be available in all locations.

(ii) The respondents may not answer questions directly.

(iii) The respondents may switch of mobiles and may recharge according to their convenience.

(iv) Detailed information may not be available immediately from the respondents.

7.5.3 Applications

(i) Community based tank management project of Government of Andhra Pradesh is successfully using this method.

(ii) Horticulture mission of Government of Andhra Pradesh is successfully using this method.

(iii) All universities in India are using this method successfully.

(iv) Many Non-Government organizations adopted this method without any difficulty.

7.6 Video Conference Method

The information collected through video conference is called video conference method. This method is an improved version of schedule method. The date and time of video conference is intimated in advance to the respondents. The information is gathered through interview with respondents by viewing through screen. In this interview, question and answers will take place and detailed information can be collected quickly. The process and analysis of data can be done quickly and remedial steps, if necessary, can be suggested immediately.

7.6.1 Merits

(i) The detailed information can be collected directly from the respondents by interview method viewing them through video.

(ii) Authentic information can be obtained quickly.

(iii) Information from third persons other than respondents can be avoided.

(iv) This is an improved method over schedule method avoiding lot of human resource involvement.

7.6.2 Demerits

(i) This method is costly and involves lot of expenditure.

(ii) The network for video conference is available only with State and Central Government departments.

(iii) The network is only available at district head quarters at present and hence it is not possible to adopt for nook and corners of the country.

(iv) Lot of preparation is needed for conducting the video conference for the respondents on both sides.

(v) Failure of network is possible at any time during the conduct of video conference.

7.6.3 Applications

(i) Prime Minister and Chief Ministers are conducting video conference for collecting information from their respective staff through video conference method successfully.

(ii) Selection of candidates and other information from candidates is being collected through this method by selection committees.

(iii) Universities, scientific organizations are using this method for collecting information from their staff at lower level.

(iv) Non-Government and private organizations are hiring video conference halls owned by Government for conducting video conferences to gather information from respondents.

7.7 Collection of Secondary Data

As already stated earlier that the secondary data is the data already available from records such as project reports journals, newspapers, books, statistical abstracts published by Directorates of State Governments, National Sample Survey Organization (NSSO), Government of India, trade journals, internet, market journals, industrial journals etc. The secondary data can be taken from the relevant source and can be used for analysis for the research project. Sometimes primary data and secondary data are both included for the project work. However, the source of obtaining secondary data has to be mentioned underneath the table containing data. For certain research projects, it is not possible to collect entire data afresh as it consumes lot of time and money. Further it is unnecessary to collect entire primary data.

However care has to be taken with respect to source, time and relevance of secondary data. The data collected by government agency and published in statistical abstracts, agricultural situation in India etc., are considered as authentic. For example, production and productivity of agricultural crops, cement, steel, population, coal output, birth and death rates, imports and exports of several commodities, area under irrigation, industrial output etc., data published in Government journals are considered as authentic. The data recorded with respect to rainfall, temperature, relative humidity, sunshine hours, wind velocity etc by meteorology department, Government of India are taken as authentic data.

CHAPTER 8

Data Organization

8.1 Introduction

When the data is collected for any research it has to be organized in such a way that it should be amenable to further analysis. Further the organization of data should be able to bring out important information from the data. If the information is of descriptive type then it should be coded for storing in the computer system. For example, the type of industries established in a particular year in the country is given in Table 8.1.

Table 8.1

Type of industry	Number
Very large	4
Large	10
Medium	18
Small	26
Ancillary	34

8.2 Inclusive Method of Grouping

The cement production (tons) on different days is presented in the following distribution.

Table 8.2

Cement (tons)	Days
4-6	4
7-9	10
10-12	7
13-15	9

The presentation of cement production according to days of a month in the format given in Table 8.2 is called 'Inclusive Method of Grouping'. In this method both lower and upper limits of the class are included in the same class or group then it is known as Inclusive method of grouping. For example, in Table 8.2 the cement production of 4 and 6 tons are both included in the first group. The figures in 'Days' column are called frequencies. The entire table is called 'Grouped frequency distribution'. The width of the class is determined by dividing the difference of highest and lowest values of the data by the number of classes required. Here the width of the class is given as $\frac{15-4}{4}=\frac{11}{4}=2.75$. The width of the class is between 2 to 3.

8.3 Exclusive Method of Grouping

If upper limits are excluded and included in next higher class then it is known as exclusive method of grouping. Table 8.2 is converted into exclusive method of grouping and presented in Table 8.3.

Table 8.3

Cement (tons)	Days
4-7	3
7-10	9
10-13	8
13-16	10

In the first group of Table 8.3, cement production of 7 tons is included in (7-10) group but not in (4-7) group and so on. Usually if the data is given in Inclusive method of grouping then it is modified into Exclusive method of grouping by subtracting 0.5 from lower limit and adding 0.5 to the upper limit for further analysis.

8.4 Diagrammatic Representation

If the data is presented in diagrams then it is known as diagrammatic representation. These are (i) Bar diagram/chart (ii) component bar diagram/chart (iii) Multiple bar diagram/chart (iv) Pie diagram/chart and (v) pictogram/pictochart.

8.4.1 Bar Diagram/Chart

In this diagram rectangles are erected such that the length of the rectangle is proportional to the magnitude of the variable. The width of each rectangle or bar is same and width between any two bars will remain same. This diagram is illustrated with an example given in Table 8.4.

Table 8.4

Year	Cement (m.t)
2006	35
2007	42
2008	50
2009	60
2010	55

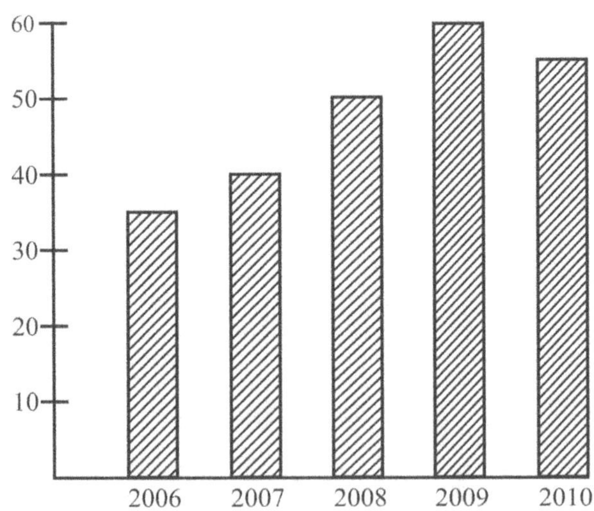

Fig. 8.1 Bar diagram.

The bars drawn in Fig. 8.1 can be coloured with same coluor for appealing to eye. The width of the bar can be chosen as per our choice depending upon the availability of space in the chart or card board.

8.4.2 Component Bar Diagram/Chart

In this diagram, the heights of the component parts of the bar are directly proportional to the magnitude of the constituent parts of the variable. In this diagram, the width of each bar should be same and also space between bars should be same. The diagram may not be much advantage if the component parts are more than four as they will become clumsy. This diagram is illustrated with an example given in Table 8.5.

Table 8.5 Cement production (m.t)

Year	Summer	Rainy	Winter	Total
2006	10	8	17	35
2007	12	9	21	42
2008	14	11	25	50
2009	18	12	30	60
2010	16	10	29	55

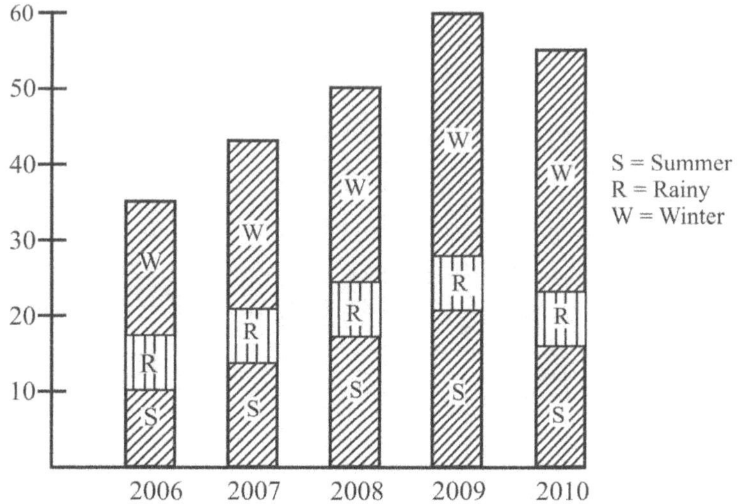

Fig. 8.2

From Fig. 8.2 comparison between total production between years and also between seasons within each year and between years can be done simultaneously.

8.4.3 Multiple Bar Diagram/Chart

In this diagram more than one bar will be attached to each other. These attached bars represent the related variables.

Example: The power consumption of domestic and industrial sectors in different years of a particular city is presented in Table 8.6

Table 8.6 Power consumption (k.w)

Year	Domestic	Industrial
2006	24	38
2007	30	44
2008	35	48
2009	40	60

The data given in Table 8.6 can be represented by multiple bar diagram in Fig. 8.3.

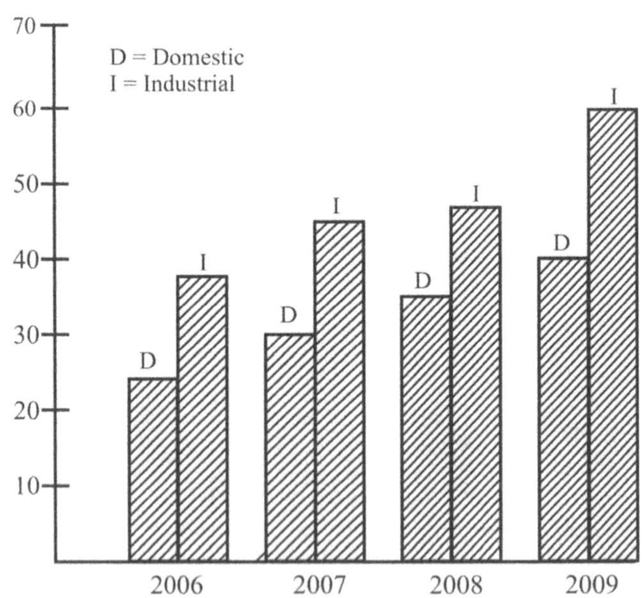

Fig. 8.3

8.4.4 Pie Diagram/Chart

When more than four components of a variable are to be represented in a diagram, the pie diagram is used instead bar diagram. This diagram is a circle wherein the areas of different sectors are directly proportional to the magnitudes of the components of a variable.

Example: The following are the amounts allocated in a year by the owner of a factory producing industrial products. Represent the data given in Table 8.7 by a pie diagram.

Table 8.7

S.No	Item	Amount (lakhs)	Sector angle
1.	Salaries of officers	30	$360^\circ \times \frac{30}{100} = 108$
2.	Salaries of labour	19	$360^\circ \times \frac{19}{100} = 68$
3.	Raw material	20	$360^\circ \times \frac{20}{100} = 72$
4.	Infrastructure and repairs	12	$360^\circ \times \frac{12}{100} = 43$
5.	Water	3	$360^\circ \times \frac{3}{100} = 11$
6.	Electricity	6	$360^\circ \times \frac{6}{100} = 22$
7.	Contingencies	10	$360^\circ \times \frac{10}{100} = 36$
	Total	100	360°

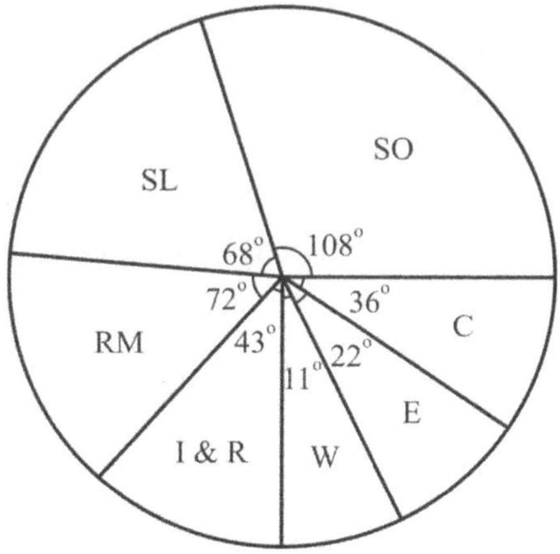

Fig. 8.4 Pie diagram.

In pie diagram, the total amount allocated is proportional to the radius of the circle. If the allocation of amount for different years are to be represented then different circles are to be drawn with radii directly proportional to the total amounts allotted to different years. From Fig. 8.4 it can be observed that major allotment has been done to salaries of officers followed by raw material and salaries of labour.

8.4.5 Pictogram/Pictochart

In this diagram, volume of picture is directly proportional to the magnitude of the variable. This diagram is useful when the magnitude of the variable is very large and the range of the values is very large. For example, the production of cement in a year is represented by the size of the bag, steel by steel bars, food production by length of the ear, army by soldier, navy by ship, air force by aeroplane etc. If the army of India is 8.5 lakhs, china 30.2 lakhs and America 15.6 lakhs then 8 and half of size soldiers represents India, 30 and 0.2 size soldiers represent china and 15 and 0.6 size soldiers for America. Here each soldier represents one lakh army.

8.4.6 Merits

(i) The diagram is more appealing to eye than numerical data for comparison in a shortest time

(ii) This is of much importance for VIPs as they find less time for going through data and also for uneducated people as they cannot compare numerical values.

8.4.7 Demerits

(i) The diagram only gives rough idea about the magnitude of the variable but not exact value

(ii) No further statistical analysis is possible with the diagrams

(iii) When the number of items are more then it will be difficult and confusing for drawing comparisons.

8.5 Graphic Representation of Data

When the data is represented by graphs then it is called graphic representation of data. These are (i) Histogram (ii) Frequency polygon (iii) Frequency curve and (iv) cumulative frequency curves (0gives).

8.5.1 Histogram

If rectangles are erected with base as class interval and height proportional to the corresponding frequency such that the area of the rectangle is directly proportional to the corresponding frequency then it is known as Histogram. Also the total area under the histogram is proportional to the total frequency.

Example: The following is the grouped frequency distribution of houses with respect to plinth areas (100 sq. m). Construct histogram for the data given in Table 8.8.

Table 8.8

Plinth area (100 sq. m)	Houses
2-6	6
6-12	10
12-16	24
16-22	16
22-25	7

The histogram is drawn for the data given in the above Table 8.8 and presented in Fig. 8.5.

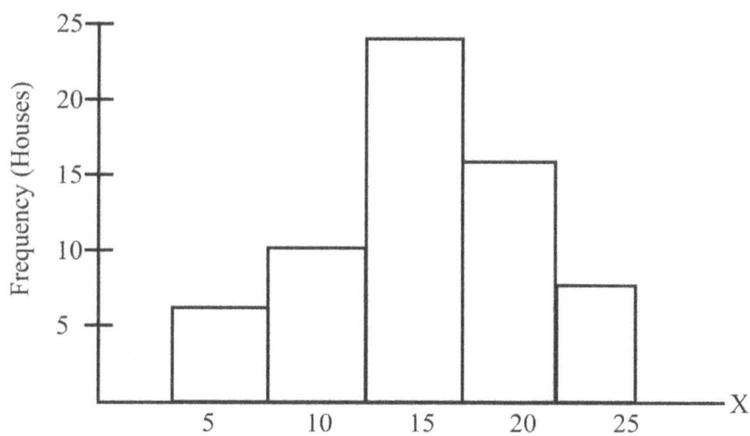

Fig. 8.5 Class limits (Plinth areas).

The histogram in Fig. 8.5 provides the trend of houses with respect to plinth areas. One may compare bar diagram with histogram as they resemble same. Here in histogram there is no gap between rectangles and width of rectangle changes as class interval changes whereas in bar diagram the width of the bars is same and there should be space left between every pair of bars. The histogram is drawn on graph sheet whereas bar diagram is drawn on card board.

8.5.2 Frequency Polygon

If the points are plotted with mid-values of the classes on X-axis and corresponding frequencies on Y-axis, the figure formed by joining these points with scale is known as frequency polygon. Usually polygon will have more than 4 sides. The area under polygon is proportional to total frequency.

Example: Draw frequency polygon for the data given in Table 8.8.

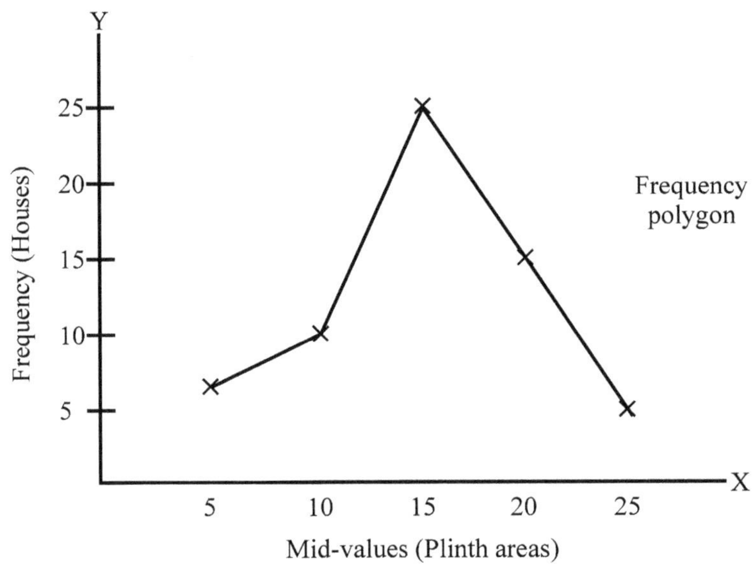

Fig. 8.6

The frequency polygon in Fig. 8.6 gives the trend of number of houses as per plinth areas.

8.5.3 Frequency Curve

If the points are plotted with mid-values of classes on X-axis and corresponding frequencies on Y-axis and the figure formed by joining these points with a smooth hand is known as frequency curve. The areas under frequency curve, frequency polygon and histogram are same. The frequency curve also gives trend of houses with respect to plinth areas.

Further it is possible to find the plinth area of a particular house from the curve by taking X-coordinate value for a given Y co-ordinate value by drawing lines parallel to X-axis and Y-axis.

Example: Draw frequency curve for the data given in Table 8.8.

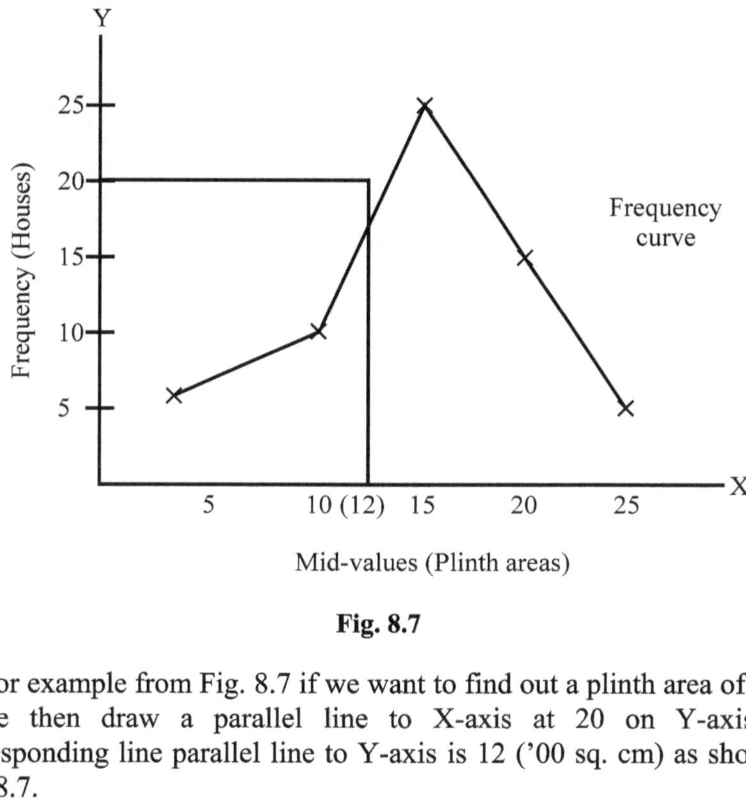

Fig. 8.7

For example from Fig. 8.7 if we want to find out a plinth area of a 20th house then draw a parallel line to X-axis at 20 on Y-axis and corresponding line parallel line to Y-axis is 12 ('00 sq. cm) as shown in Fig. 8.7.

8.5.4 Cumulative Frequency Curves (Ogives)

If the points are plotted with upper limits of classes on X-axis and corresponding cumulative frequencies (less than) On Y-axis then the figure formed by joining these points with a smooth hand is known as cumulative frequency curve (less than). Also if the points are plotted with lower limits of classes on X-axis and corresponding cumulative frequencies (more than) on Y-axis the figure formed by joining these points with a smooth hand is known as cumulative frequency curve (more than). The cumulative frequency curves are useful to find out the cumulative totals at a particular cut off point. For example in order to know the number of houses below say 15('00 sq. m) plinth area or above say 10('00 sq. m) plinth area they can be directly obtained from the corresponding cumulative frequency curves. These curves are also called a 'ogive' curves.

Example: The distribution given in Table 8.8 is considered and presented in Table 8.9 here. Represent the data by cumulative frequency curves.

Table 8.9

Plinth area ('00 sq. m)	Houses	C.f (less than)	C.f. (more than)
2-6	6	6	63
6-12	10	16	57
12-16	24	40	47
16-22	16	56	23
22-25	7	63	7

The cumulative frequency curves for the data given in Table 8.9 are presented in Fig, 8.8.

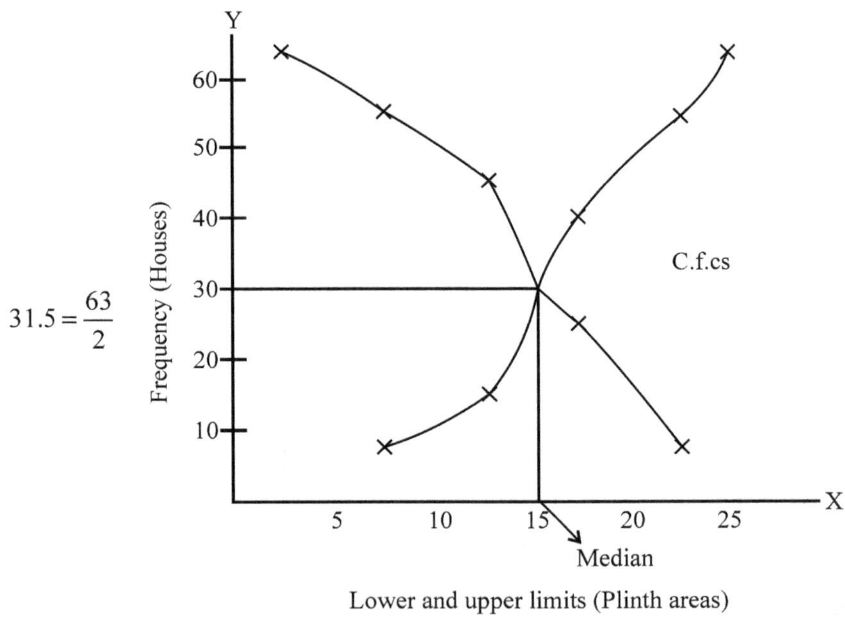

Fig. 8.8

The X-coordinate of the point of intersection of two cumulative frequency curves gives the 'Median' value. These curves can also be used to know the amount of tax to be lost if the level of income is increased to be exempted from Income tax.

CHAPTER 9

Measures of Central Tendency and Dispersion

9.1 Measures of Central Tendency

The representative value of a group of data is called central tendency. This is also called as average. The single figure which represents entire data conveys important information from the data. Instead of studying entire data it is sufficient to understand the single figure to know about the rough idea about the data. The method by which the central tendency is calculated is called measure of central tendency or Measure of location. The measures of central tendency are (i) Arithmetic mean (ii) Median (iii) Mode (iv) Geometric mean and (v) Harmonic mean.

9.1.1 Arithmetic Mean

(a) Type I data (individual observation values): It is defined as the sum of the observations divided by its number.

Def: If $x_1, x_2, \ldots, x_n$ be 'n' variate values then arithmetic mean (A.M.) is given as

$$A.M = \overline{x} = \frac{x_1 + x_2 + ... + x_n}{n} = \frac{\sum_{i=1}^{n} x_i}{n}$$

(b) Type II data: (frequency distribution)

Def: If $f_1, f_2, ..., f_n$ be n frequencies corresponding to the variate values $x_1, x_2, ..., x_n$ respectively then arithmetic mean is given as

$$A.M = \overline{x} = \frac{f_1x_1 + f_2x_2 + ... + f_nx_n}{f_1 + f_2 + ... + f_n} = \frac{\sum_{i=1}^{n} f_ix_i}{\sum_{i=1}^{n} f_i}$$

$$= \frac{\sum_{i=1}^{n} f_ix_i}{N} \quad \text{where} \quad N = \Sigma f_i$$

Example: The following is the frequency distribution of areas under parks in a city. Find the mean area under parks.

Table 9.1

Area under parks (x_i) (100 sq.m)	Parks (f_i)	$f_i x_i$
18	3	54
22	5	110
24	8	192
28	4	112
30	10	300
Total	30	768

$$A.M = \overline{x} = \frac{768}{30} = 25.6 \text{ i.e. } 25.6 \times 100 = 2560 \text{ sq.m}$$

(c) Type III data (Grouped frequency distribution)

Def: If $f_1, f_2, ..., f_n$ be n frequencies corresponding to the mid-values of the classes $x_1, x_2, ..., x_n$ respectively then arithmetic mean is given as

$$A.M = \overline{x} = \frac{f_1x_1 + f_2x_2 + ... + f_nx_n}{f_1 + f_2 + ... + f_n} = \frac{\Sigma f_ix_i}{\Sigma f_i} = \frac{\Sigma f_ix_i}{N}$$

Example: The following is the grouped frequency distribution of areas under parks in a city. Find the mean area under parks.

Table 9.2

Area under parks (100 sq.m)	Parks (f_i)	Mid-value x_i	$f_i x_i$
10-16	6	13	78
16-22	13	19	247
22-28	20	25	500
28-34	18	31	558
34-40	3	37	111
Total	**60**		**1494**

$$\text{A.M} = \overline{x} = \frac{1494}{60} = 24.9 \quad \text{i.e. } 24.9 \times 100 = 2490 \text{ sq.m.}$$

9.1.1.1 Characteristics of a satisfactory average

(i) It should have well defined formula (ii) It should be based upon all the observations (iii) It should be comprehensible (iv) It should be one among the observations (v) It should not be effected by extreme values (vi) It should be least effected by sampling fluctuations (vii) It should be easily computed and (viii) It should be capable of algebraic treatment.

9.1.1.2 Merits

(i) It possesses all the characteristics of satisfactory average. It has got two algebraic properties such as

(a) The algebraic sum of the deviations taken from A.M is zero i.e., $\sum_{i=1}^{n}(x_i - \overline{x}) = 0$

(b) If $\overline{x}_i$ be the mean of n_i observations for i = 1, 2, …, k then $\overline{x}$ be the mean of $n_1 + n_2 + \ldots + n_x$ observations, then

$$\overline{x} = \frac{n_1\overline{x}_1 + n_2\overline{x}_2 + \ldots + n_k\overline{x}_k}{n_1 + n_2 + \ldots + n_k} = \frac{\sum_{i=1}^{k} n_i\overline{x}_i}{\sum_{i=1}^{k} n_i}$$

9.1.1.3 Demerits

(i) It may not be one among the observations from which it is calculated (ii) It is effected by presence of extreme values (iii) It is difficult to calculate whenever the extreme classes in grouped frequency distribution are not well defined.

9.1.2 Median

(a) (Type I data) (individual observation values):

Def: It is defined as that value of the variate below which half of the values will lie and above which the remaining values will lie when the observations are arranged in ascending order of magnitude.

Example: The following are the heights of 10 students 162, 168, 156, 174, 170, 182, 178, 181, 169, 171. Find Median height.

The heights are arranged in ascending order as follows

S.No.	1	2	3	4	5	6	7	8	9	10
Height (cm)	156	162	168	169	170	171	174	178	181	182

$$\text{Median no.} = \frac{n+1}{2} \text{ where n = number of observations}$$

$$= \frac{10+1}{2} = 5.5$$

$$\text{Median} = 5^{th} \text{ value} + 0.5\ (6^{th} \text{ value} - 5^{th} \text{ value})$$

$$= 170 + 0.5\ (171 - 170) = 170.5 \text{ cm}$$

(b) Type II data (frequency distribution)

Example: The following is the frequency distribution of heights (cm) of students. Find the median height?

Table 9.3

Height (cm) (1)	**Students (2)**	**Height (cm) (3)**	**Students (4)**	**c.f (5)**
146	2	146	2	2
170	10	158	4	6
158	4	164	12	18
164	12	170	10	28
179	12	179	13	41
184	10	184	5	46
Total	46			

From the Table 9.3, it can be observed that the variate values i.e., heights are not given in ascending order of magnitude. Hence they are arranged in ascending order of magnitude in column (3). Then cumulative frequencies are computed and presented in column (5).

$$\text{Median} = \frac{N+1}{2} = \frac{46+1}{2} = 23.5$$

$$\text{Median} = 23^{rd} \text{ value} + 0.5\,(24^{th} \text{ value} - 23^{rd} \text{ value})$$

$$= 170 + 0.5\,(170 - 170) = 170 \text{ cm}$$

The median height is obtained as 170 cm

(c) Type III data (grouped frequency distribution)

In the case of grouped frequency distribution the median is calculated using the interpolation formula given as

$$\text{Median} = l + \frac{\left(\frac{N+1}{2} - m\right)c}{f}$$

where l = lower limit of the median class, $\frac{N+1}{2}$ = median number, m = cumulative frequency just before the median class, c = class interval of the median class and f = frequency of the median class where median class is that class wherein cumulative frequency $\frac{N+1}{2}$ exists.

Example: The following is the grouped frequency distribution of heights of students. Find the median height.

Table 9.4

Height (cm) (1)	Students (2)	Height (cm) (3)	Students (4)	c.f (5)
140-150	5	140-150	5	5
170-180	18	150-160	14	19
160-170	22	160-170	22	41
150-160	14	170-180	18	59
180-190	10	180-190	10	69
	69		69	

From Table 9.4 the groups are not given in ascending order of magnitude and hence they are arranged in ascending order of magnitude and presented in column (3).

$$\text{Median no} = \frac{69+1}{2} = 35$$

Since 35 lies between 19 and 41 of c.f. in column (5), the median class is identified as 160-170.

$$\text{Median} = l + \frac{\left(\frac{N+1}{2} - m\right)c}{f}$$

Here $l = 160, \frac{N+1}{2} = 35, m = 19, f = 22, c = 10$

$$\text{Median} = 160 + \frac{(35-19)10}{22} = 160 + 7.27 = 167.27 \text{ cm}$$

9.1.2.1 Merits

(i) It can be calculated even when the extreme values are not well defined (ii) It can be easily located on frequency curve (iii) It is comprehensible (iv) It is having one important algebraic property i.e., the sum of absolute values of the deviations is least when the deviations are taken from median.

9.1.2.2 Demerits

(i) It is not based on all the observations (ii) It is not widely used in practice.

9.1.3 Mode

(a) Type I data (individual observational values).

Def: It is defined as that value of the variate which occurs most frequently.

Example: The following are the heights (cm) of 10 students. Find modal height.

168, 150, 164, 170, 168, 159, 171, 164, 168, 180.

In the above 168 is repeated 3 times whereas other numbers are repeated only once, therefore 168 is known as modal height.

(b) Type II data (frequency distribution)

Example: The following is the distribution of heights of students. Find modal height.

Table 9.5

Height (cm)	Students
168	9
170	10
174	15
179	20
181	24
183	12

From Table 9.5 it can be seen that the height 181 cm is having the highest frequency 24 and therefore it is the modal height.

(c) Type III data (grouped frequency distribution)

If f_1, f_2, …, f_n be n frequencies corresponding to the mid-values of the classes x_1, x_2, … x_n respectively then 'mode' is given by the formula as

$$Mode = l + \frac{(f - f_p)\ c}{2f - f_p - f_s}$$

where l = lower limit of the modal class, f = frequency of modal class, f_p = frequency of the class which is just preceding the modal class, f_s = frequency of the class which is just succeeding to the modal class, c = class interval of the modal class and modal class is that class which is having maximum frequency.

Example: The following is the grouped frequency distribution of coal production (tons) on different days. Find modal production.

Table 9.6

Coal production (tons)	Days
40-50	3
50-60	10
60-70	12
70-80	4
80-100	1

Since the class (60-70) is having maximum frequency, 12 in the Table 9.6, it is known as modal class.

$$Mode = l + \frac{(f - f_p)c}{2f - f_p - f_s}$$

where $l = 60$, $f = 12$, $f_p = 10$, $f_s = 4$, $c = 10$

$$\text{Mode} = 60 + \frac{(12-10)10}{2 \times 12 - 10 - 4} = 60 + \frac{20}{10} = 62 \text{ tons}$$

Here modal coal production is 62 tons.

9.1.3.1 Merits

(i) It can be easily located on frequency curve (ii) It can be calculated even when extreme classes are not well defined except modal class (iii) It is mostly used in business as the businessman would like to keep the item in stores which is sold maximum for getting maximum profits (iv) If the maximum frequency occurs more than once then method of grouping is adopted for identifying modal class.

9.1.3.2 Demerits

(i) It is not based on all the observations (ii) It is not having algebraic properties (iii) It is not stable since different methods of grouping would lead to different modal values.

The empirical relationship between mean, median and mode is

$$\text{Mean} - \text{Mode} = 3\,(\text{Mean} - \text{Median})$$

9.1.4 Geometric Mean

(a) Type I data (individual observational values)

Def: The geometric mean of n observations is the nth root of their product. If $x_1, x_2, \ldots, x_n$ be n observations then geometric mean is given as

$$G.M = (x_1, x_2, \ldots, x_n)^{\frac{1}{n}}$$

$$\text{Log } G.M = \frac{1}{n}\log\,(x_1,\ldots,x_n)$$

$$= \frac{1}{n}\sum_{i=1}^{n}\log x_i$$

$$G.M = \text{Antilog}\left[\frac{1}{n}\sum_{i=1}^{n}\log x_i\right]$$

Example: Find G.M for the annual incomes (lakhs) of 5 companies.

2, 4, 8, 16, 32

$$G.M = (2 \times 4 \times 8 \times 16 \times 32)^{\frac{1}{5}}$$

$$= (2 \times 2^2 \times 2^3 \times 2^4 \times 2^5)^{\frac{1}{5}}$$

$$= (2^{15})^{\frac{1}{5}} = 2^3 = 8 \text{ lakhs}$$

The G.M is 8 lakhs

(b) Type II data (frequency distribution)

Def: If $f_1, f_2, \ldots, f_n$ be n frequencies corresponding to variate values $x_1, x_2, \ldots, x_n$ respectively then Geometric Mean (G.M.) is given as

$$G.M. = \left(x_1^{f1} \,.\, x_2^{f2} \ldots x_n^{fn}\right)^{\frac{1}{N}} \qquad \text{where } N = \Sigma f_i$$

$$\text{Log } G.M. = \frac{1}{N}\left[f_1 \log x_1 + f_2 \log x_2 + \ldots + f_n \log x_n\right]$$

$$= \frac{1}{N}\left[\sum_{i=1}^{n} f_i \log x_i\right]$$

$$G.M. = \text{Anti log}\left[\frac{1}{N}\Sigma f_i \log x_i\right]$$

Example: Find G.M. for the distribution of annual income of different firms given as

Annual income (Lakhs)	3	9	27	81	243	Total
Firms	4	6	8	7	5	30

$$G.M. = \left(3^4 \times 9^6 \times 27^8 \times 81^7 \times 243^5\right)^{\frac{1}{30}}$$

$$= \left[\left(3^4 \times (3^2)^6 \times (3^3)^8 \times (3^4)^7 \times (3^5)^5\right)\right]^{\frac{1}{30}}$$

$$= \left(3^{93}\right)^{\frac{1}{30}} = 3^{\frac{93}{30}} = 3^{3.1} \text{ lakhs}$$

(c) Type III data (Grouped frequency distribution)

Def: If $f_1, f_2, \ldots, f_n$ be n frequencies corresponding to the mid-values of the classes $x_1, x_2, \ldots, x_n$ respectively then G.M. is given as

$$\text{G.M.} = \left(x_1^{f_1} \, . \, x_2^{f2} \ldots x_n^{f_n}\right)^{\frac{1}{N}}$$

$$\text{Log G.M.} = \frac{1}{N} \sum_{i=1}^{n} f_i \log x_i$$

$$\text{G.M.} = \text{Anti log } \frac{1}{N} \left[\Sigma f_i \log x_i\right]$$

$$\text{G.M.} = \text{Anti log} \left[\frac{1}{N} \Sigma f_i \log x_i\right]$$

Example: Find G.M. for the following distribution of annual incomes (lakhs) of different firms.

Table 9.7

Annual income (Lakhs)	2-6	6-10	10-22	22-42	42-86	Total
Firms	4	5	8	7	6	30
Mid-value (x_i)	4	8	16	32	64	

$$\text{G. M.} = \left(4^4 \times 8^5 \times 16^8 \times 32^7 \times 64^6\right)^{\frac{1}{30}}$$

$$= \left[\left((2^2)^4 \times (2^3)^5 \times (2^4)^8 \times (2^5)^7 \times (2^6)^6\right)\right]^{\frac{1}{30}}$$

$$= \left(2^{126}\right)^{\frac{1}{30}} = 2^{\frac{126}{30}} = 2^{4.2} \text{ lakhs}$$

9.1.4.1 Merits

(i) It has well defined formula (ii) It is based upon the all the observations (iii) It is used in computing index numbers and also in time series analysis (iv) It is used in finding compound growth rate of income, population, disease cells, light rays etc. (v) It possesses algebraic properties.

9.1.4.2 Demerits

(i) It is difficult to calculate (ii) It cannot be calculated whenever zero value is present in the observations (iii) It may not be identified with any of the given observations.

9.1.5 Harmonic Mean

(a) Type I data (individual observations)

Def: It is defined as the reciprocal of the arithmetic mean of reciprocals. If $x_1, x_2, \ldots, x_n$ be n variate values then harmonic mean (H.M.) is given as

$$\text{H.M.} = \frac{1}{\frac{1}{n}\left[\frac{1}{x_1}+\frac{1}{x_2}+\ldots\frac{1}{x_n}\right]}$$

Example: The following are the number of months quoted by firms for completing a project. Find the Harmonic mean.

10, 15, 8, 12, 20

$$\text{H.M.} = \frac{5}{\frac{1}{10}+\frac{1}{5}+\frac{1}{8}+\frac{1}{12}+\frac{1}{20}}$$

$$= \frac{5}{0.1+0.2+0.13+0.08+0.05} = \frac{5}{0.56} = 9.93$$

(b) Type II data (Frequency distribution)

Def: If $f_1, f_2, \ldots, f_n$ be n frequencies corresponding to the variate values $x_1, x_2, \ldots, x_n$ respectively, then Harmonic mean is given as

$$\text{H.M.} = \frac{N}{\frac{f_1}{x_1}+\frac{f_2}{x_2}+\ldots+\frac{f_n}{x_n}} \qquad \text{where } N = \sum_{i=1}^{n} f_i$$

Example: The following is the distribution of months quoted by different firms for completing a project.

Table 9.8

Months (x_i)	5	8	12	14	15	Total
Firms (f_i)	10	40	36	28	60	174
$\frac{f_i}{x_i}$	2	5	3	2	4	16

$$\text{H.M.} = \frac{174}{16} = 10.875 \text{ months}$$

(c) Type III data (Grouped Frequency distribution)

Def: If $f_1, f_2, \ldots, f_n$ be n frequencies corresponding to the mid-values of the classes $x_1, x_2, \ldots, x_n$ respectively, then H.M. is given as

$$\text{H.M.} = \frac{N}{\frac{f_1}{x_1} + \frac{f_2}{x_2} + \ldots + \frac{f_n}{x_n}} \qquad \text{where } N = \sum_{i=1}^{n} f_i$$

Example: The following is the distribution of months quoted by different firms. Find H.M. ?

Table 9.9

Months	4-8	8-12	12-16	16-20	Total
Firms	36	70	42	90	238
Mid-value (x_i)	6	10	14	18	
$\frac{f_i}{x_i}$	6	7	3	5	21

$$\text{H.M.} = \frac{238}{21} = 11.33 \text{ months}$$

9.1.5.1 Merits

(i) It is well defined (ii) It is based upon all the observations (iii) It is useful in finding out average time to be taken for completing a project, average time taken for covering a fixed distance by a vehicle, average time taken for filling up a water tank. Here smaller values are given more importance than larger values.

9.1.5.2 Demerits

(i) It is not much used in practice except in cases where smaller values are to be given more importance.

9.2 Measures of Dispersion

The scattering or variation among the observed values in a group of data is called dispersion. The method by which the variation in the data is measured is known as measure of dispersion. Though the central tendency value gives the representation of data but it is not sufficient to describe the data. For example the average daily production of a factory will give the idea of capacity of production of a factory but it will not indicate when it touches lowest production and when it touches highest production. Measure of dispersion gives the variation among the observations and also variation from central tendency value. The measures of dispersion are (i) Range (ii) Quartile deviation (iii) Mean deviation (iv) Standard deviation and (v) Coefficient of variation.

9.2.1 Range

It is the difference between highest and lowest values.

(a) Type I data (Individual observations)

Example: Find the range for the data on minimum temperatures recorded at a hill station for 10 days in winter month

–6, 0, 1, – 4, 2, 3, – 7, – 2, 4, 5

Range = 5 – (– 7) = 12

(b) Type II data (Frequency distribution)

Example: The following is the distribution of minimum temperature at hill station.

Table 9.10

Min. Temp.	– 6	– 4	– 2	– 1	0	3	4	5	7
Days	3	6	10	4	7	2	3	4	2

Range = 7 – (–6) = 13

(c) Type III data (Grouped frequency distribution)

***Example*:** The following is the distribution of minimum temperatures at hill station.

Table 9.11

Min. Temp	– 8 – 4	– 4 – 2	– 2 – 0	0 – 4	4 – 8
Days	4	6	10	7	3

Range = 8 – (–8) = 16

Range is of much use in for meteorological data such as temperature, rainfall, relative humidity, sunshine hours, wind velocity etc. It is easy to calculate even though the data is very large. It is useful in the preparation of control charts for maintaining quality control of products produced by factories. The range may not be much useful if extreme values are present in the data.

9.2.2 Quartile Deviation (Q.D)

This is also known as semi-inter quartile range.

$$Q.D = \frac{Q_3 - Q_1}{2}$$

where $Q_1 = 1^{st}$ quartile (lower quartile)

Def: It is that value of the variate below which $1/4^{th}$ of the values will lie and above which the remaining $3/4^{th}$ values will lie when the values are arranged in ascending order of magnitude.

$Q_3 = 3^{rd}$ quartile (upper quartile)

Def: It is that value of the variate below which $3/4^{th}$ of the values will lie and above which $1/4^{th}$ values will lie when the values are arranged in ascending order of magnitude.

(a) *Type I data (individual observations)*

Example: Find Q.D. for the plinth areas (100 sq.m) of 10 houses given the data as 6, 8, 10, 7, 11, 13, 5, 12, 9, 4.

The values are arranged in ascending order of magnitude as

S.No.	1	2	3	4	5	6	7	8	9	10
Plinth area (100 sq.m)	4	5	6	7	8	9	10	11	12	13

Q_1 No: $\frac{n+1}{4}$ where n = no. of observations

$$= \frac{10+1}{4} = 2.75$$

Q_1 Value $= 2^{nd}$ value $+ 0.75$ (3rd value $- 2^{nd}$ value)

$$= 5 + 0.75\,(6 - 5) = 5.75$$

Q_3 No: $\frac{3n+1}{4} = \frac{3 \times 10 + 1}{4} = 7.75$

Q_3 Value $= 7^{th}$ value $+ 0.75$ (8th value $- 7^{th}$ value)

$$= 10 + 0.75\,(11 - 10) = 10.75$$

$$\text{Q.D.} = \frac{10.75 - 5.75}{2} = 2.5 \quad (2.5 \times 100 = 250 \text{ sq.m})$$

(b) Type II data (Frequency distribution)

Example: the following is the distribution of plinth areas (100 sq.m) of houses in a locality. Find Q.D.

Table 9.12

Plinth area (100 sq.m)	7	9	12	14	8	6	20
Houses	5	12	10	4	11	3	7

The plinth areas in Table 9.12 are not in ascending order of magnitude. Therefore the distribution is rearranged in ascending order of magnitude and presented in Table 9.13.

Table 9.13

Plinth area (100 sq.m)	6	7	8	9	12	14	20
Houses (f_i)	3	5	11	12	10	4	7
c.f.	3	8	19	31	41	45	52

(13.25) (39.25)

The cumulative frequencies are presented in row 3 of the Table 9.13.

$$Q_1 \text{ No} = \frac{n+1}{4} \text{ where N = total frequency}$$

$$= \frac{52+1}{4} = 13.25$$

$$Q_1 \text{ Value} = 13^{th} \text{ value} + 0.25\ (14^{th} \text{ value} - 13^{th} \text{ value})$$

$$= 8 + 0.25\ (8 - 8) = 8$$

$$Q_3 \text{ No} = \frac{3N+1}{4} = \frac{3 \times 52 + 1}{4} = 39.25$$

$$Q_3 \text{ Value} = 39^{th} \text{ value} + 0.25\ (40^{th} \text{ value} - 39^{th} \text{ value})$$

$$= 12 + 0.25\ (12 - 12) = 12$$

$$\text{Q.D.} = \frac{12-8}{2} = 2 \ \ (2 \times 100 \text{ sq.m} = 200 \text{ sq.m})$$

(c) *Type III data (Grouped Frequency distribution)*

In the case of grouped frequency distribution Q_1 and Q_3 values are obtained using interpolation formulae as in the case of median. Here Q_1 value is given as

$$Q_1 = l_1 + \frac{\left(\frac{(N+1)}{4} - m_1\right) C_1}{f_1}$$

where l_1 = lower limit of Q_1 class, $\frac{N+1}{4} = Q_1$ number, m_1 = cumulative frequency just preceding to the Q_1 class, f_1 = frequency of Q_1 class and C_1 = class interval of Q_1 class. Q_1 class is that class wherein cumulative frequency $\frac{N+1}{4}$ exists.

$$Q_3 = l + \frac{\left(\frac{3N+1}{4} - m_3\right) C_3}{f_3}$$

Where l_3 = lower limit of Q_3 class, $\frac{3N+1}{4} = Q_3$ number, m_3 = cumulative frequency just preceding to the Q_3 class, f_3 = frequency of Q_3 class and C_3 = class interval of the Q_3 class. Q_3 class is that class wherein cum. freq. $\frac{3N+1}{4}$ exists.

Example: The following is the distribution of parks (1000 sq.m). Find Q.D.?

Table 9.14

Area under Parks (1000 sq.m)	2-6	6-10	10-20	20-22	22-30
Parks (f)	8	14	20	13	7
c.f.	8	22	42	55	62

Since the distribution of areas under parks are in ascending order of magnitude, there is no need to rearrange the distribution.

$$Q_1 \text{ No: } \frac{N+1}{4} = \frac{62+1}{4} = 15.75$$

The Q_1 class is (6 – 10) since 15.75 lies between cum. freqs. 8 and 22.

$$l_1 = 6, \quad \frac{N+1}{4} = 15.75, \quad m_1 = 8, \quad f_1 = 14, \quad C_1 = 4$$

$$Q_1 = 6 + \frac{(15.75 - 8)\ 4}{14} = 6 + 2.21 = 8.21$$

$$Q_3 \text{ No.} = \frac{3N+1}{4} = \frac{3 \times 62 + 1}{4} = 46.75$$

Here Q_3 class is (20 – 22) since Q_3 No. (46.75) lies between cum. freqs. 42 and 55.

$$l_3 = 20, \quad \frac{3N+1}{4} = 46.75, \quad m_3 = 42, \quad f_3 = 13, \quad C_3 = 2$$

$$Q_3 = 20 + \frac{(46.75 - 42.0)\ 2}{13} = 20 + 0.73 = 20.73$$

$$\text{Q.D.} = \frac{(20.73 - 8.21)}{2} = 6.26 \qquad (6.26 \times 1000 = 6260 \text{ sq.m})$$

9.2.3 Mean Deviation (M.D.)

It is defined as the arithmetic mean of the absolute values of deviations taken from any central tendency value. The central tendency value can be taken as Arithmetic Mean, Median, Mode etc.

Type I data (Individual observation values)

Def: if $x_1, x_2, \ldots, x_n$ be n observations then the

$$\text{M.D. from Mean} = \frac{1}{n}\,\Sigma\,|x_i - \bar{x}| \qquad \text{where } \bar{x} = \text{A.M.}$$

$$\text{M.D. from Median} = \frac{1}{n}\,\Sigma\,|x_i - M| \qquad \text{where M = Median}$$

$$\text{M.D. from Mode} = \frac{1}{n}\,\Sigma\,|x_i - M_0| \qquad \text{where } M_0 = \text{Mode}$$

Example: Find M.D. from Mean, Median and Mode for the following daily production of pesticide (tons) by a pesticide factory.

8, 10, 7, 9, 8, 11, 14, 16, 12, 5

Table 9.15

S.No.	x_i	$\lvert x_i - \bar{x} \rvert$ $\bar{x} = 10$	$\lvert x_i - M \rvert$ $M = 9.5$	$\lvert x_i - M_0 \rvert$ $M_0 = 8$
1	8	2	1.5	0
2	10	0	0.5	2
3	7	3	2.5	1
4	9	1	0.5	1
5	8	2	1.5	0
6	11	1	1.5	3
7	14	4	4.5	6
8	16	6	6.5	8
9	12	2	2.5	4
10	5	5	4.5	3
Total	100	26	26.0	28
Mean	10			

In order to find out 'Median' the data given above is arranged in ascending order of magnitude as follows.

S.No.	1	2	3	4	5	6	7	8	9	10
	5	7	8	8	9	10	11	12	14	16

$$\text{Median} = \frac{10+1}{2} = 5.5$$

$$\text{Median} = 5^{th} \text{ value} + 0.5\ (6^{th} \text{ value} - 5^{th} \text{ value})$$

$$= 9 + 0.5\ (10 - 9) = 9.5$$

Since '8' value is repeated twice 8 is taken as mode value

$$\text{M.D. from Mean} = \frac{26}{10} = 2.6$$

$$\text{M.D. from Median} = \frac{26}{10} = 2.6$$

$$\text{M.D. from Mode} = \frac{28}{10} = 2.8$$

(b) Type II data (Frequency distribution)

Def: If $f_1, f_2, \ldots, f_n$ be n frequencies corresponding to the variate values $x_1, x_2, \ldots, x_n$ respectively then mean deviation is given as

$$\text{M.D. from Mean} = \frac{1}{N} \Sigma f_i \left| x_i - \bar{x} \right| \qquad \text{where } \bar{x} = \text{A.M.}$$

$$\text{M.D. from Median} = \frac{1}{N} \Sigma f_i \left| x_i - M \right| \qquad \text{where M = Median}$$

$$\text{M.D. from Mode} = \frac{1}{N} \Sigma f_i \left| x_i - M_0 \right| \qquad \text{where } M_0 = \text{Mode}$$

Example: The following is the distribution of production of urea (tons) fertilizer on different days in a fertilizer factory. Find M.D. from Mean, Median and Mode.

Table 9.16

Production (tons) (x_i)	Days (f_i)	c.f.	$f_i x_i$	$\lvert x_i - \bar{x} \rvert$	$f_i \lvert x_i - \bar{x} \rvert$	$\lvert x_i - M \rvert$	$f_i \lvert x_i - M \rvert$	$f_i \lvert x_i - M_0 \rvert$
6	3	3	18	3.9	11.7	5	15	15
9	6	9	54	0.9	5.4	2	12	12
11	12	21	132	1.1	13.2	0	0	0
12	7	28	84	2.1	14.7	1	7	7
5	2	30	10	4.9	9.8	6	12	12
Total	30		298		54.8		46	46

$$\bar{x} = \frac{298}{30} = 9.9$$

$$\text{Median No.} = \frac{30+1}{2} = 15.5$$

$$\text{Median} = 11$$

$$\text{Mode} = 11$$

$$\text{M.D. from Mean} = \frac{54.8}{30} = 1.83 \text{ tons}$$

$$\text{M.D. from Median} = \frac{46}{30} = 1.53 \text{ tons}$$

$$\text{M.D. from Mean} = \frac{46}{30} = 1.53 \text{ tons}$$

(c) Type III data (Grouped frequency distribution)

Def: If $f_1, f_2, \ldots, f_n$ be n frequencies corresponding to the mid-values of the classes $x_1, x_2, \ldots, x_n$ respectively the M.D. is given as

$$\text{M.D. from Mean} = \frac{1}{N} \sum_{i=1}^{n} f_i \left|x_i - \bar{x}\right| \quad \text{where } \bar{x} = \text{A.M.}$$

$$\text{M.D. from Median} = \frac{1}{N} \sum_{i=1}^{n} f_i \left|x_i - M\right| \quad \text{where M = Median}$$

$$\text{M.D. from Mode} = \frac{1}{N} \sum_{i=1}^{n} f_i \left|x_i - M_0\right| \quad \text{where } M_0 = \text{Mode}$$

Example: The following is the distribution of steel production (m. tons) on different days in a steel factory. Find M.D. from Mean?

Table 9.17

Production (m. tons)	Days (f_i)	M.V. x_i	$f_i x_i$	$\left\|x_i - \bar{x}\right\|$	$f_i \left\|x_i - \bar{x}\right\|$
4-8	3	6	18	6.7	20.1
8-12	10	10	100	2.7	27.0
12-16	12	14	168	1.3	15.6
16-20	4	18	72	5.3	21.2
20-24	1	22	22	9.3	9.3
	30		380		93.2

$$\bar{x} = \frac{380}{30} = 12.7$$

$$\text{M.D. from Mean} = \frac{93.2}{30} = 3.11 \text{ (m. tons)}$$

Similarly M.D. from Median and Mode can be calculated using appropriate formulae for Type III data.

9.2.4 Standard Deviation (S.D.)

It is defined as the positive square root of the arithmetic mean of the squares of deviation taken from Arithmetic mean.

(a) Type I data (Individual observational values)

Def: If $x_1, x_2, \ldots, x_n$ be n observations then S.D. is given as

$$\text{S.D.} = \sigma = \sqrt{\frac{1}{n}\sum_{i=1}^{n}(x_i - \bar{x})^2}$$

$$\text{Variance} = \sigma^2 = \frac{1}{n}\Sigma(x_i - \bar{x})^2$$

Example: The following are the daily production (tons) of coal. Find S.D.

10, 8, 12, 10, 9, 13, 14, 16, 15, 13

Table 9.18

S. No.	Production x_i	$(x_i - \bar{x})$	$(x_i - \bar{x})^2$
1	10	− 2	4
2	8	− 4	16
3	12	0	0
4	10	− 2	4
6	9	− 3	9
7	13	1	1
8	14	2	4
9	16	4	16
10	15	3	9
11	13	1	1
Total	120		64
Mean	12		

$$\text{S.D} = \sigma = \sqrt{\frac{64}{10}} = \sqrt{6.4} = 2.53 \text{ (m. tons)}$$

$$\text{Variance} = \sigma^2 = 6.4 \text{ (m. tons)}$$

(b) Type II data (Frequency distribution)

Def: If $f_1, f_2, \ldots, f_n$ be n frequencies corresponding to the variate values $x_1, x_2, \ldots, x_n$ respectively, then S.D. is given as

$$\text{S.D} = \sigma = \sqrt{\frac{1}{n}\Sigma f_i(x_i - \bar{x})^2} \qquad \text{where } N = \sum_{i=1}^{n} f_i$$

$$\text{Variance} = \sigma^2 = \frac{1}{N}\Sigma f_i(x_i - \bar{x})^2$$

Example: The following is the distribution of areas (1000 sq. m) under roads and buildings in different colonies in a city.

Table 9.19

Area (000 sq.m) (x_i)	Colonies (f_i)	$f_i x_i$	$(x_i - \bar{x})$	$(x_i - \bar{x})^2$	$f_i (x_i - \bar{x})^2$
4	6	24	– 1.5	2.25	13.50
8	10	80	2.5	6.25	62.50
12	4	48	– 3.5	12.25	49.00
9	7	63	0.5	0.25	1.75
3	3	9	– 4.5	20.25	60.75
Total	30	224			187.50

$$\bar{x} = \frac{224}{30} = 7.5$$

$$\text{S.D.} = \sigma = \sqrt{\frac{187.50}{30}} = \sqrt{12.5}$$

$$= 3.54 \quad (3.54 \times 1000 = 3540 \text{ sq. m})$$

$$\sigma^2 = 12.5 \quad (12.5 \times 1000 = 12{,}500 \text{ sq. m})$$

(c) Type III data (Grouped Frequency distribution)

Def: If $f_1, f_2, \ldots, f_n$ be n frequencies corresponding to the mid-values of the classes $x_1, x_2, \ldots, x_n$ respectively, then standard deviation is given as

$$\text{S.D.} = \sigma = \sqrt{\frac{1}{N} \Sigma f_i (x_i - \bar{x})^2} \qquad \text{where } \bar{x} = \text{A.M.}$$

$$\text{Variance} = \sigma^2$$

Example: The following is the distribution of production of fertilizer (tons) in different days by a fertilizer factory. Find S.D. and variance.

Table 9.20

Production (tons)	Days (f_i)	M.V. (x_i)	$f_i x_i$	$(x_i - \bar{x})$	$(x_i - \bar{x})^2$	$f_i (x_i - \bar{x})^2$
2-6	3	4	12	– 7.2	51.84	155.52
6-10	8	8	64	– 3.2	10.24	81.92
10-14	14	12	168	0.8	0.64	8.96

Table 9.20 *Contd...*

Production (tons)	Days (f_i)	M.V. (x_i)	$f_i x_i$	$(x_i - \bar{x})$	$(x_i - \bar{x})^2$	$f_i (x_i - \bar{x})^2$
14-18	2	16	32	4.8	23.04	46.08
18-22	3	20	60	8.8	77.44	232.32
Total	30		336		163.20	524.80

$$\bar{x} = \frac{\Sigma f_i x_i}{\Sigma f_i} = \frac{336}{30} = 11.2$$

$$\sigma = \sqrt{\frac{524.80}{30}} = \sqrt{17.49} = 4.18 \text{ tons}$$

$$\sigma^2 = \text{variance} = 17.49 \text{ (tons)}$$

It may be noted that standard deviation is used in most of the advanced statistical techniques as a basic tool for assessing the variation in the data. It is extensively used in tests of hypotheses, statistical genetics, quality control, probability distributions etc. Quartile deviation and mean deviations are not used in advanced statistical techniques as basic tools. These along with Range are generally used for secondary data.

$$\text{Coefficient of variation (C.V)} = \frac{\text{S.D}}{\text{Mean}} \times 100$$

This is used for measuring the consistency of one or more series of data. The less is the C.V. the more is the consistency.

9.3 Skewness

Skewness is known as the asymmetry in the shape of the curve. If Mean, Median and Mode are all equal then the shape the frequency curve is symmetric. The curve is depicted in Fig. 9.1.

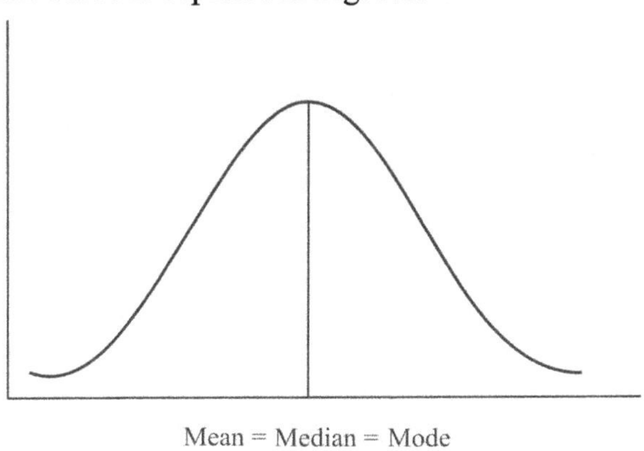

Fig. 9.1

(a) *Positively skewed curve:* If the curve bends towards left and long tail on right then it is called positively skewed curve and it is shown in Fig. 9.2

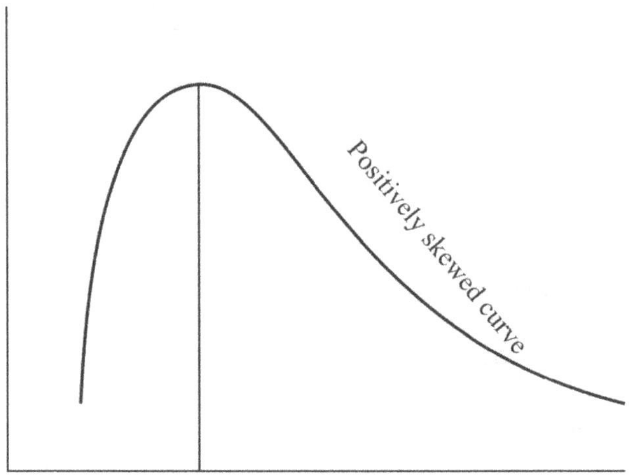

Fig. 9.2

(b) *Negatively skewed curve:* If the curve bends towards right and long tail towards left then it is known as negatively skewed curve and it is depicted in Fig. 9.3.

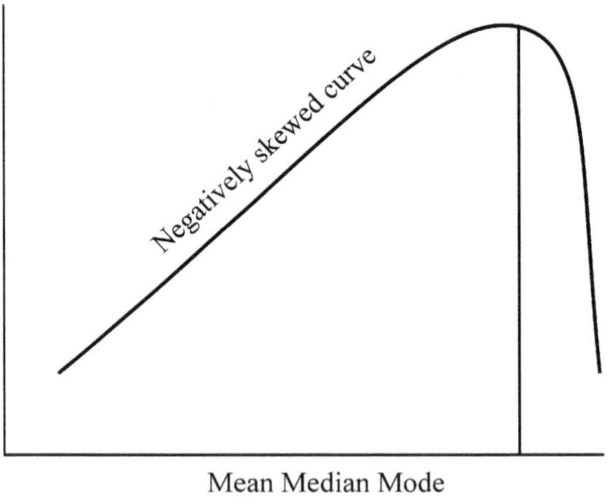

Fig. 9.3

The extent of skewness in curve is measured by coefficient of skewness, β_1. The formulae are given as

(i) Pearson's coefficient of skewness $= \dfrac{(\text{Mean} - \text{Mode})}{\text{S.D.}}$

(ii) Quartile coefficient of skewness $= \dfrac{(Q_3 - Q_2) - (Q_2 - Q_1)}{(Q_3 - Q_1)}$

where Q_1, Q_2 and Q_3 are 1st, 2nd and 3rd quartiles respectively.

(iii) Moment coefficient of skewness $\beta_1 = \dfrac{\mu_3}{\mu_2\sqrt{\mu_2}}$

where μ_2 and μ_3 are 2nd and 3rd central moments respectively and $\mu_2 = \dfrac{1}{N}\,\Sigma\,(x_i - \bar{x})^2$, $\mu_3 = \dfrac{1}{N}\Sigma\,(x_i - \bar{x})^3$ for type I data.

For a symmetric curve the coefficient of skewness is zero since mean equal to mode.

9.4 Kurtosis

The shape of the vertex of curve is denoted as kurtosis. Though the curves may be symmetric yet they may differ with respect to shape of the vertex. The distance from vertex of the curve to the x-axis is measured by coefficient of kurtosis. If this ordinate distance is equal to '3' then it is called Mesokurtic or Normal curve. If the ordinate length is more than 3 then it is known as 'Lepto Kurtic' curve and if this length is less than '3' then it is said to be 'Platy kurtic' curve. These curves are depicted in Fig. 9.4.

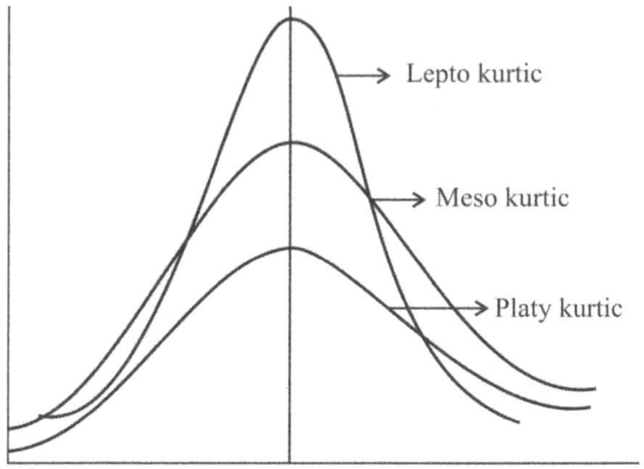

Fig. 9.4

The coefficient of kurtosis is given as

$$\beta_2 = \frac{\mu_4}{\mu_2^2}$$

where μ_2 and μ_4 are 2nd and 4th central moments respectively and

$$\mu_2 = \frac{1}{N}\,\Sigma\,(x_i - \bar{x})^2, \qquad \mu_4 = \frac{1}{N}\,\Sigma\,(x_i - \bar{x})^4$$

for type I data.

Both coefficients of skewness and kurtosis are independent of units of measurement. These tools are generally used for secondary data.

CHAPTER 10

Tests of Hypotheses

10.1 Introduction

Tests of hypotheses are used for making decisions in management. Hypothesis is a statement based on assumption formed by previous knowledge and experience. For example, a statement such as if power supply is good the production in a factory is good. This statement is considered as hypothesis. The average production in a factory over several years was found to be 34 tons per day. This average production is taken as hypothesis. If the average production for 10 days was obtained as 32 tons, now it is to be tested whether the difference of 2 tons is a real difference or due to sampling fluctuation. This is called test of hypothesis. If the difference is not due to sampling fluctuation then corrective measures are to be taken by management. If the difference is real then it is called significant difference. For testing significant difference or not, standard error is used in tests of hypotheses. In tests of hypotheses the concepts used are

(i) Null hypothesis
(ii) Alternate hypothesis
(iii) Level of significance and
(iv) Degrees of freedom

10.1.1 Null Hypothesis

It is a statement about the parameter or parameters which is likely to be rejected after testing. If two samples are to be tested then the null hypothesis is equality of means in the populations. Usually the null hypothesis is denoted by H_0.

10.1.2 Alternate Hypothesis

This is a statement about parameters or parameters when null hypothesis is rejected. If null hypothesis is rejected then alternate hypothesis is accepted. It is denoted by H_1.

10.1.3 Level of Significance

Before explaining the level of significance, the two types of errors are explained here.

Type I error: Rejecting the null hypothesis when it ought to be accepted.

Type II error: Accepting the null hypothesis when it ought to be rejected.

Usually both type I and type II errors are committed in tests of hypothesis. Though both errors are serious and should be avoided but it is not possible to avoid these two errors. Since type I error is more serious than type II error it is restricted to certain level of probability. The probability at which the type I error is restricted is called 'Level of significance'. If the probability is 0.01 then it is known as 1 percent level of significance and if it is 0.05 then it is called 5 percent level of significance. In other words the decision of rejecting the null hypothesis when it ought to be accepted will be 1 or 5 out of 100 cases respectively.

10.1.4 Degrees of Freedom

The mathematical definition for degrees of freedom is given as the total number of linearly independent contrasts that can be formed from 'n' unknowns constants. If 'n' is the total number of unknown constants and 'k' linearly independent contrasts that can be formed from them then 'k' is called the degrees of freedom.

The elementary definition is stated as the difference between total number of items and total number of constraints. If n is the total number of items and k is the total number of constraints then the degrees of freedom (d.f.) is (n – k). For example, if five numbers are to be chosen such that the total should be 100 then four numbers can be chosen at freedom and fifth number has to be chosen such that total of 5 numbers should be 100. Here the d.f. is 5 – 1 = 4.

If x follows normal distribution with mean, μ and S.D., σ then $\bar{x}$ also follows normal distribution with mean, μ and S.D., $\frac{\sigma}{\sqrt{n}}$.

Here $\frac{\sigma}{\sqrt{n}}$ is called standard error of mean.

Further, $\frac{\bar{x}-\mu}{\frac{\sigma}{\sqrt{n}}} = Z$ also follows normal distribution with mean equal to zero and S.D. as 1.

The curve of standard normal distribution is given in Fig. 10.1.

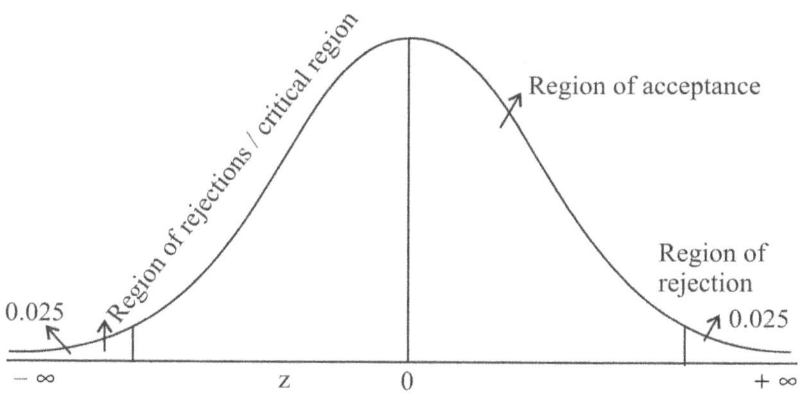

Fig. 10.1

If 'z' value falls in the regions of rejection then the null hypothesis is rejected. If z value falls in the region of acceptance then the null hypothesis is accepted. If the region of rejection area is 0.025 on both-sides of curve in Fig. 10.1 then the total area of rejection is 0.025 + 0.025 = 0.05 i.e., 5 per cent level of significance. If the region of rejection is 0.005 on both sides of the curve then the total area of rejection is 0.005 + 0.005 = 0.01

$$Z = \frac{\bar{x}-\mu}{\frac{\sigma}{\sqrt{n}}} \sim N(0, 1)$$

Z is called standard normal deviate (S.N.D.) and the test based on S.N.D. is called S.N.D. test. The confidence limits or fidicual limits for population mean can be obtained as $\bar{x} \pm 1.96\ \sigma/\sqrt{n}$. In other words the population mean, μ lies between $\bar{x}-1.96\ \sigma/\sqrt{n}$ and $\bar{x}+1.96\ \sigma/\sqrt{n}$ where 1.96 is the tabulated value of normal distribution at 5 per cent level of significance.

10.2 One Sample S.N.D. Test (Z-test)

Case (i) : Population standard deviation, σ is known

Assumption: (i) population is normal and (ii) sample is drawn at random

Conditions: (i) population S.D., σ is known and (ii) size of the sample may be small or large.

$$H_0 : \mu = \mu_0, \quad H_1 : \mu \neq \mu_0$$

where μ is the population mean and μ_0 is the population mean under null hypothesis.

$$Z = \frac{|\bar{x} - \mu|}{\frac{\sigma}{\sqrt{n}}}$$

where

$\bar{x}$ = mean of sample

n = sample size

σ = population S.D.

Conclusion

If Z (calculated) value > Z (tabulated) value at the required level of significance then null hypothesis, H_0 is rejected and alternate hypothesis H_1 is accepted. If H_0 is rejected then it can be concluded that there is significant difference between sample mean and population mean and sample may not belong to the population with respect to character under consideration. Otherwise, H_0 is accepted.

Example: The average daily production of a cement factory over several years was found to be 46 tons with a S.D. of 6 tons. On inspection for 10 days, the daily production was recorded as

38, 56, 44, 40, 36, 43, 51, 49, 37, 26

Test whether there is any significant difference between sample production and average production recorded over several years at 5 per cent level of significance.

$$H_0 : \mu = \mu_0 = 46$$

$$\bar{x} = \frac{38 + 56 + ... + 26}{10} = \frac{420}{10} = 42$$

$$\sigma = 6$$

$$Z = \frac{|42 - 46|}{\frac{6}{\sqrt{10}}}$$

$$= \frac{4\sqrt{10}}{6} = 2.11$$

Conclusion

Here Z (cal.) value i.e., 2.11 > Z (tab.) value i.e., 1.96 at 5 per cent level of significance. Therefore H_0 is rejected and H_1 is accepted. Hence it can be concluded that there is significant difference between sample average production and average production of the factory and therefore necessary steps have to be taken for restoring the production.

Case (ii) : Population S.D., σ is not known

Assumption: (i) population is normal and (ii) sample is drawn at random

Conditions: (i) population S.D., σ is not known and (ii) size of the sample is large (n > 30).

$$H_0 : \mu = \mu_0, \qquad H_1 : \mu \neq \mu_0$$

$$Z = \frac{|\bar{x} - \mu|}{\frac{s}{\sqrt{n}}}$$

where $S^2 = \frac{1}{n}\Sigma(x_i - \bar{x})^2$ for type I data

$$S^2 = \frac{1}{N}\Sigma f_i(x_i - \bar{x})^2 \text{ for type II and III data}$$

$\bar{x}$ = sample mean, n = size of sample

Conclusion

Same as in case (i)

Example: The distribution of urea production on different days in a fertilizer factory is given as follows. The daily production of urea over several years was found to be 25 tons. Test whether the sample daily production is significantly different from average production at 1 percent level of significance.

Production	10-15	15-20	20-25	25-30
Days	8	10	11	2

Table 10.1

Production	Days (f_i)	M.V. (x_i)	$f_i\, x_i$	$(x_i - \bar{x})$	$f_i\,(x_i - \bar{x})^2$
10-15	8	12.5	100.0	6.1	297.68
15-20	10	17.5	175.0	1.1	12.10
20-25	11	22.5	247.5	3.9	167.31
25-30	2	27.5	55.0	8.9	158.42
Total	31		577.5		635.51

$$\bar{x} = \frac{577.5}{31} = 18.6$$

$$S^2 = \frac{635.51}{31} = 20.5$$

$$Z = \frac{118.6 - 251}{\sqrt{\frac{20.5}{31}}} = \frac{6.4}{0.81} = 7.9$$

Conclusion

Here Z (cal.) value i.e., 7.9 > Z (tab.) value i.e., 2.58 at 1 per cent level of significance. Therefore H_0 is rejected and H_1 is accepted. Hence it can be concluded that the average sample daily production is significantly different from average production of a factory.

10.3 Two Sample S.N.D. Test (Z-test)

Case (i) : Common population S.D., σ is known

Assumptions: (i) population is normal and (ii) samples are drawn independently and at random

Conditions: (i) common population S.D., σ is known and (ii) sizes of samples may be small or large.

$$H_0 : \mu_1 = \mu_2, \qquad H_1 : \mu_1 \neq \mu_2$$

where μ_1 and μ_2 are the means of 1st and 2nd populations respectively.

$$Z = \frac{\left|\bar{x}_1 - \bar{x}_2\right|}{\sqrt{\sigma^2\left(\frac{1}{n_1} + \frac{1}{n_2}\right)}}$$

where $\bar{x}_1$, $\bar{x}_2$ are means of 1st and 2nd samples with sizes n_1 and n_2 respectively.

Conclusion

If Z (cal.) value > Z (tab.) value at the required level of significance then H_0 is rejected and H_1 is accepted. Otherwise H_0 is accepted. If H_0 is rejected then it can be concluded that there is significant difference between two sample means.

Example: The standard deviation of the daily production of steel for a corporate company was found to be 15 (m.t.) The average daily production of steel for 1st factory of the company was recorded as 126 (m.t.) based on 20 days data and for 2nd factory 137 (m.t.) based on 40 days data. Test whether 2nd factory production is significantly more than 1st factory at 5 per cent level of significance.

$$H_0 : \mu_1 = \mu_2 \; ; \; H_1 : \mu_2 > \mu_1$$

where μ_1 and μ_2 are 1st and 2nd population means respectively. Here H_1 is $\mu_2 > \mu_1$ and it is known as one-tailed test and the critical region is one side of the curve. The table value of z is taken for 10 per cent level for 5 per cent of two-tailed test.

Here $\bar{x}_1 = 126, \quad \bar{x}_2 = 137, \quad \sigma = 15$

$n_1 = 20, \quad n_2 = 40$

$$Z = \frac{|126 - 137|}{\sqrt{(15)^2\left[\frac{1}{20} + \frac{1}{40}\right]}} = \frac{11}{\sqrt{16.875}} = \frac{11}{4.1} = 2.68$$

Conclusion

Here Z (cal.) value i.e., 2.68 > Z (tab.) value i.e., 1.645 at 10 per cent level of significance. Therefore H_0 is rejected and H_1 is accepted. Hence it can be concluded the average production of 2nd factory is significantly more than the 1st factory.

Case (ii): Common population S.D., σ is not known

Assumptions: (i) populations are normal and (ii) samples are drawn independently and at random

Conditions: (i) common population S.D., σ is not known and (ii) sizes of samples are large ($n_1 > 30, n_2 > 30$)

$$H_0 : \mu_1 = \mu_2 ; \qquad H_1 : \mu_1 \neq \mu_2$$

$$Z = \frac{\left|\bar{x}_1 - \bar{x}_2\right|}{\sqrt{\left(\frac{S_1^2}{n_1} + \frac{S_2^2}{n_2}\right)}}$$

where $$S_1^2 = \frac{1}{n_1}\Sigma\left(x_1 - \bar{x}_1\right)^2, \quad S_2^2 = \frac{1}{n_2}\Sigma\left(x_2 - \bar{x}_2\right)^2$$

for type I data

$$S_1^2 = \frac{1}{N_1}\Sigma f_i\left(x_1 - \bar{x}_1\right)^2, \quad S_2^2 = \frac{1}{N_2}\Sigma f_i\left(x_2 - \bar{x}_2\right)^2$$

for type II and type III data

and $\bar{x}_1$ and $\bar{x}_2$ are the means of 1st and 2nd samples with sizes n_1 and n_2 respectively.

Conclusion

Same as in case (i)

Example: The average marks scored by 2009 batch B.Tech (planning) consisting of 48 students was 74 with a S.D. of 12 marks and the average marks of 38 students of 2010 batch was 68 with a S.D. of 10 marks. Test the hypothesis that 2009 batch students are superior to 2010 students at 1 per cent level with respect to their performance.

$$H_0 : \mu_1 = \mu_2; \qquad H_1 : \mu_1 > \mu_2$$

Here $\bar{x}_1 = 74$, $\bar{x}_2 = 68$, $n_1 = 48$

$n_2 = 38$, $S_1 = 12$, $S_2 = 10$

$$Z = \frac{|74 - 68|}{\sqrt{\left[\frac{(12)^2}{48} + \frac{(10)^2}{38}\right]}} = \frac{6}{\sqrt{5.63}} = \frac{6}{2.37} = 2.53$$

Conclusion

Here Z (cal.) value i.e., 2.53 > Z (tab.) value i.e., 2.33 at 2 per cent level of significance. Therefore H_0 is rejected and H_1 is accepted. Hence it can be concluded that 2009 batch students are superior to 2010 students based on their performance.

10.4 Student's t-distribution

This distribution is symmetrical about the origin, unimodal and extends from $-\infty$ to $+\infty$. It was developed by W.S. Gosset with pen name as 'student'. If sample size, n becomes large this distribution tends to standard normal distribution with mean equal to zero and variance equal to one. If the sample size is small ($n \leq 30$) and population S.D., σ is not known then t-distribution is used instead of standard normal distribution and the tests based on t-distribution are called t-tests.

10.4.1 One Sample t-test

Assumptions: (i) population is normal and (ii) sample is drawn at random

Conditions: (i) population S.D., σ is not known and (ii) size of the sample is small ($n \leq 30$),

$H_0 : \mu = \mu_0$; $H_1 : \mu \neq \mu_0$

$$t = \frac{|\bar{x} - \mu|}{\sqrt{\frac{s^2}{n}}}$$

where $s^2 = \frac{1}{n-1} \Sigma (x_i - \bar{x})^2$ and is the unbiased estimate of population variance, σ^2.

The confidence limits for population mean are given as

$$\bar{x} \pm t_{(n-1)} \times \sqrt{\frac{s^2}{n}}$$

In other words, the population mean, μ lies between lower limit $\bar{x} - t_{(n-1)} \times \sqrt{\frac{s^2}{n}}$ and upper limit $\bar{x} + t_{(n-1)} \times \sqrt{\frac{s^2}{n}}$ where $t_{(n-1)}$ is the tabulated value of t-distribution with $(n - 1)$ degrees of freedom.

Conclusion

If t (cal.) value > t (tab.) value with (n – 1) d.f. at the required level of significance, the H_0 is rejected and H_1 is accepted. If H_0 isrejected then it can be concluded that there is significant difference between sample mean and population mean and the sample does not belong to the population with respect to character under consideration.

Example: The average sales per day of cakes prepared by a Bakery was 5.6 (₹000) based on several years data. The sample sales for 10 days were recorded as

4.8, 5.2, 4.9, 5.7, 4.2, 5.1, 5.0, 4.8, 5.4, 5.3

Test the significant difference between sample sales and record sales at 5 per cent level and also find the confidence limits for the population mean.

Table 10.2

S.No.	x_i	$(x_i - \bar{x})$	$(x_i - \bar{x})^2$
1	4.8	– 0.24	0.0576
2	5.2	0.16	0.0256
3	4.9	– 0.14	0.0196
4	5.7	0.66	0.4356
5	4.2	– 0.84	0.7056
6	5.1	– 0.06	0.0036
7	5.0	– 0.04	0.0016
8	4.8	– 0.24	0.0576
9	5.4	0.36	0.1296
10	5.3	0.26	0.0676
	50.4		1.5040

$$\bar{x} = \frac{50.4}{10} = 5.04$$

$$s^2 = \frac{1.5040}{9} = 0.1671$$

$$t = \frac{|5.04 - 5.60|}{\sqrt{\frac{0.1671}{10}}} = \frac{0.56}{0.13} = 4.31$$

The confidence limits for population mean are given as

$$\bar{x} - t_{n-1} \times \sqrt{\frac{s^2}{n}} = 5.04 - 2.26 \times 0.13 = 4.75$$

$$\bar{x} + t_{n-1} \times \sqrt{\frac{s^2}{n}} = 5.04 + 2.26 \times 0.13 = 5.33$$

Conclusion

Here t (cal.) value i.e., 4.31 > t (tab.) value i.e., 2.26 with at (10 – 1) d.f. 5 per cent level of significance. Therefore H_0 is rejected and H_1 is accepted. Hence it can be concluded that the average sample sales are significantly lower than average sales over the years. Also it can be verified the average sales over the years does not lie between confidence limits i.e., 4.75 and 5.33.

10.4.2 Two Sample t-test (Independent t-test)

Assumptions: (i) population are normal and (ii) samples are drawn independently and at random.

Conditions: (i) common population S.D., σ is not known and (ii) sizes of samples are small ($n_1 \leq 30$, $n_2 \leq 30$)

$$H_0 : \mu_1 = \mu_2 \; ; \quad H_1 : \mu_1 \neq \mu_2$$

$$t = \frac{|\bar{x}_1 - \bar{x}_2|}{\sqrt{s_c^2 \left(\frac{1}{n_1} + \frac{1}{n_2}\right)}}$$

where $$s_c^2 = \frac{(n_1 - 1)\, s_1^2 + (n_2 - 1)\, s_2^2}{n_1 + n_2 - 2} = \frac{\Sigma(x_1 - \bar{x}_1)^2 + \Sigma(x_2 - \bar{x}_2)^2}{n_1 + n_2 - 2}$$

and $$s_1^2 = \frac{1}{n_1 - 1}\, \Sigma(x_1 - \bar{x}_1)^2, \quad s_2^2 = \frac{1}{n_2 - 1}\, \Sigma(x_2 - \bar{x}_2)^2$$

$\bar{x}_1$, $\bar{x}_2$ are the means of 1st and 2nd samples with n_1 and n_2 sizes respectively. s_c^2 is called the combined estimate of variance, σ^2.

The confidence limits for the difference of two population means are given as

$$(\bar{x}_1 - \bar{x}_2) \pm t_{(n_1+n_2-2)} \times \sqrt{s_c^2 \left(\frac{1}{n_1} + \frac{1}{n_2}\right)}$$

where $t_{(n_1+n_2-2)}$ is the tabulated value of t-distribution with $(n_1 + n_2 - 2)$ d.f. and $\sqrt{s_c^2 \left(\frac{1}{n} + \frac{1}{n_2}\right)}$ is the standard error for the difference of two sample means.

Conclusion

If t (Cal.) value > t (tab.) value with $(n_1 + n_2 - 2)$ d.f. at the required level of significance, the H_0 is rejected and H_1 is accepted. If H_0 is rejected then it can be concluded that there is significant difference between two sample means. Otherwise, H_0 is accepted.

Example: The following are the daily outputs (tons) of two kilns A and B in a cement factory.

Days

Kiln	**1**	**2**	**3**	**4**	**5**	**6**
A	12	18	20	24	21	
B	20	26	18	30	32	24

Test the significant difference between two kilns A and B at 5 per cent level and find the confidence limits for the difference of two population means.

Table 10.3

S.No.	A x_1	B x_2	$(x_1 - \bar{x}_1)$	$(x_1 - \bar{x}_1)^2$	$(x_2 - \bar{x}_2)$	$(x_2 - \bar{x}_2)^2$
1	12	20	– 7	49	– 5	25
2	18	26	– 1	1	1	1
3	20	18	1	1	– 7	49
4	24	30	5	25	5	25
5	21	32	2	4	7	49
6		24			– 1	1
Total	95	150		80		150
Mean	19	25				

Here $\bar{x}_1 = 19, \quad \bar{x}_2 = 25$

$$s_c^2 = \frac{\Sigma(x_1 - \bar{x}_1)^2 + \Sigma(x_2 - \bar{x}_2)^2}{n_1 + n_2 - 2} = \frac{80 + 150}{5 + 6 - 2} = \frac{230}{9} = 25.56$$

$$t = \frac{|19 - 25|}{\sqrt{25.56\left(\frac{1}{5} + \frac{1}{6}\right)}} = \frac{6}{\sqrt{9.37}} = \frac{6}{3.06} = 1.96$$

The confidence limits for the difference of two population means are

$$\left(\bar{x}_1 - \bar{x}_2\right) \pm t_{n_1 + n_2 - 2} \times \sqrt{s_c^2\left(\frac{1}{n_1} + \frac{1}{n_2}\right)}$$

$$6 \pm 2.26 \times 3.06 = (-0.92, 12.92)$$

Conclusion

Here t (cal.) value i.e., 1.96 < t (tab.) value with (5 + 6 – 2) d.f. i.e., 2.26 at 5 per cent level of significance. Therefore, H_0 is accepted. Hence it can be concluded that there is no significant difference between two kilns with respect to their output. Further the difference between two population means will lie between – 0.92 to 12.92.

10.4.3 Paired t-test (Dependent t-test)

Assumptions: (i) populations are normal and (ii) paired sample is drawn at random

Conditions: (i) common population S.D., σ is not known and (ii) sizes of samples are equal, small and related. ($n_1 = n_2 = n \leq 30$)

$$H_0 : \mu_1 = \mu_2 \quad ; \quad H_1 : \mu_1 \neq \mu_2$$

$$t = \frac{|\bar{d}|}{\sqrt{\frac{s_d^2}{n}}}$$

where $\quad d_i = (x_{1i} - x_{2i}), \quad \bar{d} = \frac{\sum_{i=1}^{n} d_i}{n}$

$$s_d^2 = \frac{1}{n-1} \Sigma(d_i - \bar{d})^2 = \frac{1}{n-1}\left[\Sigma d_i^2 - \frac{(\Sigma\, d_i^2)}{n}\right]$$

The paired t-test is generally used when the samples are small, equal and related. For example, comparison between the output of coal between morning and evening shifts, comparison between practical and theory marks of students of a particular course, comparison of two drugs effect on the same patients, comparison of two branches of tree with respect to bearing of fruits, comparison of two diets with respect to gain in weight of children etc., can be tested with the help of paired t-test.

Example: The following are the coal output (tons) in a coal mine for 10 days with respect to day and night shifts.

Days

Shift	**1**	**2**	**3**	**4**	**5**	**6**	**7**	**8**	**9**	**10**
Day	22	29	30	24	32	28	34	31	27	23
Night	18	22	31	22	23	24	28	26	29	25

Test the significant difference between day and night shifts with respect to coal output at 1 per cent level of significance.

Table 10.4

S.No.	Day (x_1)	Night (x_2)	$d_i = (x_{1i} - x_{2i})$	d_i^2
1	22	18	4	16
2	29	22	7	49
3	30	31	– 1	1
4	24	22	2	4
5	32	23	9	81
6	28	24	4	16
7	34	28	6	36
8	31	26	5	25
9	27	29	– 2	4
10	23	25	– 2	4
Total			32	236

$$\bar{d} = \frac{32}{10} = 3.2$$

$$s_d^2 = \frac{1}{n-1}\left[\Sigma d_i^2 - \frac{(\Sigma\, d_i)^2}{n}\right] = \frac{1}{(10-1)}\left[236 - \frac{(32)^2}{10}\right]$$

$$= 14.84$$

$$t = \frac{|\,3.2\,|}{\sqrt{\dfrac{14.84}{10}}} = \frac{3.2}{\sqrt{1.484}} = \frac{3.2}{1.22} = 2.62$$

Conclusion

Here t (cal.) value i.e., 2.62 < t (tab.) value i.e., 3.25 with (10 – 1) d.f. at 1 per cent level of significance. Therefore H_0 is accepted. Hence it can be concluded that there is no significant difference between day and night shifts outputs at 1 per cent level of significance.

10.5 S.N.D. Tests for Proportions

Sometimes there is need to test the proportions of sample and population and between proportions of two samples when population proportions is known or unknown instead of means. For example, if the proportion of defective screws produced by a factory with population proportion of defective screws or proportions of defective screws produced by two machines in a factory, SND tests for proportions are used. In these tests, standard error for proportion or between proportions are obtained with the assumption of Binomial distribution.

10.5.1 One-sample S.N.D. Test for Proportion

Assumptions: (i) population is normal and (ii) sample is drawn at random

Conditions: (i) proportion in the population, P is known and (ii) size of the sample is large. ($n > 30$)

$$H_0 : P = P_0 ; \qquad H_1 : P \neq P_0$$

$$Z = \frac{|p - P|}{\sqrt{\frac{PQ}{n}}}$$

where $\sqrt{\frac{PQ}{n}}$ is the standard error of P, the proportion in the population. P is the proportion in the sample and P_0 is the value of proportion in the population under null hypothesis. $Q_0 = 1 - P_0$ and n is the size of the sample.

Conclusion

If Z (cal.) value > Z (tab.) value at the required level of significance the H_0 is rejected and H_1 is accepted. If H_0 is rejected then it can be concluded that there is significant difference between sample and population proportions and sample may not belong to the population with respect to character under consideration. Otherwise, H_0 is accepted.

Example: In a T.V. manufacturing plant the percentage of T.V. sets were found to be defective was 2 over several years of production. In a particular day 40 were found to be defective out of 500 sets produced. Test whether there is significant difference between sample and over all record with respect to number of defective sets at 1 per cent level.

$$H_0 : P = P_0 ; \quad H_1 : P \neq P_0$$

$$Z = \frac{|40/500 - 0.02|}{\sqrt{\frac{0.02 \times 0.98}{500}}} = \frac{0.06}{\sqrt{0.000039}} = 9.52$$

Conclusion

Here Z (cal.) value i.e., 9.52 > Z (tab.) value i.e., 2.58 at 1 per cent level of significance. Therefore H_0 is rejected and H_1 is accepted. Hence it can be concluded that the percentage of defective sets in the sample is significantly different from population percentage.

10.5.2 Two-sample S.N.D. Test for Proportions

Case (i): Common population proportion, P is known

Assumptions: (i) Populations are normal and (ii) samples are drawn independently and at random

Conditions: (i) common population, P is known and (ii) sizes of the samples are large. ($n_1 > 30, n_2 > 30$)

$$H_0 : P_1 = P_2 \quad ; \quad H_1 : P_1 \neq P_2$$

$$Z = \frac{|p_1 - p_2|}{\sqrt{PQ\left(\frac{1}{n_1} + \frac{1}{n_2}\right)}}$$

where p_1, p_2 are proportions in the 1st and 2nd samples with sizes n_1 and n_2 respectively.

Conclusion

If Z (cal.) > Z (tab.) value at the required level of significance then H_0 is rejected and H_1 is accepted. If H_0 is rejected then it can be concluded that there is significant difference between proportions in the two samples.

Example: In a computer manufacturing plant, it was found that 4 per cent of the units produced were found defective over several years of production. In one unit of the factory 20 systems were found defective out of 120 systems produced in a month and 30 systems were found defective out of 140 systems produced in a month in the 2nd unit of the factory. Test whether 2nd unit is producing more defective systems compared to 1st unit at 5 per cent level of significance.

$$H_0 : P_1 = P_2 \quad ; \quad H_1 : P_2 > P_1$$

$$Z = \frac{\left|\frac{20}{120} - \frac{30}{140}\right|}{\sqrt{0.04 \times 0.96\left(\frac{1}{120} + \frac{1}{140}\right)}} = \frac{|0.17 - 0.21|}{\sqrt{0.0006}} = \frac{0.04}{0.02} = 2.0$$

Conclusion

Here Z (cal.) value i.e., 2.0 > Z (tab.) value i.e., 1.65 at 10 per cent level of significance. Here 10 per cent level is considered since it is one-tailed test. Therefore, H_0 is rejected and H_1 is accepted. Hence it can be concluded that the 2nd unit is producing more percentage of defective systems than 1st unit in the factory.

Case (ii): Population proportion is not known.

Assumptions: (i) populations are normal and (ii) samples are drawn independently and at random

Conditions: (i) population proportion, P is not known and (ii) sizes of samples are large. ($n_1 > 30$, $n_2 > 30$)

$$H_0 : P_1 = P_2 \quad ; \quad H_1 : P_1 \neq P_2$$

$$Z = \frac{| p_1 - p_2 |}{\sqrt{p\,q\left(\frac{1}{n_1} + \frac{1}{n_2}\right)}}$$

where p_1, p_2 are proportions in the 1st and 2nd samples with sizes n_1 and n_2 respectively.

$$p = \frac{| n_1 p_1 + n_2 p_2 |}{\sqrt{n_1 + n_2}}, \qquad q = (1 - p)$$

Conclusion

Same as in case (i)

Example: In a municipal corporation area it was found that 45 houses were constructed violating the approved plan outplay out of 300 houses in one locality. In another locality, 50 houses were constructed violating the approved plan outplay out of 400 houses. Test whether there is any significant difference between the two localities at 5 per cent level of significance with respect to violation of rules.

$$H_0 : P_1 = P_2 \; ; \quad H_1 : P_1 \neq P_2$$

$$Z = \frac{\left|\frac{45}{300} - \frac{50}{400}\right|}{\sqrt{0.14 \times 0.86\left(\frac{1}{300} + \frac{1}{400}\right)}} = \frac{|0.15 - 0.13|}{\sqrt{0.0007}} = \frac{0.02}{0.026} = 0.77$$

where $$p = \frac{300 \times \frac{45}{300} + 400 \times \frac{50}{400}}{300 + 400} = 0.14$$

$$q = 0.86$$

Conclusion

Here Z (cal.) value i.e., 0.77 < Z (tab.) value i.e., 1.96 at 5 per cent level of significance. Therefore H_0 is accepted. Hence it can be concluded that there is no significant difference between the proportions of two localities with respect to violation of rules.

CHAPTER 11

Chi-square Distribution

11.1 Introduction

If $x_1, x_2, \ldots, x_n$ be n independent normal variates each one of them is normally distributed with mean equal to zero and S.D equal to one, then $x_1^2 + x_2^2 + \ldots + x_n^2$ is distributed as chi-square distribution with n degrees of freedom. This distribution was given by Karl Pearson. The chi-square $\left(\chi^2\right)$ curves for d.f. n = 1, 2, ..., 6 are depicted in Fig. 11.1.

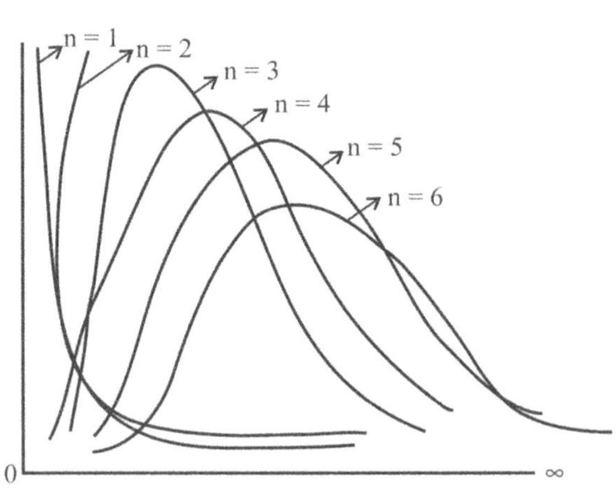

Fig. 11.1

11.2 Properties

(i) If $0 < n, \leq 2$, the curve is L-shaped and has infinite ordinate at the origin.

(ii) The curve has mode at (n-2) when $n > 2$.

(iii) If $\chi_1^2, \chi_2^2, \ldots, \chi_k^2$ are k independent chi-square variates with $n_1, n_2, \ldots, n_k$ d. f. respectively then $\chi_1^2 + \chi_2^2 + \ldots + \chi_k^2$ is also a χ^2-variate with $(n_1 + n_2 + \ldots + n_k)$ d. f.

(iv) The central moments, $\mu_2 = 2n$, $\mu_3 = 8n$, $\mu_4 = 48n + 12n^2$

(v) The coefficient of skewness $= \dfrac{4}{\sqrt{2n}}$ and

(vi) The coefficient of kurtosis $= 3 + \dfrac{12}{n}$

11.3 Chi-square Test

Chi-square test is based on chi-square distribution. Chi-square test is used for enumeration data whereas S.N.D. test and t-test are used for measurement data.

11.3.1 Measurement data

The data obtained by measurement is called measurement data. For example, height, weight, age, income, area etc.

11.3.2 Enumeration data

The data obtained by counting, is known as enumeration data. For example number of people, number of plants, number of factories etc.

11.3.3 Applications of chi-square test

(i) It is used in testing the goodness of fit of distributions like Binomial. Poisson and Normal.

(ii) It is used in testing the association between two attributes in contingency tables.

(iii) It is used in testing the segregations of characters according to Mandelian ratios in genetics and

(iv) It is useful in testing linkage problems in genetics.

11.3.4 Chi-square Test for Goodness of Fit

The application of chi-square test in goodness of fit is illustrated in the following example.

***Example*:** The following is the distribution of boxes of screws. If the number of defective screws are less than or equal to 5 the sample boxes are accepted. Otherwise the boxes are rejected. Assuming that the pattern of distribution of screws follow binomial distribution, fit the binominal distribution and test the goodness of fit.

Table 11.1

Defective screws (x_i)	**Boxes (f_i) (o_i)**	$f_i x_i$	**Probability**	**Expected frequencies (E_i)**	$\left(\frac{O_i - E_i}{E_i}\right)^2$
0	4	0	$(0.52)^5 = 0.0380$	$50 \times 0.038 = 1.90$	2.321
1	7	7	$5c_1\,(0.52)^4\,(0.48) = 0.1755$	8.775	0.359
2	10	20	$5c_2\,(0.52)^3\,(0.48)^2 = 0.3240$	16.200	2.373
3	18	54	$5c_3\,(0.52)^2\,(0.48)^3 = 0.2990$	14.950	0.622
4	6	24	$5c_4\,(0.52)\,(0.48)^4 = 0.1380$	6.900	0.117
5	5	25	$(0.48)^5 = 0.0255$	1.275	10.883
Total	50	130	1.0000	50.000	16.675

$$\bar{x} = \frac{130}{50} = 2.6 = n\,p \quad \text{and } n = 5$$

$$p = \frac{2.6}{5} = 0.52,\ q = 1 - 0.52 = 0.48$$

H_0: The distribution given in Table 11.1 follows binominal distribution

H_1: The distribution given in Table 11.1 does not follow binominal distribution

$$\chi^2 = \sum_{i=1}^{n} \frac{(O_i - E_i)^2}{E_i} \qquad .....(11.1)$$

where O_i is the observed frequency of i-th item or variate value in the distribution for i =1, 2,…, n.

and E_i is the expected frequency of i-th item or variate value in the distribution for i = 1, 2,..., n. In the example given in table 11.1, we have

$$\chi^2 = \sum_{i=1}^{6} \frac{(O_i - E_i)^2}{E_i} = \frac{(4-1.9)^2}{1.9} + \frac{(7-8.775)^2}{8.775} + \cdots + \frac{(5-1.275)^2}{1.275} = 16.675$$

Conclusion: Here χ^2 (cal.) value i.e. 16.675 > χ^2 (tab.) value i.e. 11.07 with (6 –1) d.f. at 5 percent level of significance. Therefore H_0 is rejected and H_1 is accepted. Hence it can be concluded that the given distribution does not follow binomial distribution.

11.3.5 Chi-square test in 2 × 2 contingency table

If the frequencies are arranged in 2 rows and 2 columns according to two attributes then it is called 2 × 2 contingency table.

Example: If two attributes A and B are classified into two categories each and the frequency table is given in table 11.2.

H_0: The two attributes A and B are independent

H_1: The two attributes A and B are not independent and they are associated.

Table 11.2

B \ A	A_1	A_2	Total
B_1	a	b	R_1
B_2	c	d	R_2
Total	C_1	C_2	N

where a, b, c and d are the observed frequencies in the cells, R_1, R_2 and c_1 and c_2 are the row and column totals and N is the grand total.

$$\chi^2 = \sum_{i=1}^{2}\sum_{i=1}^{2} \frac{(O_{ij} - E_{ij})^2}{E_{ij}} \qquad \text{.....(11.2)}$$

where O_{ij} is the observed frequency of (i, j)-th cell and E_{ij} is the expected frequency of (i, j)-th cell for i, j = 1, 2. The expected frequencies are obtained as follows

$$E_{11} = \frac{R_1 \times C_1}{N}, \qquad E_{12} = \frac{R_1 \times C_2}{N}$$

$$E_{21} = \frac{R_2 \times C_1}{N}, \qquad E_{22} = \frac{R_2 \times C_2}{N}$$

The c^2 (cal.) value is obtained by substituting the observed and expected frequencies in the above given formula (11.2). It may be noted that in 2 × 2 contingency table one expected frequency need to be calculated. The other expected frequencies are obtained by subtraction from corresponding marginal totals. For example if E_{11} is known then $E_{12} = (R_1 - E_{11})$ and $E_{21} = (C_1 - E_{11})$ and $E_{22} = (R_2 - E_{21}) = (C_2 - E_{12})$. Further in 2 × 2 contingency table the χ^2 (cal.) value can be obtained directly without finding expected frequencies using the following formula.

$$\chi^2 = \frac{(ad - bc)^2 N}{R_1 R_2 C_1 C_2} \quad .....(11.3)$$

Conclusion

If χ^2 (cal.) value > χ^2 (tab.) value with (2 – 1) (2 – 1) d. f. at the required level of significance then H_0 is rejected and H_1 is accepted. If H_0 is rejected then it can be concluded that there is significant association between the two attributes. Otherwise H_0 is accepted.

***Example*:** 60 children were tested in English language test who belong to Government school in a particular locality at 6th class and 40 children were tested in English language who belong to private administered school at 6th class in the same locality. The results are presented in the following 2 × 2 table given in table 11.3.

Test the association between type of administration and English language skill at 5 percent level.

Table 11.3

	Passed	**Failed**	**Total**
Government	34	26	60
Non-government	28	12	40
Total	62	38	100

H_0: Administration and language skill are independent.

H_1: Administration and learning language are associated.

The numbers in cells in Table 11.3 are observed frequencies. The expected frequencies are obtained as follows

$$E_{11} = \frac{R_1 \times C_1}{N} = \frac{60 \times 62}{100} = 37.2$$

$$E_{12} = 60 - 37.2 = 22.8$$
$$E_{21} = 62 - 37.2 = 24.8$$
$$E_{22} = 40 - 24.8 = 15.2$$

$$\chi^2 = \frac{(34-37.2)^2}{37.2} + \frac{(26-22.8)^2}{22.8} + \frac{(28-24.8)^2}{24.8} + \frac{(12-15.2)^2}{15.2}$$
$$= \frac{(3.2)^2}{37.2} + \frac{(3.2)^2}{22.8} + \frac{(3.2)^2}{24.8} + \frac{(3.2)^2}{15.2} = 1.81$$

Direct-Method:

$$\chi^2 = \frac{(34 \times 12 - 26 \times 28)^2}{60 \times 40 \times 62 \times 38} 100 = 1.81$$

Conclusion

Here χ^2 (cal.) value i.e., 1.81 < χ^2 (tab.) value i.e. 3.84 with (2-1) (2-1) d. f. at 5 percent level of significance. Therefore H_o is accepted. Hence it can be concluded that the administration of school is not associated with acquiring English language skill by children.

11.3.6 Yates Correction

In 2 × 2 contingency table if the expected frequency of any one or more cells are less than 5 then Yates Correction is used in the direct formula of chi-square test.

Example: The following 2 × 2 contingency table gives the classification of small scale industries which were rehabilitated and not rehabilitated financially. Test whether rehabilitation helped in recovering from sickness significantly at 5 percent level.

H_0: Rehabilitation has no effect in recovering from sickness of small scale industries.

H_1: Rehabilitations does effect in recovering from sickness.

Table 11.4

	Recovered	**Not-recovered**	**total**
Rehabilitated	8	4	12
Not-rehabilitated	5	15	20
Total	13	19	32

It can be observed that the expected frequency of 1st row and 1st column i.e. $E_{11} = 4.875 < 5$. Therefore Yates Correction is used with the formula given as

$$\chi^2 = \frac{\left(|ad - bc| - \frac{N}{2}\right)^2}{R_1R_2C_1C_2} N$$

$$= \frac{\left(|8 \times 15 - 4 \times 5| - \frac{32}{2}\right)^2}{12 \times 20 \times 13 \times 19} 32$$

$$= \frac{225792}{59280} = 3.81$$

Conclusion

Here χ^2 (cal.) value i.e. 3.81 < χ^2 (tab.) value i.e. 3.84 with (2-1) (2-1) d. f. at 5 percent level of significance. Therefore H_0 is accepted. Hence it can be concluded that rehabilitation has no significant effect in recovering from sickness.

11.3.7 Ch-Square Test in m × n contingency table

If each of the two attributes are classified according to m and n categories and the frequencies are presented in a two-way table then it is knows as m × n contingency table. The H_o , H_1 and formula of chi-square test and conclusion will remain same as in 2 × 2 contingency table. The procedure of computing chi-square value is illustrated in the following example.

***Example*:** The following is the table classifying industries according to size and operational status.

Table 11.5

Size	Healthy	Partially Sick	Sick	Total
Large	16 (10.8)	9 (9.9)	5 (9.3)	30
Medium	12 (12.2)	14 (11.2)	8 (10.6)	34
Small	8 (13.0)	10 (11.9)	18 (11.1)	36
Total	36	33	31	100

H_0: Size of industry and operational status are independent.

H_1: Size of industry and operational status are associated.

$$E_{11} = \frac{36 \times 30}{100} = 10.8, \qquad E_{12} = \frac{33 \times 30}{100} = 9.9,$$

$$E_{13} = 30 - (10.8 + 9.9) = 9.3$$

$$E_{21} = \frac{36 \times 34}{100} = 12.2, \qquad E_{22} = \frac{33 \times 34}{100} = 11.2,$$

$$E_{23} = 34 - (12.2 + 11.2) = 10.6$$

$$E_{31} = 36 - (10.8 + 12.2) = 13.0$$

$$E_{32} = 33 - (9.9 + 11.2) = 11.9$$

$$E_{33} = 31 - (9.3 + 10.6) = 11.1$$

$$\chi^2 = \frac{(16 - 10.8)^2}{10.8} + \frac{(9 - 9.9)^2}{9.9} + \cdots + \frac{(18 - 11.1)^2}{11.1} = 12.43$$

Conclusion

Here χ^2 (cal.) value i.e. 12.43 > χ^2 (tab.) value i.e. 9.49 with (3-1) (3-1) d. f. at 5 percent level of significance. Therefore H_o is rejected and H_1 is accepted. Hence it can be concluded that size of industry and healthyness of industry are associated.

CHAPTER 12

Correlation and Regression

12.1 Correlation

If one variable changes in accordance with another variable then they are said to be correlated. For example, if weight changes as height changes for an individual then 'height' and 'weight' are said to be correlated. The extent of correlation or the amount of relationship between the correlated variables is called correlation coefficient. It was first developed by Karl Pearson. It is denoted by 'r'. If two variables change in the same direction then they are said to be positively correlated. If the two variables change in opposite directions then they are said to be negatively correlated. 'r' always lies between –1 and +1 and it is independent of units of measurement. Correlation between two variables can be identified from the graph by plotting the points of two or bi-variate values. The graphs are shown in Fig. 12.1 to 12.5.

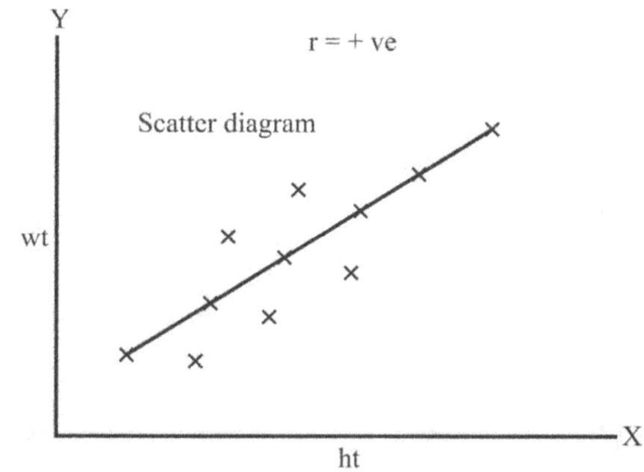

Fig. 12.1

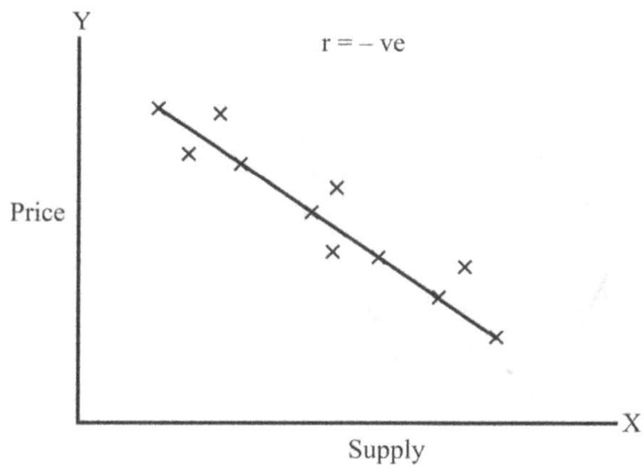

Fig. 12.2

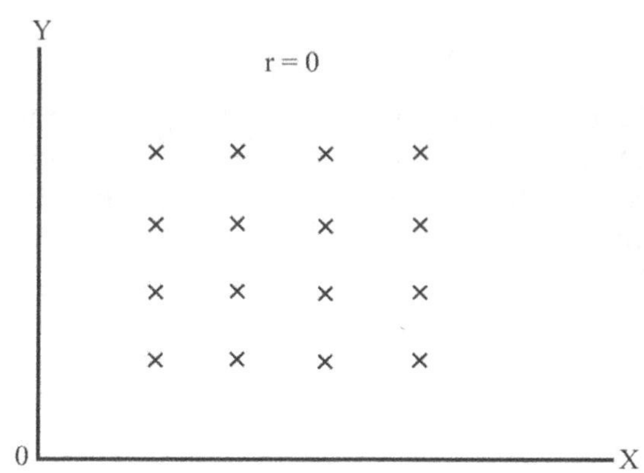

Fig. 12.3

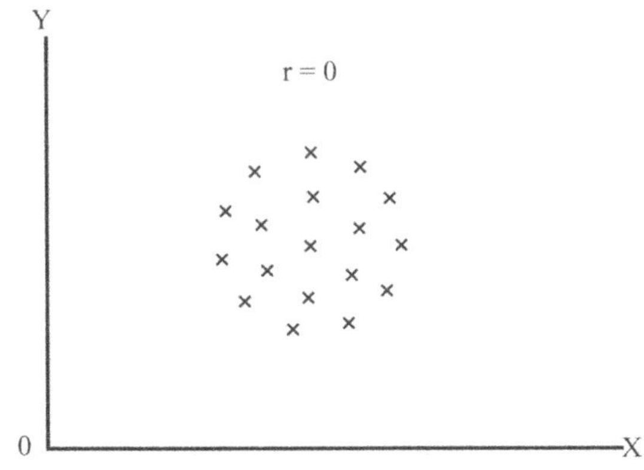

Fig. 12.4

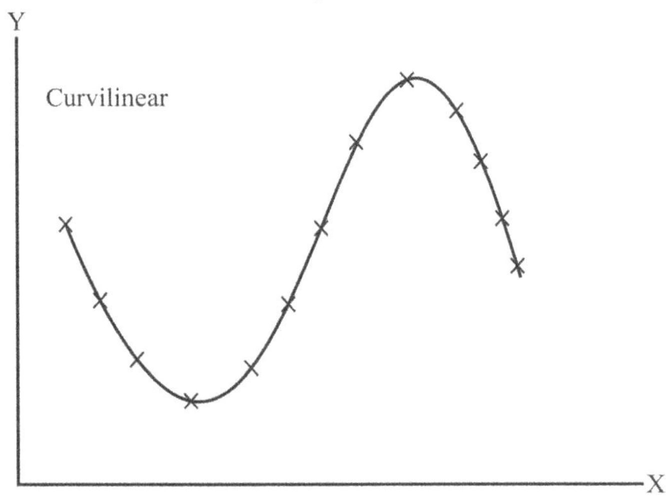

Fig. 12.5

From Fig. 12.1, it can be observed that the plotted points indicate the straight line relationship and it is also known as linear relationship and as height increased, weighs also increased. Therefore the linear relationship is positive. Similarly it is seen from Fig. 12.2 that the plotted points indicate straight line relationship and here as supply increased, price of the commodity decreased. Therefore the linear relationship is negative. In Fig. 12.3, the plotted points are in square shape. Therefore the correlation between x and y variables does not exist and hence r = 0. In Fig. 12.4 the plotted points are in a circular shaped and hence there exists no correlation between x and y variables. In Fig. 12.5 the plotted points indicate curve and not a straight line. Though there exists relationship between x and y variables but it is not linear relationship and it is non-linear or curvilinear relationship. 'r' only measures the linear relationship.

If x and y are two related variables then

$$r = \frac{\text{Covariance (xy)}}{\sqrt{\text{Variance (x). Variance (y)}}} \qquad .....(12.1)$$

where $\text{covariance (xy)} = \frac{1}{n} \Sigma(x_i - \bar{x})(y_i - \bar{y})$

$$\text{variance (x)} = \frac{1}{n} \Sigma (x_i - \bar{x})^2$$

$$\text{variance (y)} = \frac{1}{n} \Sigma (y_i - \bar{y})^2$$

$$r = \frac{\Sigma (x_i - \bar{x})(y_i - \bar{y})}{\sqrt{\Sigma (x_i - \bar{x})^2 (y_i - \bar{y})^2}} \qquad .....(12.2)$$

After simplification of numerator and denominator

$$r = \frac{\Sigma x_i y_i - \frac{(\Sigma x_i)(\Sigma y_i)}{n}}{\sqrt{\left[\Sigma x_i^2 - \frac{(\Sigma x_i)^2}{n}\right]\left[\Sigma y_i^2 - \frac{(\Sigma y_i)^2}{n}\right]}}$$

where n is the number of paired observations.

12.2 Test of Significance

The correlation coefficient 'r' can be tested for its significance. Sometimes if r value is high still it may not found significant due to large value of standard error. The value of standard error may increase due to small sample size or small value of n. Therefore it is always necessary to test the significance of 'r' value in order to establish the significant relationship between two variables.

$$H_0: \ \rho = 0 \ ; \quad H_1: \ \rho \neq 0$$

Where 'ρ' is called the population correlation coefficient

$$t = \frac{|r|}{\sqrt{\frac{(1 - r^2)}{(n - 2)}}} \qquad .....(12.3)$$

Conclusion

If t (cal.) value > t (tab) value with (n – 2) d.f. at the required level of significance, then H_0 is rejected and H_1 is accepted. If H_0 is rejected then it can be concluded that there is significant correlation between two variables x and y. Otherwise H_0 is accepted.

Example: The following are the data on 'supply' of a commodity in markets and the corresponding price. Find the correlation coefficient and test its significance at 5 percent level.

Table 12.1

S. No.	Supply (q) (x_i)	Price (₹ 000) y_i	$(x_i - \bar{x})$	$(y_i - \bar{y})$	$(x_i - \bar{x}) \cdot (y_i - \bar{y})$	$(x_i - \bar{x})^2$	$(y_i - \bar{y})^2$
1.	18	10	5	– 6	– 30	25	36
2.	22	12	9	– 4	–36	81	16
3.	10	16	– 3	0	0	9	0
4.	9	17	– 4	1	– 4	16	1
5.	7	20	– 6	4	– 24	36	16
6.	14	18	1	2	2	1	4
7.	13	15	0	– 1	0	0	1
8.	11	20	– 2	4	– 8	4	16
Total	104	128			– 100	172	90

$$\bar{x} = \frac{104}{8} = 13, \qquad \bar{y} = \frac{128}{8} = 16$$

$$r = \frac{\Sigma (x_i - \bar{x})(y_i - \bar{y})}{\sqrt{\Sigma (x_i - \bar{x})^2 \, \Sigma (y_i - \bar{y})^2}} = \frac{-100}{\sqrt{172 \times 90}} = \frac{-100}{124.42} = -0.80$$

The correlation coefficient between 'supply' and 'price' of a commodity was found to be – 0.80.

Test of significance:

$$H_0: \rho = 0, \quad H_1: \rho \neq 0$$

$$t = \frac{|r|}{\sqrt{\dfrac{(1-r^2)}{n-2}}} = \frac{|-0.80|}{\sqrt{\dfrac{1-(-0.80)^2}{(8-2)}}} = \frac{0.80}{\sqrt{0.06}} = \frac{0.80}{0.24} = 3.33$$

Conclusion

Here t (cal.) value i.e., 3.33 > t (tab.) value i.e., 2.45 with (8 – 2) d.f. at 5 percent level of significance. Therefore H_0 is rejected and H_1 is accepted. Hence it can be concluded that there exists significant negative correlation between supply and price of a commodity in the markets.

12.3 Regression

Galton studied heights of grand fathers, fathers and sons in large number of families. He observed that sons heights are more correlated to grand fathers heights than fathers heights. This type of relation he considered as backward relationship and termed it as 'Regression'. The scatter diagram between number of hours of work and daily production is presented in Fig. 12.6.

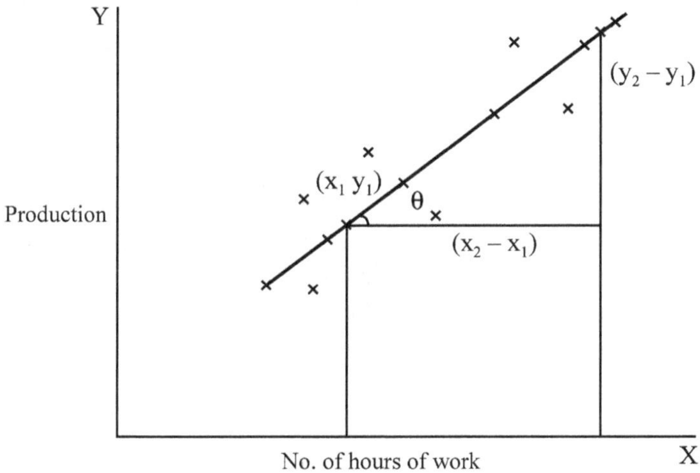

Fig. 12.6

The equation of straight line in Fig. 12.6 is taken as

$$y = a + bx \qquad .....(12.4)$$

where y is the dependent variable, x is the independent variable and the equation is known as regression equation of y on x. b is called the regression coefficient of y on x and explains the change in dependent variable, y for a unit change in independent variable, x. This is also known as 'slope' of the straight line and it is measured by 'tan θ' and which is given as

$$b = \tan\theta = \frac{(y_2 - y_1)}{(x_2 - x_1)}$$

and 'a' is called as intercept or constant. If data are available for 'x' and 'y' variables then

$$b = \frac{\text{Covariance (xy)}}{\text{Variance (x)}} \qquad .....(12.5)$$

$$\text{where covariance (x y)} = \frac{1}{n}\Sigma (x_i - \bar{x})(y_i - \bar{y})$$

$$\text{and variance (x)} = \frac{1}{n}\Sigma (x_i - \bar{x})^2$$

$$b = \frac{\sum_{i=1}^{n} (x_i - \bar{x})(y_i - \bar{y})}{\sum_{i=1}^{n} (x_i - \bar{x})^2} \qquad .....(12.6)$$

where n is the number of paired observations. Here 'b' is measured in the units of dependent variable.

$$a = \bar{y} - b\bar{x} \qquad .....(12.7)$$

where $\bar{x}$, $\bar{y}$ are the means of x and y variables.

Example: The following is the data on number of hours of work per day and the production by an individual in a factory. Fit the regression equation of production per day and number of hours of work and test the significance of regression coefficient at 5 per cent level.

Table 12.2

S. No.	No. of hours (x_i)	Production (units) (y_i)	$(x_i - \bar{x})$	$(y_i - \bar{y})$	$(x_i - \bar{x})(y_i - \bar{y})$	$(x_i - \bar{x})^2$	$(y_i - \bar{y})^2$
1.	6	14	– 4	– 7	28	16	49
2.	8	17	– 2	– 4	8	4	16
3.	12	24	2	3	6	4	9
4.	9	18	– 1	– 3	3	1	9
5.	13	28	3	7	21	9	49
6.	15	30	5	9	45	25	81
7.	10	21	0	0	0	0	0
8.	7	16	– 3	– 5	15	9	25
Total	80	168			126	68	238
Mean	10	21					

Here $\bar{x} = 10, \quad \bar{y} = 21$

$$\Sigma (x_i - \bar{x})(y_i - \bar{y}) = 126, \qquad \Sigma (x_i - \bar{x})^2 = 68$$

$$b = \frac{\Sigma (x_i - \bar{x})(y_i - \bar{y})}{\Sigma (x_i - \bar{x})^2} = \frac{126}{68} = 1.85$$

$$a = \bar{y} - b\bar{x} = 21 - 1.85 \times 10 = 2.5$$

The fitted regression equation of 'number of hours of work' and 'production' is given as

$$y = 2.5 + 1.85\, x$$

Here b = 1.85 explains that if the number of hours is increased by one hour there will be an increase of 1.85 units in production. From this equation it is also possible to predict or forecast the production for a given hours of work. For example, find the production if the number of hours of work is 14 hours. Substituting x = 14 in the fitted regression equation the production, y is obtained.

$$y = 2.5 + 1.85\,(14) = 28.4$$

12.3.1 Test of Significance of Regression Coefficient

$$H_0 : \beta = 0; \qquad H_1 : \beta \neq 0$$

where 'β' is known as population regression coefficient of y on x.

$$t = \frac{|\,b\,|}{\sqrt{\dfrac{\Sigma (y_i - \bar{y})^2 - b^2 (x_i - \bar{x})^2}{(n-2)\,(x_i - \bar{x})^2}}} \qquad .....(12.8)$$

Conclusion

If t (cal.) value > t (tab.) value with (n – 2) d.f. at the required level of significance then H_0 is rejected and H_1 is accepted. If H_0 is rejected then it can be concluded that there is significant regression between y and x. Otherwise, H_0 is accepted.

Example: Test the significance of regression coefficient obtained in the example given in Table 12.2.

$$H_0 : \beta = 0 \; ; \quad H_1 = \beta \neq 0$$

$$\text{Here } b = 1.85, \; \Sigma(y_i - \bar{y})^2 = 238, \; \Sigma(x_i - \bar{x})^2 = 68$$

$$t = \frac{|1.85|}{\sqrt{\dfrac{238 - (1.85)^2 \; 68}{(8-2) \; 68}}} = \frac{|1.85|}{\sqrt{\dfrac{5.27}{408}}} = \frac{1.85}{0.11} = 16.82$$

Conclusion

Here t (cal.) value i.e., 16.82 > t (tab.) value i.e., 2.45 with (8 – 2) d.f. at 5 per cent level of significance. Therefore, H_0 is rejected and H_1 is accepted. Hence it can be concluded that there is significant regression of 'number of hour of work' on 'production'.

12.3.2 Regression Equation of x on y

When both variables x and y are correlated and x depends on y and y depends on x then it is possible to find out the regression equations of y on x and x on y.

The regression equation of y on x is given in equation (12.4) as

$$y = a + bx$$

the regression equation of x on y is

$$x = a' + b'y \qquad .....(12.9)$$

where x is dependent variable and y is independent variable and b' is the regression coefficient of x on y and it measures the change in x for a unit change in y. b' is measured in the units of x. Both 'b' and 'b'' are having no limits.

$$b' = \frac{\text{Covariance } (x\,y)}{\text{Variance } (y)} \qquad .....(12.10)$$

$$= \frac{\Sigma\,(x_i - \bar{x})\,(y_i - \bar{y})}{\Sigma\,(y_i - \bar{y})^2}$$

$$a' = \bar{x} - b'\bar{y} \qquad .....(12.11)$$

12.3.3 Test of Significance of Regression Coefficient of x on y

$$H_0 : \beta' = 0; \qquad H_1 : \beta' \neq 0$$

where β' is the population regression coefficient of x on y.

$$t = \frac{|b'|}{\sqrt{\dfrac{\Sigma (x_i - \bar{x})^2 - b'^2 (y_i - \bar{y})^2}{(n-2)(y_i - \bar{y})^2}}} \qquad .....(12.12)$$

Conclusion

If t (cal.) value > t (tab.) value with (n – 2) d.f. at the required level of significance, the H_0 is rejected and H_1 is accepted. If H_0 is rejected then it can be concluded that there is significant regression of x on y.

The correlation coefficient is the geometric mean of two regression coefficients and which is given as

$$r = \sqrt{b \times b'} \qquad .....(12.13)$$

Here 'r', b and b' values will have same sign. The point of intersection of two regression lines y on x and x on y is $\left(\bar{x}, \bar{y}\right)$.

Example: The following are the data on number of vehicles (10) passed through a particular point on a road in an hour and the width of the road (ft.) in a city. Fit both regression equations of y on x and x on y and test the regression coefficients, find the correlation coefficient and point of intersection of two regression lines.

Table 12.3

S. No.	(x_i) traffic (10/hr)	Width of road (ft) (y_i)	$(x_i - \bar{x})$	$(y_i - \bar{y})$	$(x_i - \bar{x})(y_i - \bar{y})$	$(x_i - \bar{x})^2$	$(y_i - \bar{y})^2$
1.	18	40	1	1	1	1	1
2.	23	50	6	11	66	36	121
3.	25	60	8	21	168	64	441
4.	14	30	– 3	– 9	27	9	81
5.	10	25	– 7	– 14	98	49	196
6.	7	22	– 10	– 17	170	100	289
7.	19	45	2	6	12	4	36
8.	20	40	3	1	3	9	1
Total	136	312			545	272	1166
Mean	17	39					

The regression equation of y on x is

$$y = a + bx$$

where $$b = \frac{\Sigma(x_i - \bar{x})(y_i - \bar{y})}{\Sigma(x_i - \bar{x})^2}$$

$$= \frac{545}{272} = 2.00$$

$$a = \bar{y} - b\bar{x} = 39 - 2 \times 17 = 5$$

The fitted regression equation of y on x is

$$y = 5 + 2x$$

The regression equation of x on y is

$$x = a' + b'y$$

where $$b' = \frac{\Sigma(x_i - \bar{x})(y_i - \bar{y})}{\Sigma(y_i - \bar{y})^2}$$

$$= \frac{545}{1166} = 0.47$$

$$a' = \bar{x} - b'\bar{y} = 17 - 0.47 \times 39 = -1.33$$

The fitted regression equation of x on y is

$$x = -1.33 + 0.47\,y$$

(i) The correlation coefficient, r is

$$r = \sqrt{b \times b'} = \sqrt{2 \times 0.47} = 0.97$$

The value of 'r' can be verified by finding the value of r directly as

$$r = \frac{\Sigma(x_i - \bar{x})(y_i - \bar{y})}{\sqrt{\Sigma(x_i - \bar{x})^2\, \Sigma(y_i - \bar{y})^2}}$$

$$= \frac{545}{\sqrt{272 \times 1166}} = \frac{545}{563.12} = 0.97$$

The tests of significance of 'b' and 'b'' are given as follows

(ii) Test of significance of 'b'

$$H_0 : \beta = 0 \quad ; \quad H_1 : \beta \neq 0$$

$$t = \frac{|b|}{\sqrt{\dfrac{\Sigma (y_i - \bar{y})^2 - b^2 \Sigma (x_i - \bar{x})^2}{(n-2)\,\Sigma (x_i - \bar{x})^2}}}$$

$$= \frac{|2|}{\sqrt{\dfrac{1166 - (2)^2 \times 272}{(8-2)\,272}}} = \frac{2}{\sqrt{0.05}} = \frac{2}{0.22} = 9.09$$

Conclusion

Here t (cal.) value i.e., 9.09 > t (tab.) value i.e., 2.45 with (8 – 2) d.f. at 5 percent level of significance. Therefore H_0 is rejected and H_1 is accepted. Hence it can be concluded that there is significant regression of 'width of road' on 'Traffic'.

(iii) Test if significance of ' b' '

$$H_0 : \beta' = 0 \quad ; \quad H_1 : \beta' \neq 0$$

$$t = \frac{|b|}{\sqrt{\dfrac{\Sigma (x_i - \bar{x})^2 - b'^2\, \Sigma (y_i - \bar{y})^2}{(n-2)\,\Sigma (y_i - \bar{y})^2}}}$$

$$= \frac{|0.47|}{\sqrt{\dfrac{272 - (0.47)^2\ 1166}{(8-2)\ 1166}}} = \frac{0.47}{\sqrt{0.0021}} = \frac{0.47}{0.05} = 9.4$$

Conclusion

Here t (cal.) value i.e., 9.4 > t (tab.) value i.e., 2.45 with (8 – 2) d.f. at 5 per cent level of significance. Therefore H_0 is rejected and H_1 is accepted. Hence it can be concluded that there is significant regression of 'Traffic' on 'width of road'.

(iv) The point of intersection of two regression lines:

The two regression lines y on x and x on y, for the data given in Table 12.3 are

$$y = 5 + 2x \quad \text{and} \quad x = -\,1.33 + 0.47\, y$$

The intersection point is obtained by solving these two equations. Substitute x value in 1st equation.

$$y = 5 + 2\,(-1.33 + 0.47\,y)$$

$$y = 5 - 2.66 + 0.94\,y$$

$$y - 0.94\,y = 2.34$$

$$y\,(1 - 0.94) = 2.34, \quad y = \frac{2.34}{0.06} = 39\,(\bar{y})$$

similarly substitute y value in x on y equation to get x value

$$x = -1.33 + 0.47\,(39) = 17\,(\bar{x})$$

Therefore it is verified that the intersection point is the means of x and y i.e., 17 and 39.

12.3.4 Correlation Vs Regression

(i) Correlation coefficient is the amount of relationship between two related variable where as regression coefficient is the change in dependent variable for a unit change in independent variable

(ii) r lies between –1 and +1 whereas b and b' lie between $-\infty$ and $+\infty$.

(iii) r is independent of units whereas b and b' are measured in the units of dependent variable.

(iv) it is possible to predict the value of dependent variable in the case of regression whereas it is not so in the case of correlation.

(v) both correlation coefficient and regression coefficient will have same sign such as positive or negative.

(vi) Correlation coefficient is the geometric mean of the two regression coefficients.

12.4 Partial Correlation

If more than two variables are related among themselves then the correlation between any two variables keeping other variables at constant level is called partial correlation. For example, if x_1, x_2 and x_3 are three variables which are related among themselves then the correlation coefficient between x_1 and x_2 keeping x_3 variable at constant level is denoted by $r_{12.3}$ and which is known as partial correlation coefficient. Partial correlation coefficient is obtained by knowing the simple correlation coefficients between x_1 and x_2, x_2 and x_3 and x_1 and x_3 which are denoted as r_{12}, r_{23} and r_{13} respectively.

The partial correlation coefficient $r_{12.3}$ is

$$r_{12.3} = \frac{(r_{12} - r_{13} \, . \, r_{23})}{\sqrt{(1 - r_{13}^2)\,(1 - r_{23}^2)}} \qquad \text{.....(12.14)}$$

similarly $r_{13.2}$ and $r_{23.1}$ are the partial correlation coefficients between x_1 and x_3 keeping x_2 at constant level and partial correlation coefficient between x_2 and x_3 keeping x_1 at constant level respectively and these are given as

$$r_{13.2} = \frac{(r_{13} - r_{12} \, . \, r_{23})}{\sqrt{(1 - r_{12}^2)\,(1 - r_{23}^2)}} \qquad \text{.....(12.15)}$$

and

$$r_{23.1} = \frac{(r_{23} - r_{12} \, . \, r_{13})}{\sqrt{(1 - r_{12}^2)\,(1 - r_{13}^2)}} \qquad \text{.....(12.16)}$$

where $r_{12} = r_{21}$, $r_{13} = r_{31}$ and $r_{23} = r_{32}$.

12.4.1 Test of Significance

$H_0 : \rho_{12.3} = 0$; $\qquad H_1 : \rho_{12.3} \neq 0$

where $\rho_{12.3}$ is the population partial correlation coefficient between x_1 and x_2 keeping x_3 at constant level.

$$t = \frac{|r_{12.3}|}{\sqrt{\frac{\left(1 - r_{12.3}^2\right)}{(n - 2 - 1)}}} \qquad \text{.....(12.17)}$$

Conclusion

If t (cal.) value > t (tab.) value with (n – 2 – 1) d.f. at the required level of significance the H_0 is rejected and H_1 is accepted. If H_0 is rejected then it can be concluded that there is significant partial correlation coefficient between x_1 and x_2 variables.

Example: The simple correlation coefficient between amount of cement (x_1), amount of sand (x_2) and the curing period (x_3) for construction of a building based on 10 observations are given as

$$r_{12} = 0.8, \quad r_{13} = 0.7 \quad \text{and} \quad r_{23} = 0.6$$

Find partial correlation coefficients $r_{12.3}$, $r_{13.2}$ and $r_{23.1}$ and test the significance of $r_{12.3}$ at 5 percent level.

$$r_{12.3} = \frac{(r_{12} - r_{13} \cdot r_{23})}{\sqrt{\left(1-r_{13}^2\right)\left(1-r_{23}^2\right)}} = \frac{(0.8 - 0.7 \times 0.6)}{\sqrt{\left[1-(0.7)^2\right]\left[1-(0.6)^2\right]}}$$

$$= \frac{0.38}{\sqrt{0.51 \times 0.64}} = \frac{0.38}{\sqrt{0.3264}} \frac{0.38}{0.57} = 0.67$$

$$r_{13.2} = \frac{(r_{13} - r_{12} \cdot r_{23})}{\sqrt{\left(1-r_{12}^2\right)\left(1-r_{23}^2\right)}} = \frac{(0.7 - 0.8 \times 0.6)}{\sqrt{\left[1-(0.8)^2\right]\left[1-(0.6)^2\right]}}$$

$$= \frac{0.22}{0.48} = 0.46$$

$$r_{23.1} = \frac{(r_{23} - r_{12} \cdot r_{13})}{\sqrt{\left(1-r_{12}^2\right)\left(1-r_{13}^2\right)}} = \frac{(0.6 - 0.8 \times 0.7)}{\sqrt{\left[1-(0.8)^2\right]\left[1-(0.7)^2\right]}}$$

$$= \frac{0.04}{0.43} = 0.08$$

(i) Test of significance of $r_{12.3}$

$$H_0: \rho_{12.3} = 0 \; ; \quad H_1: \rho_{12.3} \neq 0$$

$$t = \frac{\left| r_{12.3} \right|}{\sqrt{\left(\dfrac{1-r_{12.3}^2}{(n-3)}\right)}} = \frac{|\,0.67\,|}{\sqrt{\left(\dfrac{1-(0.67)^2}{(10-3)}\right)}} = \frac{|0.67|}{\sqrt{0.6787}}$$

$$= \frac{0.67}{0.28} = 2.39$$

Conclusion

Here t (cal.) value i.e., 2.39 > t (tab.) value i.e., 2.37 with (10 – 3) d.f. at 5 per cent level of significance. Therefore H_0 is rejected and H_1 is accepted. Hence it can be concluded that the partial correlation coefficient between amount of cement (x_1) and amount of sand (x_2) is significant.

12.5 Multiple Regression and Correlation

12.5.1 Multiple Regression

This is an extension of simple regression. If more than one independent variable is considered in simple regression then it becomes multiple regression. For example, if the increase in life of building is considered as dependent variable (y) then amount of cement, (x_1) amount of sand, (x_2), amount of steel, (x_3), curing period (x_4) etc., are independent variables, then it is considered as multiple regression. The linear relationship between y and x_1, x_2, x_3 and x_4 is called multiple linear regression and is given as

$$y = b_0 + b_1 x_1 + b_2 x_2 + b_3 x_3 + b_4 x_4 \qquad .....(12.18)$$

where $b_1, b_2, \ldots b_4$ are called partial regression coefficients and b_0 is called constant.

$b_1 = by_{1.234}$ = partial regression coefficient of y on x_1 keeping x_2, x_3 and x_4 at constant level and so on. It measures the influence of x_1 on y keeping the influences of x_2, x_3 and x_4 at constant level.

The multiple regression estimates the effects of each independent variable on the dependent variable and also the over all effect of all the independent variables together on the dependent variable.

12.5.1.1 Multiple Linear Regression with two Independent Variables

If Y is the dependent variable, X_1 and X_2 are two independent variables, then the multiple linear regression is given as

$$Y = b_0 + b_1 X_1 + b_2 X_2 \qquad .....(12.19)$$

The procedure for estimating the values of b_1 and b_2 and their test of significance is presented here.

If average of 'n' observations is considered, the equation (12.19) becomes

$$\overline{Y} = b_0 + b_1 \overline{X}_1 + b_2 \overline{X}_2 \quad .....(12.20)$$

If equation (12.20) is subtracted from eqn. (12.19), then

$$(Y - \overline{Y}) = (b_0 - b_0) + b_1 \left(X_1 - \overline{X}_1\right) + b_2 \left(X_2 - \overline{X}_2\right) \quad .....(12.21)$$

Let $\left(Y - \overline{Y}\right) = y$, $\left(X - \overline{X}_1\right) = x_1$, $\left(X_2 - \overline{X}_2\right) = x_2$

the equation (12.21) becomes

$$y = b_1 x_1 + b_2 x_2 \quad .....(12.22)$$

The normal equations are obtained by using least squares technique. In this case the normal equations are

$$\Sigma x_1 y = b_1 \Sigma x_1^2 + b_2 \Sigma x_1 x_2 \quad .....(12.23)$$

$$\Sigma x_2 y = b_1 \Sigma x_1 x_2 + b_2 \Sigma x_2^2$$

The eqns. (12.23) can be solved for obtaining b_1 and b_2 values using matrix notation as

$$\underset{2 \times 2}{\begin{bmatrix} \Sigma x_1^2 & \Sigma x_1 x_2 \\ \Sigma x_1 x_2 & \Sigma x_2^2 \end{bmatrix}} \underset{2 \times 1}{\begin{bmatrix} b_1 \\ b_2 \end{bmatrix}} = \underset{2 \times 1}{\begin{bmatrix} \Sigma x_1 y \\ \Sigma x_2 y \end{bmatrix}} \quad .....(12.24)$$

$$\begin{bmatrix} b_1 \\ b_2 \end{bmatrix} = \begin{bmatrix} \Sigma x_1^2 & \Sigma x_1 x_2 \\ \Sigma x_1 x_2 & \Sigma x_2^2 \end{bmatrix}^{-1} \begin{bmatrix} \Sigma x_1 y \\ \Sigma x_2 y \end{bmatrix} \quad .....(12.25)$$

Let $$\begin{bmatrix} \Sigma x_1^2 & \Sigma x_1 x_2 \\ \Sigma x_1 x_2 & \Sigma x_2^2 \end{bmatrix}^{-1} = \begin{bmatrix} C_{11} & C_{12} \\ C_{21} & C_{22} \end{bmatrix} \quad .....(12.26)$$

where C_{11}, C_{12}, C_{21} and C_{22} are the elements in the inverted matrix given in R.H.S. of (12.26). These are also called as Gauss multipliers and which are also used later in tests of significance of b_1 and b_2 and $C_{12} = C_{21}$.

Eqn. (12.25) becomes

$$\begin{bmatrix} b_1 \\ b_2 \end{bmatrix} = \begin{bmatrix} C_{11} & C_{12} \\ C_{21} & C_{22} \end{bmatrix} \begin{bmatrix} \Sigma x_1 y \\ \Sigma x_2 y \end{bmatrix} \quad .....(12.27)$$

$$b_1 = C_{11}\, \Sigma x_1\, y + C_{12}\, \Sigma x_2\, y \quad .....(12.28)$$

$$b_2 = C_{21}\, \Sigma x_1\, y + C_{22}\, \Sigma x_2\, y$$

further $b_0 = \bar{y} - b_1 \bar{x}_1 - b_2 \bar{x}_2$ .....(12.29)

Therefore, the estimates of b_0, b_1 and b_2 are obtained by using eqns. (12.28) and (12.29).

12.5.1.2 Test of Significance of Overall Regression

Here the procedure for testing the effect of the two variables x_1 and x_2 together on variable y is presented.

$$H_0 : \beta_1 = \beta_2 = 0; \qquad H_1 : \beta_1 \neq \beta_2 \neq 0$$

Total sum of squares (T.S.S.) = $\sum_{i=1}^{n} y_i^2$

Regression sum of squares (R.S.S.) = $b_1 \Sigma x_1\, y + b_2\, \Sigma x_2\, y$

Error sum of squares (E.S.S.) = (T.S.S. – R.S.S.)

The sums of squares are presented in analysis of variable (ANOVA) table for carrying out F-test.

Table 12.4 ANOVA TABLE

Source	**d.f.**	**S.S.**	**M.S.**	**F_{cal}**	**F_{tab} (d.f.)**
Regression	2	R.S.S.	R.M.S	$\frac{\text{R.M.S}}{\text{E.M.S}}$	2, (n – 3)
Error	(n – 1) – 2	E.S.S.	E.M.S		
Total	n – 1	T.S.S			

where $\text{R.M.S.} = \frac{\text{R.S.S}}{2}$, $\qquad \text{E.M.S.} = \frac{\text{E.S.S}}{(n-3)}$

Conclusion

If F (cal.) value > F (tab.) value with [2, (n – 3)] d.f. at the required level of significance, H_0 is rejected and H_1 is accepted. If H_0 is rejected then it can be concluded that there is significant overall regression between variables x_1 and x_2 on variable y. Other wise H_0 is accepted.

12.5.1.3 Test of Significance of Partial Regression Coefficients

(i) Test of significance of b_1

$H_0 : \beta_1 = 0; \qquad H_1 : \beta_1 \neq 0$

$$t = \frac{|b_1|}{\sqrt{C_{11}\ (\text{E.M.S})}} \qquad \text{.....(12.30)}$$

Conclusion

If t (cal.) value > t (tab.) value with (n – 3) d.f. at the required level of significance, then H_0 is rejected and H_1 is accepted. If H_0 is rejected then it can be concluded that there is significant regression of x_1 variable on the variable y. Otherwise, H_0 is accepted.

(ii) Test of significance of b_2

$H_0 : \beta_2 = 0; \qquad H_1 : \beta_2 \neq 0$

$$t = \frac{|b_2|}{\sqrt{C_{22}\ (\text{E.M.S})}} \qquad \text{.....(12.31)}$$

Conclusion

Same as in (i) above.

Example: The following are the data on 'increase in life of building' (years), y; 'cement' used (tons) in the construction of building, x_1 and 'period' of curing (days), x_2 for 10 buildings. Fit the multiple linear regression on increase in life of building on cement used and period of curing and test its significance at 1 per cent level.

Table 12.5

S. No.	Y	X_1	X_2	$(X_1-\overline{X}_1)^2$	$(X_2-\overline{X}_2)^2$	$(X_1-\overline{X}_1)(X_2-\overline{X}_2)$	$(Y-\overline{Y})^2$	$(X_1-\overline{X}_1)(Y-\overline{Y})$	$(X_2-\overline{X}_2)(Y-\overline{Y})$
1	6	10	13	64	49	56	64	64	56
2	8	13	16	25	16	20	36	30	24
3	10	15	18	9	4	6	16	12	8
4	11	18	19	0	1	0	9	0	3
5	7	12	10	36	100	60	49	42	70
6	13	19	18	1	4	– 2	1	– 1	2
7	18	21	22	9	4	6	16	12	8
8	20	24	27	36	49	42	36	36	42
9	24	28	29	100	81	90	100	100	90
10	23	20	28	4	64	16	81	18	72
Total	140	180	200	284	372	294	408	313	375
Mean	14	18	20						

$$\Sigma\left(X_1-\overline{X}_1\right)^2=\Sigma\,x_1^2=284\;;\;\;\Sigma\left(X_2-\overline{X}_2\right)^2=\Sigma\,x_2^2=372\;;$$

$$\Sigma\left(Y-\overline{Y}\right)^2=\Sigma\,y^2=408\;;\quad\Sigma\left(X-\overline{X}_1\right)(Y-\overline{Y})=\Sigma\,x_1\,y=313$$

$$\Sigma\left(X_2-\overline{X}_2\right)(Y-\overline{Y})=\Sigma\,x_2y=375,\;\Sigma\left(X_1-\overline{X}_1\right)(X_2-\overline{X}_2)=\Sigma x_1x_2=294$$

Equation (12.25) can be written as

$$\begin{bmatrix} b_1 \\ b_2 \end{bmatrix}=\begin{bmatrix} \Sigma\,x_1^2 & \Sigma\,x_1x_2 \\ \Sigma\,x_1x_2 & \Sigma\,x_2^2 \end{bmatrix}^{-1}\begin{bmatrix} \Sigma\,x_1y \\ \Sigma\,x_2y \end{bmatrix}$$

$$\begin{bmatrix} b_1 \\ b_2 \end{bmatrix}=\begin{bmatrix} 284 & 294 \\ 294 & 372 \end{bmatrix}^{-1}\begin{bmatrix} 313 \\ 375 \end{bmatrix}$$

The inverted matrix is obtained as

$$\begin{bmatrix} 284 & 294 \\ 294 & 372 \end{bmatrix}^{-1}=\begin{bmatrix} 0.0194 & -0.0153 \\ -0.0153 & 0.0148 \end{bmatrix}$$

Substituting this inverted matrix, we have

$$\begin{bmatrix} b_1 \\ b_2 \end{bmatrix}=\begin{bmatrix} 0.0194 & -0.0153 \\ -0.0153 & 0.0148 \end{bmatrix}\begin{bmatrix} 313 \\ 375 \end{bmatrix}$$

$$b_1=0.3347,\;b_2=0.7611$$

$$b_0=\overline{Y}-b_1\overline{X}_1-b_2\overline{X}_2$$

$$=14-0.3347\times 18-0.7611\times 20$$

$$=-7.2466$$

The fitted multiple linear regression is

$$Y=-7.2466+0.3347\,X_1+0.7611\,X_2$$

The interpretation for the estimated partial regression coefficients in the above equation is given as follows.

Here $b_1 = 0.3347$ which indicates that if one ton of extra cement used in construction of building there will be an increase of 0.33 years of extra life in building. Similarly for $b_2 = 0.7611$ if there is one day increase in curing there will be (0.77 years) corresponding increase in life of building.

(i) Test of significance of overall regression.

Total sum of squares (T.S.S.) = $\Sigma y_i^2 = 408$

Regression sum of squares (R.S.S)

$$= b_1 \Sigma x_1 y + b_2 \Sigma x_2 y$$

$$= 0.3347 \times 313 + 0.7611 \times 375 = 390.17$$

Error sum of squares (E.S.S.) = (T.S.S – R.S.S.)

$$= 408.00 - 390.17 = 17.83$$

The above sums of squares are furnished in the ANOVA table to carry out F-test.

$$H_0 : \beta_1 = \beta_2 = 0; \qquad H_1 : \beta_1 \neq \beta_2 \neq 0$$

Table 12.6 ANOVA Table

Source	d.f.	S.S.	M.S.	F_{cal}	F_{tab}
Regression	2	390.17	195.09	76.51	(2, 7)
Error	9 – 2 = 7	17.83	2.55		9.55
Total	10 – 1 = 9	408.00			

Conclusion

Here F (cal.) value i.e., 76.51 > F (tab.) value i.e., 9.55 with (2, 7) d.f. at 1 per cent level of significance. Therefore H_0 is rejected and H_1 is accepted. Hence it can be concluded that there is significant effect of amount of cement used and number of days of curing, in increasing the life of building.

Now individual partial regression coefficiens are tested for their significance.

(ii) Test of significance of b_1

$$H_0 : \beta_1 = 0; \quad H_1 : \beta_1 \neq 0$$

$$t = \frac{|b_1|}{\sqrt{C_{11}\ (EMS)}} = \frac{|0.3347|}{\sqrt{0.0194 \times 2.55}} = \frac{0.3347}{0.2224} = 1.50$$

Conclusion

Here t (cal.) value i.e., 1.50 < t (tab.) value with 7 d.f. i.e., 3.50 (at 1 per cent level of significance. Therefore H_0 is accepted. Hence it can be concluded that there is no significant effect of amount of cement used in the increase in life of building.

(iii) Test of significance of b_2

$$H_0 : \beta_2 = 0; \quad H_1 : \beta_2 \neq 0$$

$$t = \frac{|b_2|}{\sqrt{C_{22}\ (E.M.S)}} = \frac{|0.7611|}{\sqrt{0.0148 \times 2.55}} = \frac{0.7611}{0.1943} = 3.92$$

Conclusion

Here t (cal.) value i.e., 3.92 > t (tab.) value i.e., 3.50 with 7 d.f. at 1 per cent level of significance. Therefore H_0 is rejected and H_1 is accepted. Hence it can be concluded that there is significant effect of number of days of curing on the increase in life of building.

12.6 Multiple Correlation

It is defined as the correlation between observed and expected values of y in the multiple regression equation. The amount of correlation between the observed and expected values of y is called 'Multiple correlation coefficient' and it is denoted by 'R'. R is obtained from ANOVA table as follows.

$$R^2 = \frac{\text{Regression S.S}}{\text{Total S.S}} = \frac{\text{R.S.S}}{\text{T.S.S}} \quad .....(12.32)$$

where R^2 is known as coefficient of determination and it explains the extent of variation in dependent variable, y by the effect of all independent variables to-gether.

$$R = \sqrt{R^2} = \text{coefficient of multiple correlation}$$

Both R and R^2 lie between 0 and 1.

In other words, $0 \leq R^2 \leq 1$ and $0 \leq R \leq 1$

Example: Find R^2 and R for the data given in Table 12.5

From table 12.6, R.S.S = 390.17 and T.S.S = 408.00

$$R^2 = \frac{390.17}{408.00} = 0.96$$

Both independent variables X_1 and X_2 together influence the variation in Y to the extent of 0.96 out of 1 or 96 out of 100.

$$R = \sqrt{0.96} = 0.98$$

The correlation between expected and observed values of Y in the multiple regression equation is 0.98.

12.6.1 Test of Significance of R^2

$$H_0 : \beta_1 = \beta_2 = 0; \quad H_1 : \beta_1 \neq \beta_2 \neq 0$$

$$F = \frac{R^2}{1-R^2} \frac{(n-3)}{2}$$

$$= \frac{0.96}{\left[1-(0.96)^2\right]} \cdot \frac{(10-3)}{2} = \frac{6.72}{0.16} = 42.0$$

Conclusion

Here F (cal.) value i.e., 42.0 > F (tab.) value i.e., 9.55 with (2,7) d.f. at 1 per cent level of significance. Therefore H_0 is rejected and H_1 is accepted. Hence it can be concluded that there is significant coefficient of determination in the multiple regression and hence the multiple correlation coefficient is also significant at 1 per cent level.

12.7 Multiple Linear Regression with more than Two Independent Variables

The procedure given in 12.5.1.1 for two independent variables can be extended to k variables without any difficulty. The only problem arises to invert (k – 1) × (k – 1) matrix. This can be done with the help of computer.

The multiple regression equation with 'k' independent variables can be written as

$$y = b_0 + b_1X_1 + b_2X_2 \ldots. + b_k X_k \qquad \ldots..(12.33)$$

where $X_1, X_2, \ldots., X_k$ are 'k' independent variables and y is dependent variables. If 'n' observations are considered for fitting the multiple regression equation and averaging over 'n' observations, the eqn. (12.33) becomes

$$\overline{Y} = b_0 + b_1\overline{X}_1 + b_2\overline{X}_2 + \ldots + b_k\overline{X}_k \qquad \ldots..(12.34)$$

By subtracting eqn. (12.34) from eqn. (12.33), we have

$$Y - \overline{Y} = (b_0 - b_0) + b_1 (X_1 - \overline{X}_1) + b_2(X_2 - \overline{X}_2) + ... + b_k(X_k - \overline{X}_k) \quad .....(12.35)$$

Let $y = (Y - \overline{Y})$, $x_1 = (X_1 - \overline{X}_1)$, $x_2 = (X_2 - \overline{X}_2)$, ..., $x_k = (X_k - \overline{X}_k)$

Then eqn. (12.35) becomes

$$y = b_1x_1 + b_2x_2 + ... + b_kx_k \quad .....(12.36)$$

By least squares technique, the normal equations for estimating b_1, b_2, ..., b_k are

$$\begin{aligned} \Sigma x_1y &= b_1\Sigma x_1^2 + b_2 \Sigma x_1x_2 + ... + b_k \Sigma x_1x_k \\ \Sigma x_2y &= b_1\Sigma x_2x_1 + b_2 \Sigma x_2^2 + ... + b_k \Sigma x_2x_k \\ &\vdots \\ \Sigma x_ky &= b_1\Sigma x_kx_1 + b_2 \Sigma x_kx_2 + ... + b_k \Sigma x_k^2 \end{aligned} \quad .....(12.37)$$

The eqns. (12.37) can be written in matrix notation as

$$\underset{K\times 1}{\begin{bmatrix} b_1 \\ b_2 \\ \vdots \\ b_k \end{bmatrix}} = \underset{K\times K}{\begin{bmatrix} \Sigma x_1^2 & \Sigma x_1x_2 & \cdots & \Sigma x_1x_k \\ \Sigma x_2x_1 & \Sigma x_2^2 & \cdots & \Sigma x_2x_k \\ \vdots & \vdots & & \vdots \\ \Sigma x_kx_1 & \Sigma x_kx_2 & \cdots & \Sigma x_k^2 \end{bmatrix}} \underset{K\times 1}{\begin{bmatrix} \Sigma x_1y \\ \Sigma x_2y \\ \vdots \\ \Sigma x_ky \end{bmatrix}} \quad .....(12.38)$$

After inverting the K × K matrix on R.H.S, we have

$$\begin{bmatrix} b_1 \\ b_2 \\ \vdots \\ b_k \end{bmatrix} = \begin{bmatrix} c_{11} & c_{12} & \cdots & c_{1k} \\ c_{21} & c_{22} & \cdots & c_{2k} \\ \vdots & \vdots & & \vdots \\ c_{k1} & c_{k2} & \cdots & c_{kk} \end{bmatrix} \begin{bmatrix} \Sigma x_1y \\ \Sigma x_2y \\ \vdots \\ \Sigma x_ky \end{bmatrix} \quad .....(12.39)$$

The partial regression coefficients are obtained as

$$\begin{aligned} b_1 &= c_{11}\, \Sigma x_1y + c_{12}\, \Sigma x_2y + ... + c_{1k}\, \Sigma x_ky \\ b_2 &= c_{21}\, \Sigma x_1y + c_{22}\, \Sigma x_2y + ... + c_{2k}\, \Sigma x_ky \\ &\vdots \\ b_k &= c_{k1}\, \Sigma x_1y + c_{k2}\, \Sigma x_2y + ... + c_{kk}\, \Sigma \overline{x}_k \\ b_0 &= \overline{Y} - b_1\overline{X}_1 - b_2\overline{X}_2 - ..... - b_k \overline{X}_k \end{aligned} \quad .....(12.40)$$

Hence the fitted multiple regression equation is obtained by substituting the values of $b_0, b_1, \ldots b_k$ in the original equation (12.33).

12.7.1 Test of Significance of Overall Regression

Regression sum of squares (R.S.S.) = $b_1 \Sigma x_1 y + b_2 \Sigma x_2 y + \ldots. + b_k \Sigma x_k y$

Total sum of squares (T.S.S.) = Σy_i^2

Error sum of squares (E.S.S.) = (T.S.S. – R.S.S.)

The above sums of squares are furnished in ANOVA Table (12.7) for carrying out F-test.

$$H_0 : \beta_1 = \beta_2 = \ldots. = \beta_k = 0; \qquad H_1 : \beta_1 \neq \beta_2 \neq \ldots. \neq \beta_k \neq 0;$$

Table 12.7 ANOVA Table

Source	d.f.	S.S.	M.S.	F_{cal}	F_{tab} (d.f.)
Regression	k	R.S.S.	R.M.S	$\frac{R.M.S}{E.M.S}$	k, (n – 1–k)
Error	(n – 1) – k	E.S.S.	E.M.S		
Total	n – 1	T.S.S			

$$\text{where} \quad R.M.S. = \frac{R.S.S}{k}, \qquad E.M.S. = \frac{E.S.S}{(n-1-k)}$$

Conclusion

If F (cal.) value > F (tab.) value with [k, (n – 1 – k)] d.f. at the required level of significance then H_0 is rejected and H_1 is accepted. Hence it can be concluded that there is significant influence of all the k independent variables together on the dependent variable, y.

12.7.2 Test of Significance of Partial Regression

Coefficient, b_i for i = 1, 2, …. K.

$$H_0 : \beta_i = 0; \qquad H_1 : \beta_i \neq 0$$

where β_i is the population partial regression coefficient of i-th independent variable.

$$t = \frac{|b_i|}{\sqrt{C_{ii}\ (E.M.S)}} \qquad \ldots..(12.40)$$

where C_{ii} is the i-th diagonal element in the inverted matrix and it is also called gauss multiplier.

Conclusion

If t (cal.) value > t (tab.) value with (n – 1 – k) d.f. at the required level of significance then H_0 is rejected and H_1 is accepted. If H_0 is rejected then it can be concluded that there is significant influence of i-th independent variable on the dependent variable.

12.8 Path Coefficient Analysis

It can be observed that the independent variables in multiple regression not only influence dependent variable directly but also influence indirectly through other independent variables. Path coefficient analysis gives the path in which the independent variables influence dependent variable directly and indirectly through other independent variables. For example, if the life of building is taken as dependent variable; the amount of cement, duration of curing, the amount of sand, the amount of steel, the design of the building, the skill of construction etc., are taken as independent variables. Then the amount of cement used in construction will influence the life of building directly but also indirectly through duration of curing, amount of steel used the design of building etc. In plant breeding experiment the number of panicles not only influence yield directly but also through ear length, number of tillers etc., indirectly.

Path coefficient analysis gives both direct and indirect effects of independent variables and which is not possible in multiple regression analysis.

If y is the dependent variable and $x_1, x_2, \ldots, x_k$ are 'k' independent variables, r_{iy} is the simple correlation coefficient between y and x_i, then

$$r_{iy} = P_{1y}r_{i1} + P_{2y}\, r_{i2} + \ldots + P_{iy} + P_{i+1,y}\, r_{i,\, i+1} + \ldots + P_{ky}\, r_{ik}$$

$$\text{for } i = 1,2, \ldots, k \qquad \ldots..(12.41)$$

where $P_{1y}, P_{2y}, \ldots, P_{ky}$ are the coefficients in the linear relation eq. (12.41) and are called as path coefficients. P_{iy} is the direct effect of x_i variable on y, $P_{1y}\, r_{i1}$ is the indirect effect of x_i on y through x_1 variable, $P_{2y}\, r_{i2}$ is the indirect effect of x_i on y through x_2 variable and so on.

The relation eq. (12.41) indicates that the simple correlation between x_i and y is the sum of the direct and indirect effects of x_i on y. If P_{RY} is the residual effect left over after subtracting the sum of direct and indirect effects, then

$$P_{RY} = \sqrt{1-(P_{1y}r_{1y} + p_{2y}r_{2y} + ... + P_{ky}r_{ky})}$$

In other words the residual effects will be the remaining effect of those variables which are not considered in the relationship i.e., the other than k variables $x_1, x_2, ... , x_k$. The direct effects and indirect effects can be estimated by using matrix method for a sample data as follows.

$$\begin{bmatrix} P_{1y} \\ P_{2y} \\ \vdots \\ P_{ky} \end{bmatrix} = \begin{bmatrix} 1 & r_{12} & r_{13} & \cdots & r_{1k} \\ r_{21} & 1 & r_{23} & \cdots & r_{2k} \\ \vdots & & & & \\ r_{k1} & r_{k2} & r_{k3} & \cdots & 1 \end{bmatrix} \begin{bmatrix} r_{1y} \\ r_{2y} \\ \vdots \\ r_{ky} \end{bmatrix} \quad .....(12.42)$$

From equation (12.42), P_{1y}, P_{2y}, ... P_{ky} can be obtained by solving and which are direct effects of $x_1, x_2, ..., x_k$ variables on variable y. The indirect effects are obtained using the direct effects. $P_{2y}\, r_{12}$, $P_{3y}\, r_{13}$, $P_{4y}\, r_{14}$, ... $P_{ky}\, r_{1k}$ are the indirect effects of x_1 on y through $x_2, x_3, ... , x_k$ variables respectively.

CHAPTER 13

Analysis of Variance

Analysis of variance is a technique developed by R. A. Fisher to compare more than two treatments at a time in an experiment. The 'treatment' word is used in the sense of object of comparison. For example, if more than two machines in a factory are to be compared with respect to their performance in production then machines are termed as treatments. The details of analysis of variance are described in earlier chapter. Here some examples are worked out for illustration purpose.

13.1 One-way Analysis of Variance

If one source of variation is present in the experimental data then it is known as one-way analysis of variance. The analysis of variance model in this case is given as

$$Y_{ij} = \mu + \alpha_i + \varepsilon_{ij} \qquad .....(13.1)$$

where Y_{ij} is the response value or observational value on the j-th unit having i-th treatment for $i = 1, 2,..., p$; $j = 1, 2,...n_i$ and $\sum_{i=1}^{p} n_i = n$; μ is the overall mean and ε_{ij} is the experimental error on the j-th unit having i-th treatment. The sums of squares are obtained as follows for furnishing in analysis of variance (ANOVA) table to carry out F-test.

$$\text{Correction Factor (C.F.)} = \frac{Y_{..}^2}{n}$$

where $Y_{..}$ is the grand total of all observations and n is the total number of observations.

$$\text{Total Sum of Squares (T. S. S)} = \sum_{i}^{p}\sum_{j}^{n_i} y_{ij}^2 - C.F$$

$$\text{Treatment Sum of Squares (Tr. S. S)} = \sum_{i=1}^{p}\frac{Y_{i.}^2}{n_i} - C.F$$

where $Y_{i.}$ is the total of the i-th treatment.

Error Sum of Squares (E.S.S) = (T.S.S – Tr.S.S)

$$H_o : y_1. = y_2. = \cdots = y_p.; \quad H_1 : y_1. \neq y_2. \neq \cdots \neq y_p.$$

where $y_{i.}$ is the mean of i-th treatment.

Table 13.1 ANOVA Table

Source	**d. f.**	**S. S**	**M. S**	**F cal.**	**F tab. (d. f.)**
Treatments	p – 1	Tr. S. S	Tr. M. S	$\frac{\text{Tr.M.S}}{\text{E.M.S}}$	(p – 1), (n – p)
Error	(n –1) – (p – 1)	E.S.S	E.M.S		
Total	n – 1	T.S.S			

where $\text{Tr.M.S} = \frac{\text{Tr.S.S}}{(p-1)}$, $\text{E.M.S} = \frac{\text{E.S.S}}{(n-p)}$

Conclusion

If F (cal.) value > F (tab.) value with (p –1), (n – p) d. f. at the required level of significance then H_o is rejected and H_1 is accepted. If H_o is rejected it can be concluded that there is significant difference between treatment means. Otherwise H_o is accepted.

case (i) If H_o is rejected then pair wise comparison of treatment means can be done with the help of student's t-test if the replications for each treatment is not same. The t-test is given as follows.

$$H_o : y_i. = y_j.; \quad H_1 : y_i. \neq y_j.$$

where $y_i.$ and $y_j.$ are the means of i-th and j-th treatments

$$t = \frac{|y_{i.} - y_{j.}|}{\sqrt{E.M.S\left(\frac{1}{n_i} + \frac{1}{n_j}\right)}} \quad .....(13.2)$$

where n_i, n_j are the number of observations or replications for i-th and j-th treatments.

Conclusion

If t (cal.) value > t (tab.) value with (n – p) d. f. at the required level of significance then H_o is rejected and H_1 is accepted. If H_o is rejected then it can be concluded that there is significant difference between i-th and j-th treatment means. Otherwise H_o is accepted.

case (ii) If the number of replications is equal for all treatments then the pair wise comparison between any two treatment means is done with the help of Critical Difference (C.D.) or Least Significant Difference (L.S.D) test. It is given as follows.

$$C.D. = t_{(n-p)} \times \sqrt{\frac{2(E.M.S)}{r}} \quad .....(13.3)$$

where $t_{(n-p)}$ is the tabulated value of t with (n – p) d. f. at the required level of significant and 'r' is the number of replications for each treatment. If the difference between two treatment means is greater than C.D. value then there is significant difference between those two treatment means. Otherwise there is no significant difference between them. The above method is illustrated with the following example.

***Example*:** The following are the data on daily production (tons) of tons by three Kilans A, B and C in a cement factory on different days. Test the significant difference between them with respect to their performance at 5 per cent level.

	Days	**Total**
A:	22, 23, 18, 17, 14, 21	115
B:	28, 19, 31, 34, 26	138
C:	19, 24, 29, 30, 22, 27, 16, 20, 15	202
		455

Analysis:

Correction Factor (C.F.) $= \frac{Y..^2}{n} = \left(\frac{455}{20}\right)^2 = 10351.25$

where $n = n_1 + n_2 + n_3 = 6 + 5 + 9 = 20$

$$\text{Treatment Sum of Squares (Tr.S.S)} = \frac{Y_1.^2}{n_1} + \frac{Y_2.^2}{n_2} + \frac{Y_3.^2}{n_3} - \text{C.F.}$$

$$= \frac{(115)^2}{6} + \frac{(138)^2}{5} + \frac{(202)^2}{9} - 10351.25$$

$$= 10546.74 - 10351.25 = 195.49$$

$$\text{Total Sum of Squares (T.S.S)} = \sum_i \sum_j y_{ij}^2 - \text{C.F.}$$

$$= \left[(22)^2 + (23)^2 + \cdots + (15)^2\right] - 10351.25$$

$$= 10973.00 - 10351.25 = 621.75$$

$$\text{Error Sum of Square (E.S.S)} = (\text{T.S.S} - \text{Tr.S.S})$$

$$= 621.75 - 195.49 = 426.26$$

The sums of squares obtained are furnished in the ANOVA table for carrying out F-test

Table 13.2

Source	d. f.	S.S	M.S	$F_{cal.}$	$F_{tab.}$
Kilns	3 – 1 = 2	195.49	97.75	3.89	3.59
Error	19 – 2 = 17	426.26	25.07		
Total	20 – 1 = 19	621.75			

Conclusion

Here F(cal.) value i.e. 3.89 > F (tab.) value i.e. 3.59 at 5 per cent level of significance. Therefore H_o is rejected and H_1 is accepted. Hence it can be concluded that there is significant difference between three Kilans with respect to their performance. Now the difference between each pair of Kilans are tested with the help of student's t-test.

Case (i) $H_o : y_1. = y_2.$; $H_1 : y_1. \neq y_2.$

where $y_1.$ and $y_2.$ are the means of A and B Kilans respectively.

$$t = \frac{\left|\frac{115}{6} - \frac{138}{5}\right|}{\sqrt{25.07\left(\frac{1}{6}+\frac{1}{5}\right)}} = \frac{|19.17 - 27.61|}{\sqrt{9.19}}$$

$$= \frac{8.43}{3.03} = 2.78$$

Conclusion

Here t (cal.) value i.e. 2.78 > t (tab.) value i.e. 2.11 with 17 d. f. at 5 per cent level of significance. Therefore H_o is rejected and H_1 is accepted. Hence it can be concluded that there is significant difference between A and B Kilans with respect to their production.

Case (ii) The difference between B and C Kilans is tested similarly with student's t-test as follows.

$$H_o : y_2. = y_3. \; ; \qquad H_1 : y_2. \neq y_3.$$

where $y_2.$ and $y_3.$ are the means of B and C Kilans respectively

$$t = \frac{\left|\frac{138}{5} - \frac{202}{9}\right|}{\sqrt{25.07\left(\frac{1}{5}+\frac{1}{9}\right)}} = \frac{|27.6 - 22.44|}{\sqrt{7.80}}$$

$$t = \frac{5.16}{2.79} = 1.85$$

Conclusion

Here t (cal.) value i.e. 1.85 < t (tab.) value i.e. 2.11 with 17 d. f. at 5 per cent level of significance. Therefore H_o is accepted. Hence it can be concluded that there is no significant difference between B and C Kilans.

Since A and B Kilans are significantly different hence it is necessary to compare between A and C Kilans as the mean of Kilan C is less than the mean of Kilan B.

$$H_o : y_1. = y_3. \; ; \; H_1 : y_1. \neq y_3.$$

$$t = \frac{\left|\frac{115}{6} - \frac{202}{9}\right|}{\sqrt{25.07\left(\frac{1}{6}+\frac{1}{9}\right)}} = \frac{|19.17 - 22.44|}{\sqrt{6.96}} = \frac{3.27}{2.64} = 1.24$$

Conclusion

Here t (cal.) value i.e. 1.24 < t (tab.) value i.e. 2.11 with 17 d. f. at 5 per cent level of significance. Hence H_o is accepted. Hence it can be concluded that there is no significant difference between A and C Kilns.

In order to know the conclusions at a glance the means of A, B and C are arranged in descending order of magnitude and superscripts are placed accordingly. If the difference is not significant then same superscript is used otherwise different superscripts are used as follows in Fig.13.1.

B	C	A
b	ab	a
27.60	22.44	19.17

Fig. 13.1

The underlines above indicates no difference. It can be concluded that Kiln B is having the best performance followed by C and A in that order.

13.2 Two-Way Analysis of Variance

If two sources of variation are involved in an experiment then the analysis of variance is known as two-way analysis of variance. The analysis of variance model in this case is

$$y_{ij} = \mu + \alpha_i + \beta_j + \varepsilon_{ij} \qquad .....(13.4)$$

where y_{ij} is the response value of j-th level of 2nd factor (B) and i-th level of 1st factor (A). μ is the general mean, α_i is the effect i-th level of factor A, β_j is the effect of j-th level of factor B and ε_{ij} is the experimental error effect on the (i, j)-th unit for i=1, 2,..., p; ; = 1, 2,...q.

The sums of squares are obtained as follows

$$\text{Correction Factor (C. F.)} = \frac{Y..^2}{pq}$$

where Y.. is the grand total, p and q are the levels of factors A and B respectively.

$$\text{Total Sum of Squares (T.S.S)} = \sum_{i=1}^{p}\sum_{j=1}^{q} y_{ij}^2 - \text{C.F.}$$

$$\text{A factor Sum of Squares (A.S.S)} = \left[\frac{Y_{1.}^2}{q} + \frac{Y_{2.}^2}{q} + \cdots + \frac{Y_{p.}^2}{q}\right] - \text{C.F.}$$

where $Y_{1.}$, $Y_{2.}$,..., $Y_{p.}$ are the totals of 1st, 2nd..., p-th levels of factor A.

$$\text{B factor Sum of Squares (B.S.S)} = \left[\frac{Y_{.1}^2}{p} + \frac{Y_{.2}^2}{p} + \cdots + \frac{Y_{.q}^2}{p}\right] - \text{C.F.}$$

where $Y_{.1}$, $Y_{.2}$,..., $Y_{.q}$ are the totals of 1st, 2nd ..., q-th levels of factor B.

Error Sum of Squares (E.S.S) = T.S.S – (A.S.S + B.S.S). These sums of squares are furnished in the following ANOVA table given in table 13.3

to carry, out F-test.

(i) $H_o : \alpha_1 = \alpha_2 = \cdots = \alpha_q$,; $H_1 : \alpha_1 \neq \alpha_2 \neq \cdots \neq \alpha_q$

(ii) $H_o : \beta_1 = \beta_2 = \cdots = \beta_q$,; $H_1 : \beta_1 \neq \beta_2 \neq \cdots \neq \beta_q$

Table 13.3 ANOVA Table

Source	d. f.	S. S.	M. S.	$F_{cal.}$	$F_{tab.}$
A	(p – 1)	A.S.S	A.M.S	$\frac{\text{A.M.S}}{\text{E.M.S}}$	(p – 1), (p – 1) (q – 1)
B	(q – 1)	B.S.S	B.M.S	$\frac{\text{B.M.S}}{\text{E.M.S}}$	(q – 1), (p – 1) (q – 1)
Error	(p – 1) (q – 1)	E.S.S	E.M.S		
Total	Pq – 1	T.S.S			

where A.M.S = A.S.S/(p – 1); B.M.S = B.S.S/(q – 1) and E.M.S = E.S.S/(p –1) (q –1).

Conclusion

If F (cal.) value > F (tab.) value with (p –1), (p –1) (q –1) d. f. for factor A and F (cal.) value > F (tab.) value with (q –1), (p –1) (q –1) d. f. for factor B at the required level of significance then H_o is rejected and H_1 is accepted for factor A and factor B respectively. If H_o is rejected then it can be concluded that there is significant difference between levels of factor A and factor B as the case may be. Otherwise, H_o is accepted.

If H_o is rejected then pair wise comparison between levels of A and B is done with the C.D.s (L.S.D) which are obtained as follows

$$C.D._{(A)} = t_{(p-1)(q-1)} \times \sqrt{\frac{2(E.M.S)}{q}} \quad .....(13.5)$$

$$C.D._{(B)} = t_{(p-1)(q-1)} \times \sqrt{\frac{2(E.M.S)}{p}} \quad .....(13.6)$$

where $t_{(p-1)(q-1)}$ is the tabulated value of student's t with (p –1) (q –1) d. f. at the required level of significance.

The means of levels of factors A and B are arranged in descending order of magnitude and the difference between each pair is compared with corresponding C.D. as is done in the case of one-way analysis of variance.

The two-way analysis of variance is illustrated with the following example.

Example: The following are the daily production (tons) data according to Kilns A,B and C and number of shifts I, II and III of working in a cement factory. Test the difference between Kilns as well as shifts at 5 percent level of significance.

Table 13.4

Shift	**Kiln**			**Total**
	A	B	C	
I	31	26	22	79
II	28	22	20	70
III	19	16	14	49
Total	78	64	56	198

Analysis: Correction Factor (C.F.) $= \frac{Y_{..}^2}{pq} = \frac{(198)^2}{3 \times 3}$

$= 4356.00$

$$\text{Total Sum of Squares (T.S.S)} = \sum_{i}^{3}\sum_{j}^{3} y_{ij}^2 - \text{C.F.}$$

$$= \left[(31)^2 + (26)^2 + \cdots + (49)^2\right] - 4356.00$$

$$= 4602 - 4356 = 246.00$$

$$\text{Kilns S.S.} \quad = \sum_{i=1}^{p} \frac{Y_{i.}^2}{q} - \text{C.F.}$$

$$= \frac{(78)^2}{3} + \frac{(64)^2}{3} + \frac{(56)^2}{3} - 4356.00$$

$$= 4438.67 - 4356.00 = 82.67$$

$$\text{Shifts S.S.} \quad = \sum_{i=1}^{q} \frac{Y_{.j}^2}{p} - \text{C.F.}$$

$$= \frac{(79)^2}{3} + \frac{(70)^2}{3} + \frac{(49)^2}{3} - 4356.00$$

$$= 4514.00 - 4356.00 = 158.00$$

$$\text{E.S.S.} \quad = \text{T.S.S} - (\text{A.S.S} + \text{B.S.S})$$

$$= 246.00 - (82.67 - 158.00)$$

$$= 5.33$$

The sums of squares obtained above are furnished in ANOVA table given in table 13.5

Table 13.5 ANOVA table

Source	d. f.	S.S.	M.S.	$F_{cal.}$	$F_{tab.}$
Kilns	$3 - 1 = 2$	82.67	41.34	31.08	5.21
Shifts	$3 - 1 = 2$	158.00	79.00	59.40	5.21
Error	$2 \times 2 = 4$	5.33	1.33		
Total	$9 - 1 = 8$	246.00			

Conclusion

Here F(cal.) value i.e. 31.08 for kilns and 59.40 for shifts > F (tab.) value i.e. 5.21 with (2, 4) d. f. at 5 per cent level of significance. Therefore H_o is rejected for kilns and shifts. Hence it can be concluded that there is significant difference between kilns as well as shifts. In order to compare the difference between pairs of means of kilns and shifts, the C.D.s are computed as follows.

$$C.D._{(kilns)} = t_4 \times \sqrt{\frac{2(EMS)}{3}}$$

$$= 2.78 \times \sqrt{\frac{2 \times 1.33}{3}} = 2.61$$

$$C.D._{(shifts)} = t_4 \times \sqrt{\frac{2(E.M.S)}{3}}$$

$$= 2.78 \times \sqrt{\frac{2 \times 1.33}{3}} = 2.61$$

The means of kilns and shifts are arranged in descending order of magnitude as follows

Kilns

$\bar{A}$	$\bar{B}$	$\bar{C}$
c	b	a
26.00	21.33	18.67

Fig. 13.2

From fig. 13.2, it can be seen that there is significant difference between the three kilns with respect to daily production of cement.

Shifts

I	II	III
c	b	a
26.33	23.33	16.33

Fig. 13.3

From fig. 13.3, it can be noticed that there is significant difference between the three shifts of working with respect to production.

13.3 Three-way Analysis of Variance

If three factors are the sources of variation in the experimental data then three-way analysis of variance is used. This analysis can be done using layout of Latin square design as explained in the earlier chapter. Here the number of observations can be only 16 if 4 kilns, 4 shits and 4 inspectors will inspect the quality of cement. The difference between kilns, shifts and inspectors can be tested using analysis of variance technique. The analysis of variance model in this case is

$$Y_{ijk} = \mu + \alpha_i + \beta_j + \gamma_k + \varepsilon_{ijk} \qquad .....(13.7)$$

where Y_{ijk} is the response value of k-th column in the j-th row of i-treatment for i, j, k = 1, 2,...,r. α_i, β_j, γ_k are the effects of i-th treatment, j-row and k-th column respectively and ε_{ijk} is the experimental error effect on (i, j, k) th-unit.

The sums of squares are obtained as follows

$$\text{Correction Factor (C.F.)} = \frac{Y_{...}^2}{r^2}$$

where Y... is the grand total and r is the number of treatments, rows and columns.

$$\text{Total Sum of Squares (T.S.S)} = \sum_{i=1}^{r}\sum_{j=1}^{r}\sum_{k=1}^{r} y_{ijk}^2 - \text{C.F.}$$

$$\text{Treatment Sum of Squares (Tr.S.S)} = \sum_{i=1}^{r}\frac{Y_{i..}^2}{r} - \text{C.F.}$$

$$\text{Row Sum of Squares (R.S.S)} = \sum_{j=1}^{r}\frac{Y_{.j.}^2}{r} - \text{C.F.}$$

$$\text{Column Sum of Squares (C.S.S)} = \sum_{k=1}^{r}\frac{Y_{..k}^2}{r} - \text{C.F.}$$

Error Sum of Squares (E.S.S) = T.S.S – (R.S.S + C.S.S + Tr.S.S)

The sums of squares obtained above are furnished in the following ANOVA table for carrying out F-test.

$$H_o: \begin{array}{ll} (i) & \alpha_1 = \alpha_2 = ... = \alpha_r;\ H_1: \alpha_1 \neq \alpha_2 \neq \alpha_3 ... \neq \alpha_r \\ (ii) & \beta_1 = \beta_2 = ... = \beta_r;\ H_1: \beta_1 \neq \beta_2 \neq ... \neq \beta_r \\ (iii) & \gamma_1 = \gamma_2 = ... = \gamma_r;\ H_1: \gamma_1 \neq \gamma_2 \neq ... \neq \gamma_r \end{array}$$

Table 13.6 ANOVA table

Source	d. f.	S.S.	M.S.	$F_{cal.}$	$F_{tab.}$
Treatments	r – 1	Tr.S.S	Tr.M.S	Tr.M.S/E.M.S	(r – 1), (r – 1) (r – 2)
Rows	r – 1	R.S.S	R.M.S	R.M.S/E.M.S	(r – 1), (r – 1) (r – 2)
Columns	r – 1	C.S.S	C.M.S	C.M.S/E.M.S	(r – 1), (r – 1) (r – 2)
Error	(r – 1) (r – 2)	E.S.S	E.M.S		
Total	$r^2 - 1$	T.S.S			

where Tr.M.S. = T.S.S./(r – 1), R.M.S. = R.S.S/(r – 1),

C.M.S. = C.S.S/(r – 1), E.M.S = E.S.S./(r – 1) (r – 2)

Conclusion

If F (cal.) value > F (tab.) value with (r – 1), (r – 1) (r – 2) d. f. at the required level of significance for Treatments, Rows and Columns then H_o is rejected and H_1 is accepted. If H_o is rejected then it can be concluded that there is significant difference between treatments, rows and columns. If H_o is rejected then the difference between pairs of means of treatments, row and columns are compared with the corresponding C.D. value which is obtained as

$$\text{C.D.} = t_{(r-1)(r-2)} \times \sqrt{\frac{2(\text{E.M.S})}{r}} \qquad .....(13.8)$$

where $t_{(r-1)(r-2)}$ is the tabulated value of student's t with (r – 1) (r – 2) d. f. The procedure of analysis of variance in this case is explained through the following example.

***Example*:** The following are the data in percentage of the quality of cement inspected by 4 inspectors (A, B, C and B) at 4 kilns (K_1, K_2, K_3 and K_4) for 4 timings (T_1, T_2, T_3 and T_4) with Latin square layout.

Table 13.7

Timings	kiln				Total
	K_1	K_2	K_3	K_4	
T_1	B (62)	D (58)	C (46)	A (40)	206
T_2	C (56)	A (47)	D (43)	B (38)	184
T_3	D (49)	B (38)	A (34)	C (30)	151
T_4	A (40)	C (35)	B (31)	D (25)	131
Total	207	178	154	133	672

***Analysis*:** Correction Factor (C.F.) $= \frac{Y_{...}^2}{r^2} = \frac{(672)^2}{(4)^2} = 28224$

Total Sum of Squares (T.S.S)

$$= \sum_i \sum_j \sum_k Y_{ijk}^2 - \text{C.F.}$$

$$= \left[(62)^2 + (58)^2 + \ldots + (25)^2\right] - 28224.00$$

$$= 30102.00 - 28224.00 = 1878.00$$

Inspector Sum of Squares (I.S.S) $= \sum_{i=1}^{r} \frac{Y_{i..}^2}{r} - \text{C.F.}$

Here wherever A, B, C and D are there they are added to obtain the totals of Inspectors A, B, C and D) respectively.

$$= \frac{(161)^2}{4} + \frac{(169)^2}{4} + \frac{(167)^2}{4} + \frac{(175)^2}{4} - 28224.00$$

$$= 28249.00 - 28224.00 = 25.00$$

Timings Sum of Squares (Ti.S.S)

$$= \sum_{j=1}^{r} \frac{Y_{.j.}^2}{r} - \text{C.F.}$$

$$= \frac{(206)^2}{4} + \frac{(184)^2}{4} + \frac{(151)^2}{4} + \frac{(131)^2}{4} - 28224.00$$

$$= 29063.50 - 28224.00 = 839.5$$

Kilns Sum of Squares (K.S.S)

$$= \sum_{k=1}^{r} \frac{Y_{..k}^2}{r} - C.F.$$

$$= \frac{(207)^2}{4} + \frac{(178)^2}{4} + \frac{(154)^2}{4} + \frac{(133)^2}{4} - 28224.00$$

$$= 28984.50 - 28224.00 = 760.50$$

Error Sum of Squares

$$= E.S.S = T.S.S. - [I.S.S + K.S.S + Ti.S.S]$$

$$= 1878.00 - [25.00 + 839.50 + 760.5]$$

$$= 253.00$$

The sums of squares are furnished in the following ANOVA table given in Table 13.8 to carry out F-test.

Table 13.8 ANOVA Table

Source	**d. f.**	**S.S.**	**M.S.**	$\mathbf{F_{cal.}}$	$\mathbf{F_{tab.}}$
Inspectors	$4 - 1 = 3$	25.00	8.33	0.20	4.76
Kilns	$4 - 1 = 3$	760.50	253.50	6.01	4.76
Timings	$4 - 1 = 3$	839.50	279.83	6.64	4.76
Error	$3 \times 2 = 6$	253.00	42.17		
Total	$16 - 1 = 15$	1878.00			

Conclusion

Here F (cal.) value i.e. 0.20 < F (tab.) value i.e. 4.76 with (3, 6) d. f. at 5 per cent level of significance for Inspectors, F (cal.) value i.e. 6.01 and 6.64 > F (tab.) value i.e. 4.76 with (3, 6) d. f. for kilns and Timings at 5 per cent level of significance. Therefore, H_o is accepted for inspectors and rejected for kilns and Timings. Hence it can be concluded that there is no significant difference between Inspectors and there is significant difference between Kilns and Timings with respect to quality of cement.

Since H_o is rejected for Kilns and Timings the difference between pairs of means of Kilns and Timings are compared with the C.D. value which is obtained as

$$C.D. = t_6 \times \sqrt{\frac{2(EMS)}{4}}$$

$$= 2.45 \times \sqrt{\frac{2 \times 42.17}{4}} = 11.25$$

The means of Kilns are arranged as

$\overline{K_1}$	$\overline{K_2}$	$\overline{K_3}$	$\overline{K_4}$
b	ab	a	a
51.75	44.50	38.50	33.25

Fig. 13.4

From fig. 13.4, it can be observed that Kiln K_1 is the best and Kiln K_2 is next best with respect to quality of cement produced. The means of timings are arranged as

$\overline{T_1}$	$\overline{T_2}$	$\overline{T_3}$	$\overline{T_4}$
c	bc	ab	a
51.50	46.00	37.75	32.75

Fig. 13.5

From fig. 13.5, it can be seen that timings T_1 and T_2 are the best compared to others with respect to quality of cement.

CHAPTER 14

Time Series and Index Numbers

14.1 Time Series

The series of data based on time is known as time series or time series data. Usually this data is obtained from secondary source. For example, food production, coal production, steel production, rainfall etc., in different years as a country wide or state wide are considered as time series data.

The yearly business of Banks, and LIC etc., are also considered as time series data.

14.1.1 Analysis of Time Series Data

The objective of analysis of time series data is to know the different causes of variation effecting the behaviour of the data over a period of time. Further, analysis is useful for deeper understanding of the inner behaviour of the character under study as well as for forecasting the future time dependent observed value. For example, if the time series data on power production is studied thoroughly then it can be known how it is changing with respect to short time such as summer, winter and rainy season, long time for every three or four years and how it is changing in long years over a period of 20 years or so. This type of study is known as time series analysis.

The observed value in the time series is effecting by four components such as:

(i) Long time trend or secular trend

(ii) Seasonal variation,

(iii) Cyclical variation and

(iv) Irregular variation or random variation.

If y is the observed value, T is the longtime trend, S is the seasonal variation, C is the cyclical variation and R is the random variation, then the relation between them is given as

$$Y = T * S * C * R \qquad \text{.....(14.1)}$$

Here '*' is called convolution which represents both '+' and '×' whenever the time series follows additive law and whenever it follows exponential law respectively. T, S, C and R are called components of time series data. T indicates general trend of the data over entire period of time series data, S represents the seasonal variation i.e., variation occurs due to effect of seasons such as summer, rainy and winter and which occurs in less than a year, C is the cyclical variation and which happens usually in more than one year in cyclical way or systematic way such as drought, floods, boom and recession in economy say share markets etc., and R is the random variation which occurs randomly. Random variation may occur within a year or in more than one year. The occurrence of earth quakes, tsunami, terrorist attacks, pest attacks on crops, wars etc are some of the examples of random variation. These four components of time series data are depicted in Fig. 14.1 to 14.3.

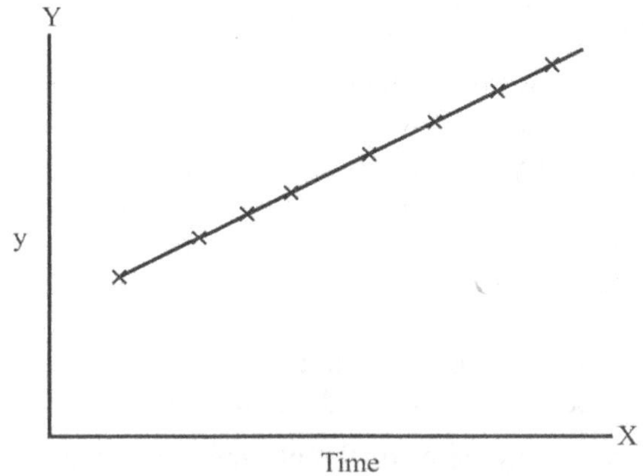

Fig. 14.1 Long time trend (T)

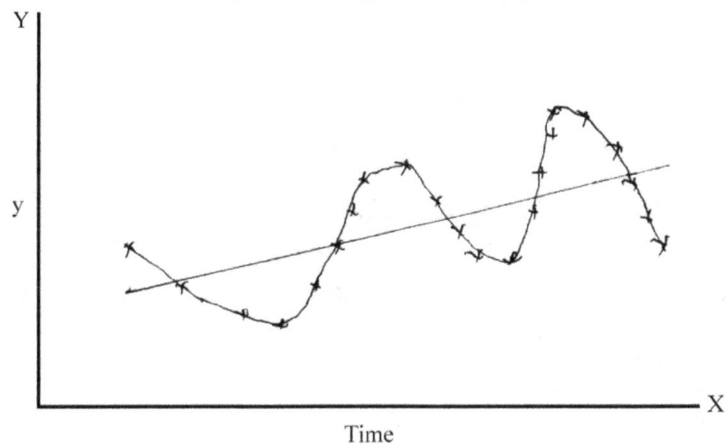

Fig. 14.2 T with cyclical variation

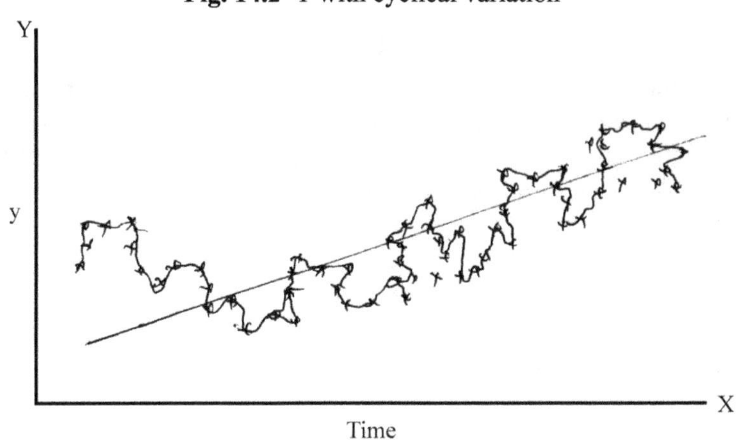

Fig. 14.3 T,C with seasonal variation

14.1.2 Secular Trend or Long Time Trend

It is desirable to know the behaviour of observed characteristic over a long period. The factory owner would like to know whether the production in the factory is increasing or decreasing or remains stationery in the long range of time. Similarly the policy maker at country level would be interested whether the power production or consumption is increasing or decreasing or remains stationary for the last 20 years or so. Further he may be interested to know the power production after 5 years taking into consideration for the last 20 years data. The graph connecting all points of time series data is called 'Historigram'.

Long time trend may be of different types like straight line, parabola, third degree polynomial etc., or curvilinear. The equations of the polynomials are given as

1st degree polynomial : $y = a + bt$

2nd degree polynomial : $y = a + bt + ct^2$ .....(14.2)

3rd degree polynomial : $y = a + bt + ct^2 + dt^3$

14.1.2.1 Trend Fitting by Observation

This is the easiest method since it is drawn by a person based on his experience. If the 'historigram' appears to be a straight line nature a straight line will be drawn with the help of a scale in such a way that upper and lower phases of cyclical curves may cancel each other. If 'historigram' appears to be a non-linear form then a smooth curve is drawn close to the points canceling seasonal variations. This is a subjective method since it is based on individual's experience.

14.1.2.2 Method of Semi Averages

In this method the data is divided into two equal parts and means are calculated for each part. Two points are plotted by taking mid-points of two time intervals are taken on x-axis and corresponding means of variate values on y-axis and joining these two points with the help of a scale is called method of semi-averages.

For example if the data is from 2001 to 2010th year then it is divided into two equal parts i.e., from 2001 to 2005 and from 2006 to 2010 and averages are calculated for these two periods. The points are plotted with mid-point of 2001 to 2005 i.e., 2003 and its average value and mid-point of 2006 to 2010 i.e., 2008 and its average value. These two points will be joined with the help of a scale. If the total number of observations is odd then the middle value is excluded for taking means of two parts to make total number of observations is even.

14.1.2.3 Method of Least Squares

If the equations are to be fitted for 1st, 2nd, 3rd etc., degree polynomials 'Least squares method' is used. The fitted equations are useful for forecasting the variate values for future.

14.1.2.4 Fitting of 1st Degree Polynomial or Straight Line

The equation of straight line is given as

$$y = a + bt \qquad .....(14.3)$$

where y is dependent value and 't' is time variable. Least squares method gives the estimates of 'a' and 'b' in eqn. (14.3) in such a way that the sum of squares of deviation of observed and expected values should be minimum. The normal equations are

$$\Sigma y = na + b\Sigma t$$

$$\Sigma ty = a\Sigma t + b\Sigma t^2 \qquad .....(14.4)$$

Since time variable 't' is changing with equally spaced interval, it is possible to simplify the calculations by transforming 't' to 'u; such that

$$u = t - A$$

where A is mid-value of the time variable if n is odd and average of the two middle values if n is even where n is the number of observations. Then

$$t = u + A \qquad .....(14.5)$$

substituting 't' in eqn. (14.3), we have

$$y = a + b\,(u + A)$$

$$y = a + bA + bu$$

Let $a' = a + bA$,

$$y = a' + bu \qquad .....(14.6)$$

The normal equations for estimating a' and 'b' are

$$\Sigma y = na' + b\Sigma u$$

$$\Sigma uy = a'\Sigma u + b\Sigma u^2 \qquad .....(14.7)$$

The advantage in solving the eqns. (14.7) in preference to eqn. (14.4) is that Σu will be zero.

Therefore 'a'', and 'b' values are directly obtained by substituting $\Sigma u = 0$ in eqns. (14.7).

$$a' = \frac{\Sigma y}{n} \quad .....(14.8)$$

$$b = \frac{\Sigma uy}{\Sigma u^2} \quad .....(14.9)$$

The fitted equation of a straight line is obtained by substituting the values of 'a'' and 'b' in eqn. (14.6). If forecasting is to be done for particular 't' then it is to be transformed to u using relation (14.5) and then 'u' value is substituted in the fitted equation for obtaining 'y' value. The above method is illustrated here with an example.

Example: The following are the data on coal output (mt.) in ten years i.e., from 2001 to 2010. Fit the 1st degree polynomial.

Table 14.1

S.No.	Year (t)	Coal (y) (m.t.)	u = 2 (t – 2005.5)	uy	u^2	Trend values
1	2001	20	– 9	– 180	81	21.07
2	2002	23	– 7	– 161	49	24.61
3	2003	28	– 5	– 140	25	28.15
4	2004	34	– 3	– 102	9	31.69
5	2005	37	– 1	– 37	1	35.23
6	2006	39	1	39	1	38.77
7	2007	42	3	126	9	42.31
8	2008	44	5	220	25	45.85
9	2009	49	7	343	49	49.39
10	2010	54	9	486	81	52.93
Total		370	0	594	330	

using eqns. (14.8) and (14.9), we have

$$a' = \frac{\Sigma y}{n} = \frac{370}{10} = 37.0; \quad n = 10$$

$$b = \frac{\Sigma uy}{\Sigma u^2} = \frac{594}{330} = 1.8$$

The fitted 1st degree polynomial is

$$y = 37 + 1.8\,u$$

suppose the coal output for the year 2015 is to be forecasted then

$$u = 2\,(t - 2005.5) = 2\,(2015 - 2005.5) = 19$$

$$y = 37 + 1.8\,(19) = 71.2 \text{ (m.t.)}$$

The forecasted output of coal for the year 2015 is 71.2 (m.t.). The trend values in Table 14.7 are obtained by substituting u values in the fitted equation.

14.1.2.5 Fitting of 2nd Degree Polynomial

If 2nd degree polynomial is to be fitted for the time series data it is given on the similar lines of fitting 1st degree polynomial.

The equation of 2nd degree polynomial is

$$y = a + bt + ct^2 \qquad \text{.....(14.10)}$$

The normal equations by least squares method are

$$\Sigma y = na + b\Sigma t + c\Sigma t^2$$

$$\Sigma ty = a\Sigma t + b\Sigma t^2 + c\Sigma t^3$$

$$\Sigma t^2 y = a\Sigma t^2 + b\Sigma t^3 + c\Sigma t^4$$

If $u = t - A$, then

$$y = a' + b'u + cu^2 \qquad \text{.....(14.11)}$$

The normal equations for estimating a', b' and c in eqn. (14.11) are

$$\Sigma y = na' + b'\Sigma u + c\Sigma u^2$$

$$\Sigma uy = a'\Sigma u + b'\Sigma u^2 + c\Sigma u^3 \qquad \text{.....(14.12)}$$

$$\Sigma u^2 y = a'\Sigma u^2 + b'\Sigma u^3 + c\Sigma u^4$$

Here $\Sigma u = \Sigma u^3 = 0$, therefore eqns. (14.12) become

$$\Sigma y = na' + c\Sigma u^2$$

$$\Sigma uy = b'\Sigma u^2 \qquad \text{.....(14.13)}$$

$$\Sigma u^2 y = a'\Sigma u^2 + c\Sigma u^4$$

The estimate of b' is obtained directly as

$$b' = \frac{\Sigma u\,y}{\Sigma u^2} \qquad \text{.....(14.14)}$$

and a' and c are obtained by solving 1st and 3rd equations in (14.13).

The above procedure is explained with the help of the following example.

Example: The following are the data on cement production (m.t.) for the years from 2001 to 2010. Fit the 2nd degree polynomial and forecast the cement production for the year 2016.

Table 14.2

S. No (1)	Year (t) (2)	Cement (m.t.) (y) (3)	u = 2 (t – 2005.5) (4)	uy (5)	u^2 (6)	u^2y (7)	u^4 (8)	Trend values (9)
1	2001	18	– 9	– 162	81	1458	6561	17.30
2	2002	25	– 7	– 175	49	1225	2401	24.55
3	2003	32	– 5	– 160	25	800	625	30.98
4	2004	37	– 3	– 111	9	330	81	36.58
5	2005	40	– 1	– 40	1	40	1	41.35
6	2006	43	1	43	1	43	1	45.29
7	2007	48	3	144	9	144	81	48.40
8	2008	50	5	250	25	1250	625	50.68
9	2009	51	7	357	49	2499	2401	52.13
10	2010	56	9	504	81	4536	6561	52.76
	Total	400	0	650	330	12325	19338	

From eqn. (14.14), we have

$$b' = \frac{\Sigma u\ y}{\Sigma u^2} = \frac{650}{330} = 1.97$$

From eqns. (14.13), we have

$$\Sigma y = na' + c\Sigma u^2$$

$$\Sigma u^2 y = a'\Sigma u^2 + c\Sigma u^4$$

$$400 = 10\,a' + 330\ c \qquad .....(14.15)$$

$$12325 = 330\ a' + 19338\ c$$

Solving eqns. (14.15), we have

$$c = -\,0.1036,\ a' = 43.42$$

The fitted 2nd degree polynomial is

$$y = 43.42 + 1.97\ u - 0.1036\ u^2$$

In order to forecast the cement production for the year 2016, we substitute u value for 2016 and which is obtained as

$$u = 2\,(2016 - 2005.5) = 21$$

in the fitted 2nd degree polynomial.

$$y = 43.42 + 1.97\,(21) - 0.1036\,(21)^2$$
$$= 39.10$$

The forecasted cement production for the year 2016 is 39.10 (m.t.). The trend values are obtained by substituting u values starting from year 2001 to 2010 in the fitted equation and presented in column (9) in Table 14.2.

The important point to be considered is that which degree polynomial will be appropriate to fit the trend equation. The approximate procedure is to compute the first differences from successive values, second differences, third differences etc. If the first differences are constant or equal then 1st degree polynomial is appropriate, if the 2nd differences are equal then 2nd degree polynomial is appropriate and so on.

14.1.2.6 Fitting of Exponential Curve

If the 'historigram' of time series data indicates non-linear relation then the data may be examined for fitting non-linear curves such as exponential curve. If the data indicate constant ratio of change instead of constant amount of change then the exponential curve is appropriate one. The equation of the curve is given as

$$y = ab^t \qquad .....(14.16)$$

where y is the dependent variable and t (time) is the independent variable. If the data plotted on semi log paper where t is taken on x-axis and log y on y-axis and the graph shows straight line relationship then the exponential curve of the type is appropriate as given in (14.16).

The estimates of 'a' and 'b' are obtained by using least squares method.

$$y = ab^t$$

Taking logarithms on both sides of the equation

$$\log y = \log a + t \log b \qquad .....(14.17)$$

The normal equations are

$$\Sigma \log y = n \log a + \log b\ \Sigma t$$
$$\Sigma t \log y = \log a\ \Sigma t + \log b\ \Sigma t^2 \qquad .....(14.18)$$

Solving two equations given in (14.18), log a and log b values can be obtained. By taking antilogarithm values of log a and log b, a and b values can be obtained.

The exponential curve is useful when the growth of variable is in geometric progression.

14.1.2.7 Fitting of 2nd Degree Exponential Curve

If the data plotted on semi-log paper shows a parabolic curve, a second degree exponential curve is appropriate one. The equation of the curve is

$$y = ab^t c^{t^2} \qquad \text{.....(14.19)}$$

The procedure of fitting this curve is on the similar lines of fitting 1st degree exponential curve by taking logarithms on both sides and using least squares method.

It may be noted that the 1st degree and 2nd degree exponential curves are appropriate for fitting whenever 1st and 2nd differences of logarithms are equal respectively.

14.1.2.8 Fitting of Modified Exponential Curve

If the data show the amount of growth declines by a constant percentage and the curve asymptotically approaches to a certain upper limit then the appropriate curve for trend is modified exponential curve. The equation of the modified exponential curve is

$$y = a + bc^t \qquad \text{.....(14.20)}$$

where 'a' is called asymptote, b and c are constants. The fitting of this curve is illustrated with the data given in Table 14.3. However, this method of fitting is only approximate one.

Table 14.3

t	y	Partial total	y increment	Percent of preceding increment
0	26			
1	46	72	20	
2	61		15	75.0
3	72	133	11	73.3
4	80		8	72.7
5	86	166	6	75.5

The modified exponential curve is depicted in Fig. 14.1 for the data given in Table 14.3.

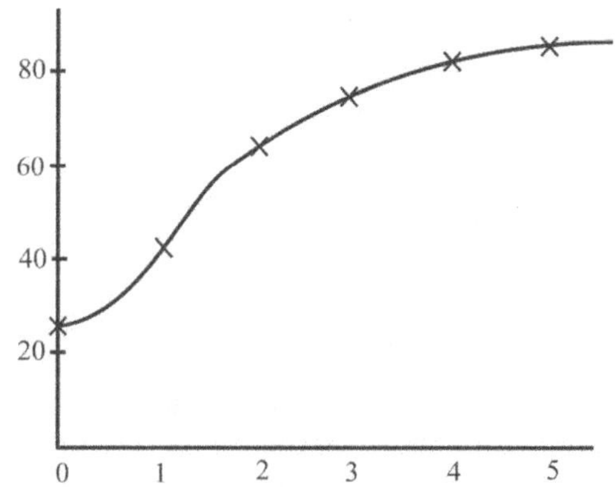

Fig. 14.1

The expressions for obtaining estimates of a, b and c are given as

$$c = \left(\frac{S_3 - S_2}{S_2 - S_1}\right)^{1/n}$$

$$b = (S_2 - S_1)\,\frac{c-1}{(c^n - 1)^2} \quad \text{and} \qquad .....(14.21)$$

$$a = \frac{1}{n}\left[\frac{S_1S_3 - S_2^2}{S_1 + S_3 - 2S_2}\right]$$

where S_1, S_2 and S_3 are the partial totals of 1st, 2nd and 3rd parts of y values in the time series data when it is divided into three equal parts and n is the total number of observations in each part.

Here $S_1 = 72$, $S_2 = 133$, $S_3 = 166$, $n = 2$

From eqns. (14.21), we have

$$a = \frac{1}{2}\left[\frac{72 \times 166 - (133)^2}{72 + 166 - 2 \times 133}\right] = \frac{1}{2}\left[\frac{-5737}{-28}\right] = 102.45$$

$$c = \left[\frac{(166 - 133)}{(133 - 72)}\right]^{1/2} = \left(\frac{33}{61}\right)^{1/2} = 0.74$$

$$b = (133 - 72)\left(\frac{0.74 - 1}{\left[(0.74)^2 - 1\right]^2}\right)$$

$$= 61\left(\frac{-0.26}{0.20}\right) = -79.3$$

The fitted modified exponential curve is therefore given as

$$y = 102.45 - 79.3\,(0.74)^t$$

14.1.2.9 Fitting of Gompertz Curve

If the data show a trend in which the logarithms of the increasing values decline by a constant percentage then Gompertz curve is appropriate for fitting. If the data plotted on a semi log graph paper resembles modified exponential curve then Gompertz curve is appropriate for fitting. The equation of the Gompertz curve is given as

$$y = a\,b^{c^t} \qquad \text{.....(14.22)}$$

where y is the dependent variable, t is the time variable, a, b and c are constants.

By taking logarithms on both sides of the equation (14.22),

$$\text{Log } y = \log a + c^t \log b \qquad \text{.....(14.23)}$$

This curve will have two asymptotes and the lower asymptote is equal to zero.

The estimates of a, b and c are obtained on the similar lines of modified exponential curve by considering log y values instead of y values. Let S_1 be the sum of 1st n observational data, S_2 be the sum of the 2nd n observational data and S_3 be the sum of the third n observational data when the total number of observations are divided into three equal parts. The estimates of constants are obtained using the following expressions

$$C^n = \frac{(S_3 - S_2)}{(S_2 - S_1)}$$

$$\log b = (S_2 - S_1)\,\frac{(c-1)}{(c^n - 1)^2} \qquad \text{.....(14.24)}$$

$$\log a = \frac{1}{n}\left[S_1 - \frac{(C^n - 1)}{(C - 1)}\,\log b\right]$$

If $c > 1$, there will be no upper asymptote and if $c < 1$, there will be both upper and lower asymptote and lower asymptote will be zero.

This curve is useful in the study of growth of industries.

14.1.2.10 Fitting of Logistic Curve

If the first differences of the reciprocals of y values decline by a constant percentage, the logistic curve is appropriate to fit to the time series data. The formula of this curve is given as

$$\frac{1}{y} = a + bc^t \qquad \text{.....(14.25)}$$

where a, b and c are constants. The fitting of this curve is done on the similar lines of modified exponential curve by using S_1, S_2 and S_3 as the sums of reciprocals of y for the 1st, 2nd and 3rd part of the time series of data when it is divided into 3 equal parts each consisting of n observations. This curve is useful in the study of population growth, growth of drosophila and yeast.

14.1.3 Seasonal Variation

The variation in the time series data may occur due to effect of seasons like summer, winter and rainy. For examples the power consumption may vary with season as it will be more in summer, less in rainy and least in winter season. Similarly sales of ice creams, umbrellas, occupancy in hotels, construction of buildings, production of cement, sales in grocery shops, expenditure of monthly income etc., vary with season, month, week etc. The most common method of isolating and measuring seasonal variation is the method of moving averages. Each average is expected to eliminate seasonal influence and will be located at the centre of period to which it pertains. In this method, the arithmetic means are calculated successively by taking a specified number of values, say p at a time and then adding the next value and dropping the initial value until all values are exhausted. The averages are written against the middle values of two corresponding observations if p is odd number and against the middle of the two middle values when p is even number where p is called the period of moving average. If y_i be the i-th observational value in the time series data for i = 1, 2, …., n and p be the period of moving average, then 1st moving average is

$$m_1 = \frac{1}{n} = (y_1 + y_2 + ... + y_p)$$

$$m_2 = \frac{1}{n} = (y_2 + y_3 + ... + y_{p+1}) \quad \text{and so on.}$$

The method of finding seasonal variation through moving average method is illustrated with the following example.

Example: The following are the data of hotel occupancy (hundreds) in a star hotel in a city for four quarters starting from January to March, April to June, July to September and October to December in a year taking as 1st, 2nd, 3rd and 4th quarters respectively in different years. Find seasonal index for each quarter.

Table 14.4

Year (1)	Quarter (2)	Occupancy (100) (3)	4-Quarter M.A.* (4)	Centred average (5)	Seasonal Index (6)
2006	I	14			
	II	28			
			22.00		
	III	24		22.75	
			23.50		105.5
	IV	22		24.50	
			25.50		89.8
2007	I	20		26.00	
			26.50		76.9
	II	36		27.00	
			27.50		133.3
	III	28		27.63	
			27.75		101.3
	IV	26		28.00	
			28.25		92.9
2008	I	21		29.00	
			29.75		72.4
	II	38		30.00	
			30.25		126.7
	III	34		30.63	
			31.50		111.0
	IV	28		31.25	
			32.00		89.6
2009	I	24		32.25	
			32.50		75.6
	II	40		33.00	
			33.50		124.0
	III	36		34.00	
			34.50		109.1
	IV	30		35.00	
			35.50		88.2
2010	I	28		36.00	
			36.50		80.0
	II	44			
					122.2
	III	40			
	IV	34			

* Moving Average

In Table 14.4, 4-quarterly moving averages are computed by taking 4-values at a time successively as described earlier and entered in column (4). Since the period of moving average is 4 and which is even number the moving average values are placed in the middle place of two mid-value i.e., in between 2nd and 3rd values and so on. Since these moving average values are not corresponding to either 2nd or 3rd value and so on and therefore further 2-period moving averages are computed for 4-period moving averages to make them correspondence with original values in Col.(3). Seasonal indices are computed by dividing values in col. (3) by values in col. (5) and then converted into percentage values. These values are entered in col. (6). The seasonal indices values are further classified according to year and quarter and furnished in Table 14.5

Table 14.5

Year	Quarter I	Quarter II	Quarter III	Quarter IV	Total
2006			105.5	89.8	
2007	76.9	133.3	101.3	92.9	
2008	72.4	126.7	111.0	89.6	
2009	75.6	124.0	109.1	88.2	
2010	80.0	122.2			
Total	152.5	250.7	214.6	179.4	
Mean	76.25	125.35	107.30	89.70	398.6
Seasonal Index	76.52	125.79	107.68	90.01	400.0

In Table 14.5 the highest and lowest values of seasonal indices in each quarter are deleted to avoid extreme values in calculation of seasonal indices. After deleting these values the averages are calculated for the remaining observations in each column of quarters. The total of these means is obtained as 398.6 but it should be ideally equal to 400. To make this total 400 a ratio, $\frac{400}{398.6} = 1.0035$ is calculated and multiplied with each mean in Table 14.5. This ratio is called 'adjustment' factor. The seasonal indices are entered into last row of Table 14.5 and the total of these indices is 400 since these indices are percentages and there are four quarters and therefore the total should be equal to 400.

The logic of obtaining seasonal indices is explained here. The values in Col (3) can be written as

$$y = T \times S \times C \times I$$

where as the values in Col (6) are moving averages which eliminated or smoothed out seasonal and irregular movements. Let y_m be the moving average value col (5), then

$$y_m = T \times C$$

Since the seasonal indices in col. (6) are obtained as the percentage ratios of col. (3) to col. (5), we have

$$\frac{y}{y_m} = \frac{\text{col.(3)}}{\text{col.(5)}} = \frac{T \times S \times C \times I}{T \times C} = S \times I$$

The values in col. (3) are S × I values which contain irregular variations. These are removed by deleting highest and lowest values in each column of quarters in Table 14.5.

14.1.3.1 Deseasonalisation of time Series data

Sometimes it is necessary to deseasonalize the time series data i.e., the effect of season has to be removed from the original data. This is done simply by dividing the values in col. (3) by corresponding seasonal index in the last row of Table 14.5.

For example the deseasonalised value of 1st quarter of 2006 year is

$$\frac{y}{S} \times 100 = \frac{14}{76.52} \times 100 = 18.3$$

The deseasonalised value for quarter III of 2007 is

$$\frac{28}{107.68} \times 100 = 26.0$$

14.1.3.2 Forecasting the value of any Season

In order to forecast the value of any season the following procedure is followed.

The equation of straight line trend is given as

$$y = a' + bu$$

where u = (t – A). If there are m seasons then let u be the difference between mid-point of a given season and mid-point of total time series data. If y' be the trend value of any given season, then

$$y' = \frac{a'}{m} + \frac{b}{m^2} u^1 \qquad \text{.....(14.26)}$$

using eqn. (14.26), the trend values of any season can be obtained. The forecasted value for a particular season is obtained as

$$\frac{T \times S}{100} \qquad \text{.....(14.27)}$$

The forecasting of different quarters or seasons are illustrated by taking data given in Table 14.4 and presented in Table 14.6.

Table 14.6

Quarter / Year	I	II	III	IV	Total
2006	14	28	24	22	88
2007	20	36	28	26	110
2008	21	38	34	28	121
2009	24	40	36	30	130
2010	28	44	40	34	146
Total	107	186	162	140	595

Let the straight line trend equation be

$$y = a' + bu$$

where $a' = \frac{\Sigma y}{n}$, $b = \frac{\Sigma uy}{\Sigma u^2}$

where u = t – A and A is the mid-point of year i.e., 2008 and t is the year. The estimates of 'a'' and 'b' are obtained as given in Table 14.7.

Table 14.7

t	y	u = (t – 2008)	u y	u^2	y_e
2006	88	– 2	– 176	4	91.8
2007	110	– 1	– 110	1	105.4
2008	121	0	0	0	119.0
2009	130	1	130	1	132.6
2010	146	2	292	4	146.2
Total	595		136	10	

$$a' = \frac{595}{5} = 119, \qquad b = \frac{136}{10} = 13.6$$

The fitted trend equation is

$$y = 119 + 13.6\,u$$

The trend values (y_e) are calculated by substituting u values in the fitted trend equation and furnished in Table 14.7.

The fitted trend equation season wise is obtained as

$$y^1 = \frac{119}{4} + \frac{13.6}{(4)^2}\,u'$$

$$= 29.75 + 0.85\,u'$$

where u' is the difference between mid-point of a quarter and mid-point of a total time series data. Here there are 5 × 4 = 20 quarters, the values of u' will be $\frac{20-1}{2} = 9.5$ i.e., starting from – 9.5 to 9.5. That is 1st quarter of 2006 will have u' value as – 9.5, 2nd quarter will have u' value as –8.5 and so on and the 4th quarter of 2010 will have u' value as 9.5.

The y' and u' values are presented in Table 14.8.

Table 14.8

Year	Quarter	u'	y'
2006	I	– 9.5	21.7
	II	– 8.5	22.5
	III	– 7.5	23.4
	IV	– 6.5	24.4
2007	I	– 5.5	25.1
	II	– 4.5	25.9
	III	– 3.5	26.8
	IV	– 2.5	27.6
2008	I	– 1.5	28.5
	II	– 0.5	29.3
	III	0.5	30.2
	IV	1.5	31.0
2009	I	2.5	31.9
	II	3.5	32.7
	III	4.5	33.6
	IV	5.5	34.4
2010	I	6.5	35.3
	II	7.5	36.1
	III	8.5	37.0
	IV	9.5	37.8

The forecasted value for the 1st quarter of 2006 year is obtained as

$$\frac{y^1 \times S}{100} = \frac{21.7 \times 76.52}{100} = 16.6$$

Similarly

$$\text{II quarter, 2006} = \frac{22.5 \times 125.79}{100} = 28.3$$

$$\text{III quarter, 2010} = \frac{37.0 \times 107.68}{100} = 39.8$$

Here 'S' values are already obtained and taken from Table 14.5.

Also the forecasted values of different quarters can be obtained for future years such as 2011 etc. For example if the hotel occupancy for II quarter of 2011 is to be forecasted then substitute

$u^1 = 11.5$ in the fitted trend equation

$$y^1 = 29.75 + 0.85\, u^1$$

$$y^1 = 29.75 + 0.85\,(11.5) = 39.53$$

with seasonal index II quarter as 125.79.

The forecasted value of II quarter, 2011 is

$$\frac{39.53 \times 125.79}{100} = 49.7$$

14.1.4 Cyclical Variation

The cyclical variation can be isolated from the time series by using the relationship between y and T, S, C, R in eqn. (14.1) where

$$y = T \times S \times C \times R$$

Divide by T × S values, we have

$$\frac{y}{T \times S} = \frac{T \times S \times C \times R}{T \times S} = CR$$

By smoothening CR values with short term moving averages of appropriate period the 'C' values can be isolated.

14.2 Index Numbers

Index numbers are ratios for measuring change in prices, quantities, total value of the commodities, educational characteristics etc., over a period of time. These are known as 'Economic barometers'. These are ratios of same units of measurement. Hence they are independent of units of measurement.

14.2.1 Uses of Index Numbers

Index numbers are useful in measuring :

(i) change in price of a commodity or commodities over a period of time,

(ii) change in quantity or quantities of commodity or commodities over a period of time,

(iii) change in total commodity values over a period of time like cost of living index numbers,

(iv) change in educational efficiency such as attendance in primary and secondary level of education etc.

14.2.2 Price Relative

If p_{ki} is the price of i-th commodity in k-th year and p_{oi} is the price of i-th commodity in o-th year or base year with which k-th year is compared. The base year may be normal year or any year with which we are interested to compare k-th year or present year. The choice of base year depends upon the investigator. The price relative (P.R.) for the i-th commodity of k-th year is given as

$$\text{P.R.} = \frac{p_{ki}}{p_{0i}} \times 100 \qquad \text{.....(14.28)}$$

14.2.3 Price Index Number

In computing price index number, prices of more than one commodity are considered. If p_{ni} is the price of i-th commodity in the n-th year and p_{oi} is the price of same commodity in the base year for i = 1, 2, …, k then price index is given as

$$P_{0,n\,(p)} = \frac{\sum_{i=1}^{k} p_{ni}}{\sum_{i=1}^{k} p_{0i}} \times 100 \qquad \text{.....(14.29)}$$

This index number is also known as aggregative index number. Here $n > 0$. In other words n-th year will be more than base year.

14.2.4 Laspeyre's Price Index Number

In this index number prices are weighted with quantities which are either produced or consumed in the base for the respective commodities. Let $L_{0,n}$ is the Laspeyre's price index number, then

$$L_{o,n} = \frac{\sum_{i=1}^{k} p_{ni}\, q_{0i}}{\sum_{i=1}^{k} p_{0i}\, q_{0i}} \times 100 \qquad \text{.....(14.30)}$$

The summation in (14.30) is over 'k' commodities. Where p_{ni}, p_{0i} are the prices of i-th commodity in the n-th year and base year respectively and q_{0i} is the quantity produced or consumed of i-th commodity in the base year. This index number is also known as cost of living index number since it measures the change in total value of commodities which are produced or consumed in base year. This index number gives some upward bias.

14.2.5 Paasche's Price Index Number

In this index number prices are weighted with quantities produced or consumed in the n-th year for the respective commodities. Let $P_{0,\,n(p)}$ is the Paasche's price index number, then

$$P_{o,n(p)} = \frac{\sum_{i=1}^{k} p_{ni}\ q_{ni}}{\sum_{i=1}^{k} p_{0i}\ q_{ni}} \times 100 \qquad \ldots..(14.31)$$

The summation in (14.31) is over 'k' commodities. Where p_{ni}, p_{0i} are the prices of i-th commodity in the n-th year and base year respectively and q_{ni} is the quantity produced or consumed for the i-th commodity in the n-th year.

This index number may give some down ward bias. This index number is also known as cost of living index number.

14.2.6 Marshall-Edgeworth Price Index Number

In this index number prices are weighted with average of quantities produced or consumed in the n-th year as well as base year. Let $M_{0,n(p)}$ is the Marshall-Edgeworth price index number, then

$$M_{0,n(p)} = \frac{\sum_{i=1}^{k} p_{ni}\ (q_{oi} + q_{ni})}{\sum_{i=1}^{k} p_{0i}\ (q_{oi} + q_{ni})} \times 100 \qquad \ldots..(14.32)$$

The summation is over 'k' commodities.

This index number has no known bias towards either upward or downward bias since both quantities at n-th and base years are used as weights. This method is not much used in practice since every time the weights are to be revised as the year changes.

14.2.7 Fishers Price Index Number

This index number is obtained by taking the geometric mean of Laspeyre's and Paasche's price index numbers.

Let $F_{0,n(p)}$ is the Fishers price index number, then

$$F_{0,n(p)} = \sqrt{L_{0,n(p)} \times P_{0,n(p)}}$$

$$= \sqrt{\frac{\Sigma\, p_{ni}\, q_{0i}}{\Sigma\, p_{0i}\, q_{0i}} \times \frac{\Sigma\, p_{ni}\, q_{ni}}{\Sigma\, p_{0i}\, q_{ni}}} \times 100 \qquad .....(14.32)$$

This index number is also known as ideal index number since it satisfies 'time' and 'factor' reversal tests.

14.2.7.1 Time Reversal Test

It states that the index number obtained by interchanging years from 'n' to 'zero' and 'zero' to 'n' then it should be the reciprocal of the original index number. If $F_{0,n(p)}$ is the Fisher's price index number and $F_{n,\,0(p)}$ is the index number obtained by interchanging n to 0 and 0 to n then

$$F_{0,\,n\,(p)} \times F_{n,\,0\,(p)} = 1 \text{ or } 100^2$$

This can be verified by taking the original formulae, where

$$F_{0,\,n\,(p)} = \sqrt{\frac{\Sigma\, p_{ni}\, q_{0i}}{\Sigma\, p_{0i}\, q_{0i}} \times \frac{\Sigma\, p_{ni}\, q_{ni}}{\Sigma\, p_{0i}\, q_{ni}}}$$

$$F_{n,\,0\,(p)} = \sqrt{\frac{\Sigma\, p_{0i}\, q_{ni}}{\Sigma\, p_{ni}\, q_{ni}} \times \frac{\Sigma\, p_{oi}\, q_{oi}}{\Sigma\, p_{ni}\, q_{oi}}}$$

Hence $\quad F_{0,\,n\,(p)} \times F_{n,\,0\,(p)} = 1$

Therefore Fishers price index number satisfies time reversal test.

14.2.7.2 Factor Reversal Test

The factor reversal test states that the product of the index number obtained by interchanging factors price, p and quantity q and the original index number should give the value index number. If $V_{0,n}$ is the value index number then

$$V_{0,n} = \frac{\Sigma\, p_{ni}\, q_{ni}}{\Sigma\, p_{0i}\, q_{0i}}$$

If $F_{0,n}$ is the Fisher's price index number and $F'_{0,n}$ is the index number obtained by changing factors from p to q and q to p in $F_{0,n}$ then

$$F_{0,n\,(p)} = \sqrt{\frac{\Sigma\, p_{ni}\, q_{oi}}{\Sigma\, p_{0i}\, q_{0i}} \times \frac{\Sigma\, p_{ni}\, q_{ni}}{\Sigma\, p_{0i}\, q_{ni}}}$$

$$F'_{0,n(p)} = \sqrt{\frac{\Sigma\, q_{ni}\, p_{oi}}{\Sigma\, q_{0i}\, p_{0i}} \times \frac{\Sigma\, q_{ni}\, p_{ni}}{\Sigma\, q_{0i}\, p_{ni}}}$$

$$F_{0,n(p)} \times F'_{0,n(p)} = \frac{\Sigma\, p_{ni}\, q_{ni}}{\Sigma\, p_{0i}\, q_{0i}} = V_{0,n}$$

Therefore, Fishers price index number satisfies factor reversal test.

The computation of Laspeyre, Paasche, Marshall-Edgeworth and Fisher's price numbers are illustrated with an example.

Example: compute Laspeyre's, Paasche's, Marshall-Edgeworth and Fishers' price numbers given the data in Table 14.9 for the year 2010 with base year as 2006.

Table 14.9

S.No.	Item	Price (p_{0i})	Quantity (q_{0i})	Price (p_{ni})	Quantity (q_{ni})
1	Cement	20	15	24	17
2	Sand	15	21	22	23
3	Steel	41	9	46	13
4	Bricks	52	13	58	15
5	Wood	120	12	132	14

For computing index numbers the following table is formed.

Table 14.10

S.No.	Item	$p_{0i}\, q_{0i}$	$p_{ni}\, q_{0i}$	$p_{ni}\, q_{ni}$	$p_{0i}\, q_{ni}$
1	Cement	300	360	408	340
2	Sand	315	462	506	345
3	Steel	369	414	598	533
4	Bricks	676	754	870	780
5	Wood	1440	1584	1848	1680
	Total	3100	3574	4230	3678

Laspeyre's price index number, $L_{0,n\,(p)} = \frac{\Sigma\, p_{ni}\, q_{oi}}{\Sigma\, p_{oi}\, q_{oi}} \times 100$

$$= \frac{3574}{3100} \times 100 = 115.3\%$$

Paasche's price index number, $P_{0,n\,(p)} = \frac{\Sigma\, p_{ni}\, q_{ni}}{\Sigma\, p_{oi}\, q_{ni}} \times 100$

$$= \frac{4230}{3678} \times 100 = 115.0\%$$

Marshall-Edgeworth price index number, $M_{0,n(p)}$ is

$$\frac{\Sigma\, p_{ni}\, (q_{0i} + q_{ni})}{\Sigma\, p_{0i}\, (q_{0i} + q_{ni})} \times 100 = \frac{\Sigma\, (p_{ni}\, q_{0i} + p_{ni}\, q_{ni})}{\Sigma\, (p_{oi}\, q_{0i} + p_{oi}\, q_{ni})} \times 100$$

$$= \frac{\Sigma\, p_{ni}\, q_{0i} + \Sigma\, p_{ni}\, q_{ni}}{\Sigma\, p_{0i}\, q_{0i} + \Sigma\, p_{oi}\, q_{ni}} \times 100$$

$$= \frac{(3574 + 4230)}{(3100 + 3678)} \times 100$$

$$= \frac{7804}{6778} \times 100 = 115.1\%$$

Fisher's price index number,

$$F_{0,n} = \sqrt{L_{0,n(p)} \times P_{0,n(p)}}$$

$$= \sqrt{115.3 \times 115.0} = 115.1\%$$

14.2.8 Chain Index Number

This index number is calculated by taking preceding yeas as the base year. Let $L_{0,1}$, $L_{1,2}$, $L_{2,3}$, $L_{3,4}$ be four chain index numbers of Laspeyre's type.

Then $\quad L_{0,4} = L_{01} \times L_{12} \times L_{23} \times L_{34}$

where $L_{0,4}$ is the index number of 4th year taking '0' year as the base year. The computation of chain index numbers are illustrated with an example given in Table 14.11 with quantities of items for the year 2007 as weights.

Table 14.11

S.No.	Item	2007		2008	2009	2010
		Price p_{07}	Quantity p_{07}	Price p_{08}	Price p_{09}	Price p_{10}
1	Paddy	16	8	18	21	22
2	Wheat	12	6	13	16	18
3	Jowar	7	4	12	13	14
4	Maize	9	3	10	11	12

For computing chain index numbers $L_{07,08}$, $L_{08,09}$, $L_{09,10}$ the table is formed and given in Table 14.12.

Table 14.12

S.No.	Item	$p_{07}\,q_{07}$	$p_{08}\,q_{07}$	$p_{09}\,q_{07}$	$p_{010}\,q_{07}$
1	Paddy	128	144	168	176
2	Wheat	72	78	96	108
3	Jowar	28	48	52	56
4	Maize	27	30	33	36
	Total	255	300	349	376

$$L_{07,08} = \frac{\Sigma\, p_{08}\, q_{07}}{\Sigma\, p_{07}\, q_{07}} = \frac{300}{255}$$

$$L_{08,09} = \frac{\Sigma\, p_{09}\, q_{07}}{\Sigma\, p_{08}\, q_{07}} = \frac{349}{300}$$

$$L_{09,10} = \frac{\Sigma\, p_{010}\, q_{07}}{\Sigma\, p_{09}\, q_{07}} = \frac{376}{349}$$

$$L_{07,\,09} = L_{07,\,08} \times L_{08,\,09} = \frac{300}{255} \times \frac{349}{300} = \frac{349}{255}$$

$$L_{07,\,10} = L_{07,\,08} \times L_{08,\,09} \times L_{09,\,10}$$

$$= \frac{300}{255} \times \frac{349}{300} \times \frac{376}{349} = \frac{376}{255}$$

14.2.9 Quantity Index Numbers

Quantity index numbers are computed by taking prices as weights. The Laspeyre's, Paasche's, Marshall-Edgeworth and Fishers quantity index numbers are obtained with the formulae as

Laspeyre's quantity index number, $L_{0,n\,(q)} = \dfrac{\Sigma\, q_{ni}\; p_{oi}}{\Sigma\, q_{oi}\; p_{oi}} \times 100$

Paasche's quantity index number, $P_{0,n\,(q)} = \dfrac{\Sigma\, q_{ni}\; p_{ni}}{\Sigma\, q_{oi}\; p_{ni}} \times 100$

.....(14.33)

Marshall-Edgeworth quantity index number,

$$M_{0,n\,(q)} = \frac{\Sigma\, q_{ni}\;(p_{0i} + p_{ni})}{\Sigma\, q_{oi}\;(p_{0i} + p_{ni})} \times 100$$

Fisher's quantity index number,

$$F_{0,n\,(q)} = \sqrt{\frac{\Sigma\, q_{ni}\; p_{0i}}{\Sigma\, q_{oi}\; p_{0i}} \times \frac{\Sigma\, q_{ni}\; p_{ni}}{\Sigma\, q_{oi}\; p_{ni}}}$$

14.2.10 Points of Construction of Index Numbers

Points to be considered in the construction of index numbers:

(i) The objective of construction of index number

(ii) Items to be included in the construction of index number

(iii) Sources of data

(iv) Selection of base period or base year

(v) Choice of weights and

(vi) Determination of the formula

(i) *Objective construction of index number:* If the objective of constructing index number is to measure the cost of living index then the level of employees with respect to skilled or non-skilled, the food items they consume, the area they live, the region they belong to have to be taken into account.

(ii) *Items to be included:* All the items are to be included according to their importance in the study. For example for construction of cost of building index number, all items such as cement, steel, sand, bricks, granite, wood, labour charges, architect charges, water curing charges, small boulder (kankar) charges, engineer charges, interior fittings etc., are to be considered.

(iii) *Sources of data:* Usually secondary source of data is used for collecting data in the construction of index numbers. 'Statistical abstract' published by Directorate of Economics and Statistics at state level, 'Agricultural situation in India' published by Ministry of Agriculture and Irrigation, Govt. of India, Economic Times, Financial Times, Price etc., news papers and internet are some of the sources of finding data. As far as possible it is desirable to use Govt. source of data to make the index number more authentic and reliable.

(iv) *Selection of base period or base year:* The base year is taken as normal year wherein extremities like floods, drought, earthquakes, wars etc., did not occur. Sometimes base period can be considered as average of some years. Base year will be shifted to more recent year due to more changes in prices, fashions, food habits, quality of goods etc., to make comparisons more realistic. However it is advisable to use same base period for all types of commodities.

(v) *Choice of weights:* The weights to be used in index number is based upon objective, time, availability of data and cost involved in collecting the data etc.

(vi) *Determination of the formula:* Choice of formula whether Laspeyre, Paasche, Marshall-Edgeworth etc., depends on objective, availability of data, time and money etc., for collecting data etc. For exports and imports index numbers, quantity index numbers are used. For cost of production of fertilizer, cement, pesticide index numbers, price index numbers are appropriate.

CHAPTER 15

Non-Parametric Tests

15.1 Introduction

In tests of hypothesis the concepts covered are :

(i) Null hypothesis

(ii) Level of significance

(iii) Distribution of the population

(iv) Degrees of freedom and

(v) Decision

However the concept of power of the test is not explained in that chapter.

15.1.1 Power of the Test

It is defined as the probability of rejecting null hypothesis H_0 when it is false. Type I error is defined as rejecting H_0 when it is true and type II error is defined as accepting H_0 when it is false. Let α and β are the probabilities of committing Type I and Type II errors respectively then the power of the test is given as

$$\text{Power} = 1 - \beta$$

In order to make a particular statistical test with less stringent assumptions as powerful as another statistical test then the sample size of the former test should be considerably increased.

If test A with sample size n_a is as powerful as test B with sample size n_b, then

$$\text{Power efficiency of test B} = \frac{n_a}{n_b} \times 100$$

15.2 Parametric Vs Non-Parametric Tests

Parametric tests depend upon the conditions of the parameters. The measurement level of the data to be used in parametric tests should be at least at interval scale. The parametric tests are more powerful tests. The inferences drawn from parametric tests are applicable to restricted population as per assumptions. For example, standard normal deviate tests, t-tests given in chapter on 'Tests of Hypotheses' are parametric tests since the population in those tests was assumed to follow normal distribution. Similarly F-test used in 'Analysis of Variance' chapter is a parametric test as one of the assumptions used in Analysis of Variance model is experimental errors are assumed to follow normal distribution.

Non-parametric tests do not depend upon the parameters though weaker assumptions such as observations are independent and continuous are to be satisfied. Non-Parametric tests can be used for the data with measurement level at 'Nominal' or 'Ordinal'. These tests are applicable in social sciences research or behaviourial sciences research such as sociology, Planning, Psychology, Agricultural extension wherein the research data will be usually at nominal or ordinal level. Further the power of these tests can be made as efficient as parametric tests by simply increasing the sample size. The inferences drawn from Non-parametric tests are applicable to large population since the assumptions are weak.

15.3 One-sample Tests

In this section one-sample tests are considered.

15.3.1 Chi-square Test

Chi-square test also can be used as a non-parametric test. It can be used to test whether frequencies are distributed uniformly in different classes or not.

H_0 : Observed frequencies are in agreement with expected frequencies

H_1 : Observed frequencies are not in agreement with expected frequencies

$$\chi^2 = \sum_{i=1}^{k} \frac{(O_i - E_i)^2}{E_i} \qquad .....(15.1)$$

where O_i, E_i are the observed and expected frequencies respectively of the i-th class for i = 1, 2, …, K.

Conclusion

If χ^2 (Cal.) value > χ^2 (tab.) value with (K – 1)d.f. at the required level of significance, then H_0 is rejected and H_1 is accepted. Otherwise, H_0 is accepted.

Example: The following is the distribution of defective screws found in 10 boxes where each box contained 100 screws. Test whether the defective screws are uniformly distributed over the boxes.

Table 15.1

Box No.	1	2	3	4	5	6	7	8	9	10
Defective screws (O_i)	3	4	2	6	5	8	1	7	3	1
Exp.fr.	4	4	4	4	4	4	4	4	4	4

H_0 : The defective screws are uniformly distributed over all the boxes.

H_1 : The defective screws are not uniformly distributed over all the boxes.

The expected frequency of each box is calculated as total observed frequency divided by total number of boxes.

$$\text{Exp. Frequency} = \frac{40}{10} = 4$$

The expected frequency, 4 is included in Table 15.1 itself against each observed frequency.

$$\chi^2 = \frac{(3-4)^2}{4} + \frac{(4-4)^2}{4} + \ldots + \frac{(1-4)^2}{4} = 13.5$$

Conclusion

Here χ^2 (Cal.) value i.e., $13.5 < \chi^2$ (tab.) value i.e., 16.92 with (10 – 1) d.f. at 5 percent level of significance. Therefore H_0 is accepted. Hence it can be concluded that the defective screws are uniformly distributed over 10 boxes.

15.3.2 Run-Test

Repetition of the same symbol followed and preceded by different symbol or no symbol is called a 'run'. This test is used for testing the randomness of a sample. The following is the sequence of 10 runs with symbols indicated by '+' and '–' signs.

+ + – – + – + + + – – – + – – + – –

1 2 3 4 5 6 7 8 9 10

Fig. 15.1

In the above sequence given in Fig. 15.1, the first two signs will be one run, next two signs will be 2nd run and soon.

Case (i) Small Samples ($n_1 \leq 20$, $n_2 \leq 20$)

Let n_1 be the number of symbols of 1st type and n_2 be the number of symbols of 2nd type such that $n_1 + n_2 = n$ be the total sample size. Let r be the number of runs in a sample. The sampling distribution of r was found and the critical values to test the null hypothesis were tabulated and given in Appendix Table for different values of n_1 and n_2 at 5 percent level of significance. The first table gives the lower limit values of r and second table refers to the upper limit values of r.

H_0 : The observations in the sample are in random order

H_1 : The observations in the sample are not in random order.

The values of r, n_1 and n_2 can be obtained from the sample.

Conclusion

If r (cal.) number $\leq$ r (tab.) number with n_1, n_2 at 5 per cent level of significance in the first table then H_0 is rejected. It can be concluded that the observations given in the sequence are not in random order. If r (cal.) number $\geq$ r (tab.) number with n_1, n_2 at 5 per cent level of significance in the second table then H_0 is rejected. If 'r' lies between two values of r given in first and second tables then H_0 is accepted.

Example: The following is the sequence of cars (C) and other than cars (N) entering at a toll gate point in a particular lane on a national high way in 10 minutes. Test whether the sequence of cars entering at a toll gate point is in random order or not at 5 percent level of significance. The sequence of cars (C) and other than cars (N) is given in Fig. 15.2.

C	N	CC	NNN	CCCC	NN	C	NN	CC	N	CCC	NNN
1	2	3	4	5	6	7	8	9	10	11	12

Fig. 15.2

H_0: Cars are entering at toll gate point in a particular lane in random order

H_1: Cars are not entering at toll gate point are not in random order

From Fig. 15.2, the number of runs, r is counted.

$$r = 12, \qquad n_1 = 13, \qquad n_2 = 12$$

Conclusion

Here r (cal.) number i.e., 12 lies between r (tab.) number i.e., 8 from the first table and r (tab.) number i.e., 19 from the second table for the values of $n_1 = 13$ and $n_2 = 12$ at 5 percent level of significance. Therefore H_0 is accepted. Hence it can be concluded that cars are entering at toll gate point in a random order.

Case (ii) Large Samples ($n_1, n_2 > 20$)

Even when one of n_1 or n_2 is greater than 20 then small sample case i.e., case (i) is not applicable.

H_0: The observations in the given sample are in random order

H_1: The observations in the given sample are not in random order

$$Z = \frac{\left| r - \left(\frac{2\, n_1 n_2}{n_1 + n_2} + 1 \right) \right|}{\sqrt{\frac{2\, n_1 n_2\, (2\, n_1 n_2 - n_1 - n_2)}{(n_1 + n_2)^2\, (n_1 n_2 - 1)}}} \qquad \text{.....(15.2)}$$

Conclusion

If Z (cal.) value > Z (tab.) value at the required level of significance, H_0 is rejected and H_1 is accepted. If H_0 is rejected then it can be concluded that the given observations in the sample are not in random order.

Example: The following is the sequence of cars (C) and other than cars (N) entering at a toll gate point in a particular lane on a national highway in 30 minutes (Fig. 15.3). Test whether the sequence of cars entering at a toll gate point is in random order or not at 5 percent level of significance.

The sequence of cars (C) and other than cars (N) entering at a toll gate point is

CC	N	C	NNN	CCC	NNNN	C	N	CC	N	CCCC	NN	C	N
1	2	3	4	5	6	7	8	9	10	11	12	13	14

C	NN	CCCC	N	CC	NN	C	NNN
15	16	17	18	19	20	21	22

Fig. 15.3

H_0 : The sequence of cars entering at toll gate point is in random order

H_1 : The sequence of cars entering at toll gate point is not in random order

Here $r = 22, \quad n_1 = 22, \quad n_2 = 21$

$$Z = \frac{\left| 22 - \left(\frac{2 \times 22 \times 21}{43} + 1 \right) \right|}{\sqrt{\frac{2 \times 22 \times 21\,(2 \times 22 \times 21 - 22 - 21)}{(22 + 21)^2\,(22 \times 21 - 1)}}}$$

$$= \frac{1.49}{\sqrt{0.9550}} = 1.52$$

Conclusion

Here Z (cal.) value i.e., 1.52 < Z (tab.) value i.e., 1.96 at 5 per cent level of significance. Therefore H_0 is accepted. Hence it can be concluded that cars are entering at toll gate point in random order.

15.4 Two Related Samples Test (Wilcoxon Test)

In two related samples case Wilcoxon test is used. This test considers the overall direction of differences between the pairs as well as magnitude of the individual differences of pairs.

Case (i) Small Samples (n < 25)

In this method the ranks are given based on the magnitude of the differences of scores for each pair irrespective of the negative or positive differences. If two or more differences are equal then the ranks will be given as in the case of tied observations. For example, if the two differences are – 4 and – 4 then the rank will be given as $\frac{1+2}{2}=1.5$ for both the difference and next difference will get rank '3'. Let d_i be i-th difference of scores for i = 1, 2, …, n. The ranks will be given to all the differences. After effecting the ranks positive or negative signs will be given to positive and negative differences respectively. Let S be the total of ranks of positive or negative ranks whichever is smaller.

H_0 : Sum of the negative ranks is equal to sum of the positive ranks

H_1 : Sum of the negative ranks is not equal to the sum of the positive ranks

In consulting tabulated value for effective number of pairs the differences with $d_i = 0$ is excluded from the total number of pairs.

Conclusion

If S (cal.) value $\leq$ S (tab.) value at the required level of significance, H_0 is rejected and H_1 is accepted. If H_0 is rejected then it can be concluded that there is significant difference between two treatments with respect to character under consideration. The tabulated value is obtained from Table G [Siegel (1956)].

Example: One of the two brothers of each of 10 business families was randomly selected and sent for training on management course for 6 months at Management institute. The other one remained at home looking after family business with his traditional knowledge. After completion of training both the brothers were interviewed in each family on the knowledge on management and the scores were awarded based on their performance in the interview. Test the significant difference between the two brothers with respect to their knowledge on management of business.

H_0 : There is no significant difference between the two brothers with respect to knowledge on management

H_1 : There is significant difference between the two brothers with respect to knowledge on management.

Table 15.2

Pair	T	UT	Difference	Rank	S
1	65	62	3	2.5	
2	70	74	– 4	– 4.5	4.5
3	69	60	9	10	
4	59	61	– 2	– 1	1.0
5	78	70	8	8.5	
6	80	76	4	4.5	
7	70	64	6	6.5	
8	84	76	8	8.5	
9	71	74	– 3	– 2.5	2.5
10	75	69	6	6.5	
				Total	8.0

T = Trained, UT = Un trained

Conclusion

Here S (cal.) value i.e., 8 = S (tab.) value i.e., 8 at 5 percent level of significance. Therefore H_0 is rejected and H_1 is accepted. Hence it can be concluded that there is significant impact of training on the knowledge of management.

Case (ii) Large samples (n > 25)

H_0 : There is no significant difference between treatments.

H_1 : There is significant difference between two treatments.

$$Z = \frac{\left| S - \frac{n(n+1)}{4} \right|}{\sqrt{\frac{n(n+1)(2n+1)}{24}}} \qquad .....(15.3)$$

where S is the total of the positive or negative ranks whichever is smaller and n is the number of pairs of observations.

Conclusion

If Z (cal.) value > Z (tab.) value with the required level of significance then H_0 is rejected and H_1 is accepted. If H_0 is rejected then it can be concluded that there is significant difference between two treatments.

Example: The following are the scores awarded by psychologist to the families residing in the houses built with knowledge on 'Vassthu' (V) and without knowledge on 'Vaasthu' (NV) in the same street based on their experience on living with respect to happiness. The scores are given in Table 15.3. Test the significant difference between 'Vaasthu' and Non-vaasthu houses with respect to happiness in living at 5 per cent level of significance.

Table 15.3

Street No.	V	NV	Difference	Rank	Street No.	V	NV	Difference	Rank
1	60	54	6	23	16	40	36	4	16.5
2	70	62	8	27	17	37	39	– 2	– 6
3	58	60	– 2	– 6	18	46	41	5	19.5
4	54	52	2	6	19	59	52	7	26
5	68	69	– 1	– 1.5	20	69	60	9	28
6	70	58	12	30	21	43	41	2	6
7	46	40	6	23	22	58	55	3	12
8	59	60	– 1	– 1.5	23	63	60	3	12
9	62	59	3	12	24	67	61	6	23
10	61	63	– 2	– 6	25	59	64	– 5	– 19.5
11	40	43	– 3	– 12	26	38	44	– 6	– 23
12	54	52	2	6	27	56	50	6	23
13	60	64	– 4	– 16.5	28	69	59	10	29
14	52	49	3	12	29	44	40	4	16.5
15	48	52	– 4	– 16.5	30	47	49	– 2	– 6

H_0: There is no significant difference between 'Vaasthu' and 'Non-vasthu' houses

H_1: There is significant difference between 'Vaasthu' and 'Non-vaasthu' houses

Here S = 114.5 and which is the total of negative ranks and which is smaller than total of positive ranks given in Table 15.3 and n = 30.

using formula of Z given in eqn. (15.3), we have

$$Z = \frac{\left|114.5 - \frac{30(30+1)}{4}\right|}{\sqrt{\frac{30(30+1)\ (2 \times 30+1)}{24}}}$$

$$= \frac{118}{\sqrt{2363.75}} = 2.43$$

Conclusion

Here Z (cal.) value i.e., 2.43 > Z (tab.) value i.e., 1.96 at 5 per cent level of significance. Therefore H_0 is rejected and H_1 is accepted. Hence it can be concluded that there is significant difference between scores of 'Vaasthu' and 'Non-vaasthu' houses.

15.5 Two Independent Samples Test (Mann-Whitney Test)

This test is used to test the significant difference between two treatments when the data is at nominal or ordinal level of measurement. This is a powerful non-parametric test corresponding to two sample t-test in parametric case.

Case (i) Small Samples (n_1, $n_2 \leq 20$)

H_0 : There is no significant difference between two treatments

H_1 : There is significant difference between the two treatments

Let n_1 and n_2 be the sizes of 1st and 2nd samples respectively. Common ranking will be done for all the (n_1 + n_2) scores taken together. Then ranks will be placed in their respective groups. Let T_1 be the total of the ranks in the 1st sample group.

$$W = \left[n_1\ n_2 + \frac{n_1\ (n_1+1)}{2}\right] - T_1 \qquad .....(15.4)$$

If W is larger than the values given in the Table (Appendix) the actual value will be taken as $W_1 = n_1n_2 - W$. Then W_1 will be taken as calculated value for comparing with tabulated value.

Conclusion

If the probability value for given W, n_1 and $n_2 \leq 0.05$ then H_0 is rejected and H_1 is accepted at 5 per cent level of significance. Otherwise H_o is accepted.

Example: The following are the average scores given by judges for 'Maintained' and 'Not-maintained' parks in a particular city (Table 15.4). Test whether there is any significant difference between the two types of parks at 5 percent level of significance.

H_0 : There is no significant difference between the two types of parks

H_1 : There is significant difference between the two types of parks

Table 15.4

Maintained Parks	60 (3)	69 (2)	58 (4)	36 (10)	42 (8)	70 (1)	
Not - Maintained Parks	38 (9)	46 (6)	52 (5)	20 (13)	29 (12)	45 (7)	30 (11)

The figures in parantheses are the ranks given to scores by considering all the scores in the two samples together.

Here $T_1 = 28, \quad n_1 = 6, \quad n_2 = 7$

$$W = 6 \times 7 + \frac{6(6+1)}{2} - 28 = 35$$

$$W_1 = n_1 n_2 - W = 6 \times 7 - 35 = 7$$

Since w = 35 is not available in the tabulated values W_1, is obtained as 7 and which is available in the tabulated values. Now tabulated values are consulted for $W_1 = 7$, $n_1 = 6$ and $n_2 = 7$. The value of the probability is 0.026 from the Table of Appendix.

Conclusion

Here the probability obtained from the table for calculated value of $W_1 = 7$, $n_1 = 6$, $n_2 = 7$ is $0.026 \leq 0.05$. Therefore H_0 is rejected and H_1 is accepted. Hence it can be concluded that the maintained parks are significantly different from Not-maintained parks with respect to scoring.

Case (ii) Large Samples ($n_2 > 20$)

H_0 : There is no significant difference between two treatments

H_1 : There is significant difference between two treatments

$$Z = \frac{\left| W - \frac{n_1 n_2}{2} \right|}{\sqrt{\frac{n_1 n_2 (n_1 + n_2 + 1)}{12}}} \qquad .....(15.5)$$

where n_1, n_2 are sizes of 1st and 2nd samples respectively and W is the value obtained by using expression given in (15.4) of small samples case.

Conclusion

If Z (cal.) value > Z (tab.) value at the required level of significance then H_0 is rejected and H_1 is accepted. If H_0 is rejected then it can be concluded that there is significant difference between the treatments. Otherwise, H_0 is accepted.

15.6 Test of P-related Samples (Friedman's Test)

In order to test the significant difference between more than two treatments when the data is at the level of ordinal then Friedman's test is used. In this test, the ranks are given based on the scores in each of the treatment row wise then the total of the ranks will be computed for each treatment or sample group.

H_0 : There is no significant difference between the treatments

H_1 : There is significant difference between the treatments

$$\chi^2 = \frac{12}{n\,p\,(p+1)} \sum_{j=1}^{p} C_j^2 - 3\,n\,(p+1) \qquad .....(15.6)$$

where n, p are the number of observations in each sample and number of samples or treatments respectively and C_j is the total of ranks in j-th treatment for j = 1, 2, ..., p. Further χ^2 is approximately distributed with (p – 1) d.f.

Conclusion

If χ^2 (Cal.) value > χ^2 (tab.) value with (p – 1) d.f. at the required level of significance then H_0 is rejected and H_1 is accepted. If H_0 is rejected then it can be concluded that there is significant difference between treatments.

Example: In pilgrim centres, sanitation (S), transport facility (T) and accommodation (A) are important factors to be considered. For ten pilgrim cities in the country the scores are awarded for the said three facilities and are presented in Table 15.5.

Table 15.5

Factor / City	S	T	A
1	40 (3)	48 (2)	51 (1)
2	62 (2)	56 (3)	66 (1)
3	51 (3)	64 (2)	68 (1)
4	48 (2)	49 (1)	40 (3)
5	54 (2)	46 (3)	58 (1)
6	65 (2)	60 (3)	66 (1)
7	38 (3)	47 (2)	49 (1)
8	32 (3)	54 (1)	36 (2)
9	50 (3)	61 (2)	64 (1)
10	47 (2)	39 (3)	48 (1)
C_j	25	22	13

The ranks are given row wise for the three facilities for each pilgrim centre based on the scores given by judges. The lowest rank is given to the highest score. The total of the ranks C_j are computed as column totals in Table 15.5.

H_0 : There is no significant difference between the three facilities provided to the pilgrims.

H_1 : There is significant difference between the three facilities provided to the pilgrims.

$$\chi^2 = \frac{12}{n\,p\,(p+1)} \sum_{j=1}^{p} C_j^2 - 3\,n\,(p+1)$$

here $n = 10, \quad p = 3, \quad C_1 = 25, \quad C_2 = 22, \quad C_3 = 13$

$$= \frac{12}{10 \times 3\,(3+1)} \left[(25)^2 + (22)^2 + (13)^2\right] - 3 \times 10\,(3+1)$$

$$= 127.8 - 120.0 = 7.8$$

Conclusion

Here χ^2 (cal.) value i.e., 7.8 > χ^2 (tab.) value i.e., 5.99 with (3 – 1) d.f. at 5 per cent level of significance. Therefore H_0 is rejected and H_1 is accepted. Hence it can be concluded that there is significant difference between the three facilities provided to the pilgrims. In other words the three facilities are not given equal priority by the administration.

15.7 Test of P-independent Samples (Kruskal-Wallis Test)

When more than two independent samples or treatments are to be tested and when the data is at the level of ordinal measurement then kruskal-Wallis test can be used. This test is corresponding to the one-way analysis of variance in the parametric case. In this test the scores are ranked taking all the scores of treatments are taken into consideration. In other words common ranking is done for all the scores. The number of observations in each sample may not be equal.

H_0: There is no significant difference between the p samples or p treatments

H_1: There is significant difference between p samples or p treatments

$$\chi^2 = \frac{12}{n\,p\,(p+1)} \sum_{j=1}^{p} \frac{C_j^2}{n_j} - 3\,(n+1) \qquad .....(15.7)$$

where C_j be the sum of the ranks in the j-th sample or j-th treatment for $j = 1, 2, \ldots, p$; n_j be the number of observations in the j-th sample and $\sum_{j=1}^{p} n_j = n$. Here χ^2 in eqn. (15.7) follows χ^2 distribution with (P – 1) d.f. when the number of observations in j-th sample i.e., n_j is at least 5 for $j = 1, 2, \ldots, p$.

Conclusion

If χ^2 (cal.) value > χ^2 (tab.) value at the required level of significance then H_0 is rejected and H_1 is accepted. If H_0 is rejected then it can be concluded that there is significant difference between p-treatments. Otherwise H_0 is accepted. This test is illustrated with the following example.

Example: The following are the scores given to three types of interior designing in Banquet halls of hotels in metropolitan city. Test whether there is any significant difference between the three types of designing at 1 percent level of significant. The scores are presented in Table 15.6.

Table 15.6

S.No.	Type I	Rank	Type II	Rank	Type III	Rank
1	64	19.5	70	15.0	60	22.0
2	72	13.0	64	19.5	71	14.0
3	80	3.5	58	24.0	73	11.5
4	79	5.0	69	16.0	78	6.0
5	66	17.0	56	25.0	74	9.5
6	82	2.0	55	26.0	75	7.5
7	74	9.5	61	21.0	80	3.5
8	75	7.5	65	18.0	73	11.5
9	89	1.0	59	23.0		
	Total	78.0		187.5		85.5

Here the ranks are given in such a way that the highest score will get lowest rank. For example a score of 89 is given rank '1', 82 is given rank '2' and soon.

H_0: There is no significant difference between the three types of interior designing

H_1: There is significant difference between the three types of interior designing

here $n = n_1 + n_2 + n_3 = 9 + 9 + 8 = 26; p = 3$

$C_1 = 78.0, C_2 = 187.5, C_3 = 85.5$

$$\chi^2 = \frac{12}{n\,p\,(p+1)} \sum_{j=1}^{p} \frac{C_j^2}{n_j} - 3\,(n+1)$$

$$= \frac{12}{26 \times 3(3+1)} \left[\frac{(78.0)^2}{9} + \frac{(187.5)^2}{9} + \frac{(85.5)^2}{8}\right] - 3\,(26+1)$$

$$= 211.39 - 81.00 = 130.39$$

Conclusion

Here χ^2 (cal.) value i.e., 130.39 > χ^2 (tab.) value i.e., 9.21 with (3 – 1) d.f. at 1 per cent level of significance. Therefore H_0 is rejected and H_1 is accepted. Hence it can be concluded that there is significant difference between the three types of interior designing.

15.8 Rank Correlation

Sometimes it is not possible to have the data at the interval or ratio level of measurement for finding the extent of relationship between the two related variables. If the measurement of data is at ratio level, the pearson's coefficient of correlation between the two related variables i.e., r is used for finding the extent of correlation between the two variables. However if the measurement of data is at ordinal level 'rank correlation coefficient' is used for measuring the extent of correlation between the two related variables. The rank correlation coefficient is denoted by 'r_s'. For example, in preparing questionnaire the questions are to be arranged in order of their importance in studies of 'planning' and social sciences. The questions will be sent to experts to give the ranking of these questions. The correlation between the ranks given by two judges can be assessed with rank correlation coefficient. The rank correlation coefficient was developed by 'spearman'. Therefore it is also known as Spearman's rank correlation coefficient. If there is a tie in scores, the average of ranks will be given to all the tied observations by first giving ranks as if they are not tied.

$$rs = 1 - \frac{6\,\Sigma(x_i - y_i)^2}{n(n^2-1)} \qquad .....(15.8)$$

where x_i, y_i be the ranks given to the i-th pair of scores for i = 1, 2, …, n.

15.8.1 Test of Significance

The test of significance of rank correlation coefficient is done on the similar lines of simple correlation coefficient 'r'.

$$H_0 : \rho_s = 0; \qquad H_1 ; \rho_s \neq 0$$

where ρ_s is the population rank correlation coefficient

$$t = \frac{|\,r_s\,|}{\sqrt{\dfrac{(1-r_s^2)}{(n-2)}}}$$

where n is the number of pairs of ranks.

Conclusion

If t (cal.) value > t (tab.) value with (n – 2) d.f. at the required level of significance then H_0 is rejected and H_1 is accepted. If H_0 is rejected then it can be concluded that there is significant correlation between the ranks of the two variables under study.

Example: In an industrial exhibition two judges A and B gave ranks for 10 stalls as shown in Table 15.7. Find the correlation coefficient between the ranks of two judges and test its significance at 5 percent level.

Table 15.7

S.No.	A (x_i)	B (y_i)	($x_i - y_i$)	$(x_i - y_i)^2$
1	3	5	– 2	4
2	8	6	2	4
3	4	3	1	1
4	7	8	– 1	1
5	10	9	1	1
6	5	2	3	9
7	2	1	1	1
8	1	4	– 3	9
9	9	10	– 1	1
10	6	7	– 1	1
Total				32

$$r_s = 1 - \frac{6\Sigma(x_i - y_i)^2}{n(n^2 - 1)}$$

here $\quad n = 10, \Sigma\,(x_i - y_i)^2 = 32$

$$r_s = 1 - \frac{6 \times 32}{10\ (100 - 1)} = 0.81$$

(i) Test of significance of r_s

$H_0 : \rho_s = 0; \qquad H_1: \rho_s \neq 0$

$$t = \frac{|\,r_s\,|}{\sqrt{\frac{(1 - r_s^2)}{(n-2)}}} = \frac{0.81}{\sqrt{\frac{1-(0.81)^2}{(10-2)}}} = \frac{0.81}{0.04} = 20.25$$

Conclusion

Here t (cal.) value i.e., 20.25 > t (tab.) value i.e., 2.31 with (10 – 2) d.f. at 5 per cent level of significance. Therefore H_0 is rejected and H_1 is accepted. Hence it can be concluded that there is significant correlation between the ranks given by two judges A and B.

CHAPTER 16

Elementary Queuing Theory

16.1 Introduction

The number of persons standing in line to get reservation of a berth or seat in a train, number of persons standing to get their work of one in post office or bank, number of aeroplanes are circling around the city to land at airport, number of persons standing in line to have a darshan at temple, number of vehicles standing in order to have gas at gas filling station, number of patients standing or waiting at hospital to have consultation with doctor etc., are some of the examples of queues. Queuing problem arises when the service counter takes more time than the time a customer enters a que. In other words service rate falls short of rate of flow of customer. If service facility provides immediately facility to the customer who arrives then the queuing problem will not arise. If service counter or facility takes 20 minutes for each customer and customers are coming for every 15 minutes then queue will build up.

16.2 Concepts of Queuing Theory

The concepts used in queuing theory are :

(i) input process of customers

(ii) Queue discipline and

(iii) Service mechanism

16.2.1 Input Process

It is defined as

(i) The probability distribution of time interval between two successive customers or units and

(ii) The probability distribution of number of units or customers arrive during that time interval

For example, the customers arrive in banks or post offices individually or single person at a time is an example of the distribution of time interval between two customers and the persons entering in a group in a hotel is an example for the distribution of number of customers or units arrive during the time interval.

16.2.2 Queue Discipline

It is defined as the first come first served. Usually if the customer arrives first and he is served first then problem will not arise from the other customers. If this procedure is violated then problem arises. However, in certain cases this discipline is violated in the case of lift wherein the last person entering in the lift will leave the first.

16.2.3 Service Mechanism

The type of service to customer or customers is called service mechanism. The customers may be served as an individual or in groups. The time required for service depends upon the nature of the customer as well as the nature of service required. The server may hasten the process of servicing depending upon the length of the queue is more or relax process if the length of the queue is less.

16.3 Terms used in Queuing Theory

Some of the terms used in queuing theory are listed here. These are :

(i) Arrival rate
(ii) Service rate
(iii) Customer
(iv) Service station
(v) Waiting time
(vi) Time spent by customer in the queue system
(vii) Number of customers in the system
(viii) Queue length
(ix) Jockeying
(x) Reneging
(xi) Balking and
(xii) Queuing System

16.3.1 Arrival Rate

It is the time taken at which the customers arrive at the service. This rate is assumed to follow Poisson distribution. The mean of poisson distribution is taken as 'λ'.

16.3.2 Service Rate

The time taken by one service channel to serve the customer is called service rate and it is assumed to follow poisson distribution and mean service rate is termed as 'μ'.

The arrival and service pattern is given as

customers arrival $\rightarrow$ waiting in queue $\rightarrow$ service $\rightarrow$ departure of customers.

The queue need not always physical presence of persons in line. The queue may be persons who booked berths in train, aeroplane etc., who are not physically present in a line.

16.3.3 Customers

Persons or units who are arriving at a service place are called customers.

16.3.4 Service Station

The place or point where service is provided called service station.

16.3.5 Waiting Time

The time spent by a customer in a queue before being serviced.

16.3.6 Time Spent by a Customer in the Queue System

The total of time spent by a customer in waiting as well as for getting serviced is considered as time spent by a customer.

16.3.7 Number of Customers in the Queue System

The total number of persons or customers in the queue and number of customers being serviced.

16.3.8 Queue Length

The number of customers waiting in the queue.

16.3.9 Jockeying

If a customer is waiting in one queue and joining the other queue by leaving the first queue is called 'jockeying'.

16.3.10 Reneging

If a customer is waiting in a queue and leaving the queue later is known as 'reneging'.

16.3.11 Balking

If a customer decides not to join the queue is called 'balking'.

16.3.12 Queuing System

Arrival of customers, waiting in queue and then getting serviced and leave the queue as per queuing discipline is known as 'queuing system'.

The object of queuing theory is to achieve a balance between the cost of providing extra counter and waiting time involved by the customer in queue. The probability distribution of arrival in queue by a customer or object is assumed to follow exponential distribution and which is the zero term in the poisson distribution.

16.3.12.1 Model 1

Let a and s be the average arrival rate and average service rates respectively where $s > a$, then p_o be the probability of zero units in the queue is $1-\frac{a}{s}$ or $\frac{s-a}{s}$. If $\frac{a}{s}$ be the probability of having a que then p_r be the probability of having 'r' units in the que and is given as

$$P_r = \left(\frac{a}{s}\right)^r p_o$$

$$= \left(1-\frac{a}{s}\right)\left(\frac{a}{s}\right)^r$$

The average queue length is given as $\frac{a^2}{s\,(s-a)}$ i.e., the number of units waiting in line for getting serviced. The average length of non empty queue is $\frac{s}{(s-a)}$. The total number of units in the queue system which include the unit which is being serviced is $\frac{a}{(s-a)}$. The average waiting time of an arrival of unit is $\frac{a}{s\,(s-a)}$ and the average waiting time of an arrival which include service time is $\frac{1}{(s-a)}$. Further $\frac{a}{s}$ is called the traffic intensity. These expressions are derived based on the assumption that the arrival and service rates follow exponential distribution.

Example 1: Find

(i) average number of customers waiting for service

(ii) average time a customer must wait in the que and

(iii) the average time to be spent by the customer in the queue system if the customer arrive at average rate of 6 minutes and average service rate is 8 minutes per customer.

Let E (r) be the expected number of customers waiting for service, then

$$E(r) = \frac{a^2}{s(s-a)} = \frac{(6)^2}{8(8-6)} = \frac{36}{16} = 2.25 \text{ pesons}$$

Let E (t_w) be the expected time to be spent by the customer in the queue is

$$E(t_w) = \frac{a}{s(s-a)} = \frac{6}{8(8-6)} = \frac{6}{16} = 0.375 \text{ hours}$$

Let E (t_q) be the expected to be spent by the customer in the queue system is

$$E(t_q) = \frac{1}{(s-a)} = \frac{1}{(8-6)} = \frac{1}{2} = 0.5 \text{ hours}$$

Example 2: The customers arrive at a gas station with an average time of 4 minutes and the average time taken to service a unit is 6 minutes. Assuming that arrival rate and service rate follow exponential distribution, find

(i) expected average que length

(ii) average number of customers in the queue system

(iii) time taken by the customer in the queue and

(iv) time taken by the customer in the queue system.

(i) Expected number of customers waiting for service or average queue length is

$$E(r) = \frac{a^2}{s(s-a)} = \frac{(4)^2}{6(6-4)} = \frac{16}{12} = 1.33$$

(ii) Average number of customers in the queue system

$$E(\bar{r}) = \frac{a}{(s-a)} = \frac{(4)}{(6-4)} = 2 \text{ persons}$$

(iii) Time taken by the customer in the queue is

$$E\ (t_w) = \frac{a}{s(s-a)} = \frac{4}{6(6-4)} = \frac{4}{12} = 0.33 \text{ hours}$$

(iv) Time taken by the customer in the queue system is

$$E\ (t_q) = \frac{1}{(s-a)} = \frac{1}{(6-4)} = \frac{1}{2} = 0.5 \text{ hours}$$

16.3.12.2 Model 2

Erlang's Model

In this method the service consists of m phases is considered. The average time taken for each phase is $\frac{1}{ma}$ and the average services time taken for each customer is $\frac{1}{s}$. Here also the exponential distribution is assumed for the actual time taken at each phase of service.

(i) The expected number of units in the system is given as

$$E(r_q) = \frac{m+1}{2m} \cdot \frac{a^2}{s(s-a)} + \frac{a}{s}$$

(ii) The expected number of units in the queue is

$$E(r) = \frac{m+1}{2m} \cdot \frac{a^2}{s(s-a)}$$

(iii) The average waiting time in the queue is

$$E(t_w) = \frac{m+1}{2m} \cdot \frac{a}{s(s-a)}$$

(v) The average time spent by a unit in the system is

$$E(t_q) = \frac{m+1}{2m} \frac{a}{s(s-a)} + \frac{1}{s}$$

Example: The repair of a vehicle requires four steps to be done one after another in a certain order. The time taken for completion of each work with an average of 2 hours and is independent of other steps. If the vehicle breaks down at a mean rate of 4 per day, find

(i) expected waiting time of a vehicle assuming that there is one mechanic at each step

(ii) average waiting time of breakdown vehicle in the queue and

(iii) expected number of breakdown vehicles in the queue.

The average breakdown = 4 per day

Average number serviced per day = 12

No. of steps or phases = 4

Here $a = 4, \ s = 12, m = 4$

(i) Expected time spent by a vehicle in the queue system is

$$E\,(t_q) = \frac{m+1}{2m} \cdot \frac{a}{s(s-a)} + \frac{1}{s}$$

$$= \frac{4+1}{2\times 4} \cdot \frac{4}{12(12-4)} + \frac{1}{12}$$

$$= \frac{20}{768} + \frac{1}{12} = 0.11 \text{ hours}$$

(ii) Expected time spent by a vehicle in the queue is

$$E(t_w) = \frac{m+1}{2m} \cdot \frac{a}{s\,(s-a)}$$

$$= \frac{4+1}{2\times 4} \cdot \frac{4}{12\,(12-4)} = \frac{20}{768} = 0.03 \text{ hours}$$

(iii) Expected number of breakdown vehicles in the queue is

$$E(r) = \frac{m+1}{2m} \cdot \frac{a^2}{s\,(s-a)}$$

$$= \frac{4+1}{2\times 4} \cdot \frac{(4)^2}{12\,(12-4)} = \frac{80}{768} = 0.10$$

CHAPTER 17

Multivariate Statistical Methods

17.1 Introduction

In this chapter the statistical methods based on several characters instead of single character are dealt. For example, in testes of hypotheses such as z-tests and t-tests single character was considered for testing the equality of means. In multivariate case, the equality of means are tested based on several characters simultaneously. For example, in testing the productivity of two cement factories if the characters such as number of working hours, number of kilns, availability of raw material, number of labour hours put in, number of hours of power available, availability of water etc., are also considered besides productivity, then it can be considered as multivariate case. Similarly in comparing two institutions, several parameters like number of admissions, budget allotment, number of courses, number of degree and P.G. programmes, number of campuses, strength of faculty, infrastructure facilities like buildings, hostels, playgrounds etc., are to be considered simultaneously. Therefore the statistical method to be used for testing will become multivariate statistical technique.

17.2 Hotelling – T^2

This test is used for testing the two population means under multivariate case whereas t-test is used in univariate case. In this case the characters are assumed to follow multivariate normal distribution.

17.2.1 One Sample Case

If one sample mean vector is tested against population mean vector, this test is used.

$$H_0 : \underline{\mu} = \underline{\mu}_0 \quad \text{and} \quad H_1 : \underline{\mu} \neq \underline{\mu}_0$$

$$\text{where} \quad \underline{\mu} = \begin{bmatrix} \mu_1 \\ \mu_2 \\ \vdots \\ \mu_p \end{bmatrix}, \quad \underline{\mu}_0 = \begin{bmatrix} \mu_{01} \\ \mu_{02} \\ \vdots \\ \mu_{op} \end{bmatrix} \quad .....(17.1)$$

where $\underline{\mu}$ is the column vector of population means and $\underline{\mu}_0$ is the column vector of population means under null hypothesis.

$$T^2 = n\left(\underline{\bar{x}} - \underline{\mu}\right)^1 S^{-1}\left(\underline{\bar{x}} - \underline{\mu}\right) \quad .....(17.2)$$

$$\text{where} \quad \underline{\bar{x}} = \begin{bmatrix} \bar{x}_1 \\ \bar{x}_2 \\ \vdots \\ \bar{x}_p \end{bmatrix}, \quad S = \begin{bmatrix} s_{11} & s_{12} & \cdots & s_{1p} \\ s_{21} & s_{22} & \cdots & s_{2p} \\ s_{p1} & s_{p2} & \cdots & s_{pp} \end{bmatrix} \quad .....(17.3)$$

$\underline{\bar{x}}$ and S are the estimates of mean $\underline{\mu}$ and variance covariance matrix Σ respectively based on n sample observations on each of p-characters. For example, $\bar{x}_1$ is the mean of n observations of 1st character and s_{11} is the variance of 1st character based on n observations and T^2 is called Hotelling– T^2.

17.2.1.1 Test of Significance

The test of significance between sample mean vector and population mean vector is done with the help of F-test.

$$F = \frac{n-p}{p(n-1)} T^2 \qquad \text{.....(17.4)}$$

Conclusion

If F (cal.) value > F (tab.) value with (p, n – p) d.f. at the required level of significance then H_0 is rejected and H_1 is accepted. If H_0 is rejected then it can be concluded that there is significant difference between sample mean vector and population mean vector. Otherwise H_0 is accepted.

17.2.2 Two Sample Case

If two sample mean vectors are tested with respect to their equality this test is used.

$$H_0 : \underline{\mu}_1 = \underline{\mu}_2, \qquad H_1 : \underline{\mu}_1 \neq \underline{\mu}_2$$

where $\underline{\mu}_1$ and $\underline{\mu}_2$ are the population mean vectors for 1st and 2nd populations respectively.

$$\underline{\mu}_1 = \begin{bmatrix} \mu_{11} \\ \mu_{12} \\ \vdots \\ \mu_{1p} \end{bmatrix}, \qquad \underline{\mu}_2 = \begin{bmatrix} \mu_{21} \\ \mu_{22} \\ \vdots \\ \mu_{2p} \end{bmatrix} \qquad \text{.....(17.5)}$$

The Hotelling – T^2 is given as

$$T^2 = \frac{n_1 \, n_2}{n_1 + n_2} \left(\underline{\bar{x}}_1 - \underline{\bar{x}}_2\right)^1 S^{-1} \left(\underline{\bar{x}}_1 - \underline{\bar{x}}_2\right) \qquad \text{.....(17.6)}$$

where n_1, n_2 are sizes of 1st and 2nd samples respectively and

$$\underline{\bar{x}}_1 = \begin{bmatrix} \bar{x}_{11} \\ \bar{x}_{12} \\ \vdots \\ \bar{x}_{1p} \end{bmatrix}, \qquad \underline{\bar{x}}_2 = \begin{bmatrix} \bar{x}_{21} \\ \bar{x}_{22} \\ \vdots \\ \bar{x}_{2p} \end{bmatrix} \qquad \text{.....(17.7)}$$

and $$S = \frac{S_1 + S_2}{n_1 + n_2 - 2}$$

where S_1 and S_2 are the variance and covariance matrices for the 1st and 2nd samples respectively and

$$S_1 = \begin{bmatrix} s_{11}^{(1)} & s_{12}^{(1)} & \cdots & s_{1p}^{(1)} \\ s_{21}^{(1)} & s_{22}^{(1)} & \cdots & s_{2p}^{(1)} \\ \vdots & \vdots & & \vdots \\ s_{p1}^{(1)} & s_{p2}^{(1)} & \cdots & s_{pp}^{(1)} \end{bmatrix}, \quad S_2 = \begin{bmatrix} s_{11}^{(2)} & s_{12}^{(2)} & \cdots & s_{1p}^{(2)} \\ s_{21}^{(2)} & s_{22}^{(2)} & \cdots & s_{2p}^{(2)} \\ \vdots & \vdots & & \vdots \\ s_{p1}^{(2)} & s_{p2}^{(2)} & \cdots & s_{pp}^{(2)} \end{bmatrix} \quad .....(17.8)$$

The Hotelling – T^2 is tested with the help of F-test

$$F = \frac{n_1 + n_2 - p - 1}{p\,(n_1 + n_2 - 2)}\, T^2 \quad .....(17.9)$$

Conclusion

If F (Cal.) value > F (tab.) value with (p, $n_1 + n_2 - p - 1$) d.f. at the required level of significance then H_0 is rejected and H_1 is accepted. If H_0 is rejected then it can be concluded that there is significant difference between two sample mean vectors. Otherwise, H_0 is accepted. For further reading please refer to Rao (2007).

17.3 Classification by Discriminant Function

It is sometimes necessary to classify an individual or object into-one or other groups. For example, a botanist may like to classify a new plant into one or other recognized species of a plant in plant taxonomy. An administrator wants to classify an industrial unit as sick or non-sick industry. Tourism department may be interested to classify a Hotel as star hotel or non-star hotel. A funding agency may be interested to classify farmers into progressive or non-progressive categories etc.

If an individual or object is classified into different groups based on more than one character then linear discriminant function is used. This linear function is constructed by taking all characters into consideration.

17.3.1 Classification for Two Groups

Here two linear functions are constructed for two samples which are drawn from two groups respectively. Let y_1, y_2 be two linear functions based on p character for the 1st and 2nd groups respectively.

Let $y_1 = l_{11} x_1 + l_{21} x_2 + l_{31} x_3 + \ldots + l_{p1} x_p$ .....(17.10)

and $y_2 = l_{12} x_1 + l_{22} x_2 + l_{32} x_3 + \ldots + l_{p2} x_p$

then $\bar{y}_1$ and $\bar{y}_2$ are the means of two samples using discriminant function and are written in matrix notation as

$$\bar{y}_1 = \left(\bar{\underline{x}}_1 - \bar{\underline{x}}_2\right)^1 S^{-1} \bar{\underline{x}}_1 \qquad .....(17.11)$$

$$\bar{y}_2 = \left(\bar{\underline{x}}_1 - \bar{\underline{x}}_2\right)^1 S^{-1} \bar{\underline{x}}_2$$

The mid-point of the two means $\bar{y}_1$ and $\bar{y}_2$ is given as

$$\frac{\bar{y}_1 + \bar{y}_2}{2} = \frac{1}{2}\left(\bar{\underline{x}}_1 - \bar{\underline{x}}_2\right)^1 S^{-1} \left(\bar{\underline{x}}_1 + \bar{\underline{x}}_2\right) \qquad .....(17.12)$$

where $\bar{\underline{x}}_1$ and $\bar{\underline{x}}_2$ are the vectors of means of two samples and S^{-1} is the inverse of common variance covariance matrix.

The individual unit is assigned to population 1 if

$$\left(\bar{\underline{x}}_1 - \bar{\underline{x}}_2\right)^1 S^{-1} \underline{x} > \frac{1}{2}\left(\bar{\underline{x}}_1 - \bar{\underline{x}}_2\right)^1 S^{-1} \left(\bar{\underline{x}}_1 + \bar{\underline{x}}_2\right) \qquad .....(17.13)$$

and it is assigned to population 2 if

$$\left(\bar{\underline{x}}_1 - \bar{\underline{x}}_2\right)^1 S^{-1} \underline{x} \le \frac{1}{2}\left(\bar{\underline{x}}_1 - \bar{\underline{x}}_2\right)^1 S^{-1} \left(\bar{\underline{x}}_1 + \bar{\underline{x}}_2\right) \qquad .....(17.14)$$

In other words, the individual units are assigned to the group with closer discriminant score.

$$\text{If } W = \underline{x}^1 S^{-1} \left(\bar{\underline{x}}_1 - \bar{\underline{x}}_2\right) - \frac{1}{2}\left(\bar{\underline{x}}_1 + \bar{\underline{x}}_2\right)^1 S^{-1} \left(\bar{\underline{x}}_1 - \bar{\underline{x}}_2\right) \qquad .....(17.15)$$

then $\underline{x}$ is assigned to population 1 if $W > 0$ and to population 2 if $W \le 0$. W is called Wald-Anderson classification statistic. For further reading please refer to Rao (2007).

17.4 Principal Component Analysis

If $x_1, x_2, \dots, x_p$ are p characters studied on the sample drawn from a population which follows multivariate distribution with mean μ and variance-covariance matrix Σ. Let the rank of Σ is $r \le p$ and the q largest characteristic roots λ_i of Σ are are written as

$$\lambda_1 > \lambda_2 > \lambda_3 > \dots > \lambda_q$$

These characteristic roots are all distinct. Suppose that a sample of n independent units are drawn from the population then the n units each having p characteristic values are presented in matrix form of size n × p as

$$X = \begin{bmatrix} x_{11} & x_{12} & \vdots & x_{1p} \\ x_{21} & x_{22} & & x_{2p} \\ \vdots & \vdots & & \vdots \\ x_{n1} & x_{n2} & & x_{np} \end{bmatrix} \quad .....(17.16)$$

Let S be the estimate of Σ and which is the sample variance-covariance matrix. If the observations recorded for different characters are in different units of measurement then these observations will be standardized before finding the sample variance-covariance matrix. The first principal component of the sample values of the characters $x_1, x_2, \ldots, x_p$ is the linear function

$$y_1 = l_{11} x_1 + l_{21} x_2 + \ldots. + l_{p1} x_p \quad .....(17.17)$$

The coefficients l_{i1}'s in the first principal component are the elements of the characteristic vector associated with greatest characteristic root λ_1 of the sample variance covariance matrix S. The characteristic root λ_1 is the sample variance of first principal component y_1. In other words the first principal component extracts maximum variation from variance covariance matrix S. The second principal component can be written as

$$y_2 = l_{12} x_1 + l_{22} x_2 + \ldots. + l_{p2} x_p \quad .....(17.18)$$

The coefficients in y_2 i.e., l_{i2}'s are the elements of the characteristic vector associated with second largest characteristic root λ_2 of sample variance covariance matrix S. Similarly the j-th principal component is

$$y_j = l_{ij} x_1 + l_{2j} x_2 + \ldots + l_{pj} x_p \quad .....(17.19)$$

The l_{ij}'s in (17.19) are the elements of the characteristic vector associated with j-th largest characteristic root λ_j.

Here $\lambda_1 + \lambda_2 + \ldots + \lambda_p = \text{trace S}$ .....(17.20)

The importance of j-th principal component is measured as

$$\frac{\lambda_j}{\text{trace S}} \quad .....(17.21)$$

The correlation coefficient between i-th character and j-th principal component is

$$\frac{l_{ij}\ \sqrt{\lambda_i}}{s_{ii}} \qquad \text{.....(17.22)}$$

where s_{ii} is the i-th diagonal element of matrix S. For further reading please refer to Rao (2007).

17.5 Factor Analysis

In this method the total number of characters will be reduced to small number of factors where each factor comprises of some characters which are having some common relationship. The identification of factors involves overlapping of characters among themselves. In other words factors containing characters are not mutually exclusive. Factor analysis provides the identification of factors which are effecting the dependent variable.

In principal component analysis, the different principal components are not invariant under changes in the scales of the characters. Further it is not well defined when to stop the process of extracting principal components and what is the maximum limit of extracting maximum variance from variance-covariance matrix. Factor analysis will meet some of the deficiencies in principal component analysis by way of representing each character as a linear function of small number of unobservable common factor variables and a single latent variate. The common factor variables provide the covariance among the observable responses, while the specific terms contribute only to the variances of their particular responses.

17.5.1 Model for Factor Analysis

Let $x_1, x_2, \ldots, x_p$ be p random variables which are represented as

$$\begin{aligned} x_1 &= l_{11}\, y_1 + l_{12}\, y_2 + \ldots. + l_{1m}\, y_m + e_1 \\ x_2 &= l_{21}\, y_1 + l_{22}\, y_2 + \ldots. + l_{2m}\, y_m + e_2 \qquad \text{.....(17.23)} \\ &\vdots \\ x_p &= l_{p1}\, y_1 + l_{p2}\, y_2 + \ldots. + l_{pm}\, y_m + e_m \end{aligned}$$

where y_j is the j-th common factor variable, l_{ij} is the coefficient of j-th common factor with i-th random variable and is called as the loading of i-th random variable on the j-th common factor and e_i is the effect of i-th specific random variable.

The equations given in (17.23) can be written in matrix notation as

$$\underline{X} = L\,\underline{Y} + \underline{E} \qquad .....(17.24)$$

where $\underline{X}' = [x_1, x_2, \ldots, x_p]$, $\underline{Y}' = [Y_1, Y_2, \ldots Y_m]$, $\underline{E}' = [e_1, e_2, \ldots e_m]$

$$L = \begin{bmatrix} l_{11} & l_{12} & \cdots & l_{1m} \\ l_{21} & l_{22} & \cdots & l_{2m} \\ \vdots & & & \\ l_{p1} & l_{p2} & \cdots & l_{pm} \end{bmatrix} \qquad .....(17.25)$$

$\underline{Y}'$ is assumed to be independently and normally distributed with mean as 0 and variance-covariance matrix I where 0 is the vector of m elements having zeros and I is the m × m identity matrix with elements of zeros in off diagonal and 1s in diagonals. Similarly $\underline{E}'$ is normally distributed with mean as 0 and variance Σ where

$$0_{p,1} = \begin{bmatrix} 0 \\ 0 \\ \vdots \\ 0 \end{bmatrix}, \quad \Sigma_{p,p} = \begin{bmatrix} \Sigma_1 & 0 & \cdots & 0 \\ 0 & \Sigma_2 & \cdots & 0 \\ 0 & 0 & \cdots & \Sigma_p \end{bmatrix} \qquad .....(17.26)$$

The variance of the i-th response can be written as

$$\sigma_i^2 = l_{11}^2 + l_{12}^2 + \ldots + l_{1m}^2 + \Sigma_1 \qquad .....(17.27)$$

The covariance between i-th and j-th responses is

$$\sigma_{ij} = l_{i1}\, l_{j1} + l_{i2}\, l_{j2} + \ldots + l_{im}\, l_{jm} \qquad .....(17.28)$$

For further reading please refer to Rao (2007).

CHAPTER 18

Report Writing

18.1 Introduction

Report writing is an important aspect of research methodology since based on report writing only the value and utility of research work is assessed. In report writing, all components of research work has to be presented in proper format for easy understanding by the examiner as well as other readers. If the report writing is not properly presented then the report may likely to be rejected even though it contains valuable material of research significance.

The language should be good and simple and the presentation of research material in logical sequence avoiding confusion.

18.2 Results and Discussion

Results and discussion will occupy as one of the important chapters of thesis writing for degrees like M.Sc., M.Phil and Ph.D.

18.2.1 Results

The results obtained after statistical analysis of data are presented in tables in logical sequence as per the objectives of the research work. The conclusions drawn after applying statistical methods are presented underneath each of the tables. If 10 parameters or characters are studied then 10 tables will be presented with conclusions in logical sequence. The values of statistical tools are presented in the tables. These tables should be consolidated tables. The original data should not be presented in these tables. If the number of parameters or characters is large then the results may be presented in few tables or single table to avoid repetition. The values of statistical tools like z, t, r, etc., are presented in the same tables. The values of partial regression coefficients b_i s. R^2, R, SEs are presented in one table. The statistical packages like SPSS, SAS can be used for statistical analysis.

The presentation of results of statistical analysis can be done with the help of these packages. The titles of the tables should be appropriate and brief as per objectives of the survey or research work either in laboratory or experimental field. While presenting results in tables we should be conscious of meeting the objectives of the research work.

18.2.2 Discussion

Discussion of the results should go along with results in this chapter. Discussion includes interpretation of results properly and discussion about the implications, establishment of hypothesis of the present and past and collaborating with other research work done by earlier authors etc. In discussion the limitations about the size of the sample, assumptions involved in using statistical tools used in drawing conclusions have to be mentioned. If the results obtained are supporting the previous research work then reasons of supporting should be indicated. Similarly if the results of present research work are going against the previous research then reasons should be established. If the results are entirely new then it should be mentioned that further research work has to be carried out to establish or confirm the new results obtained in the present research. It is always necessary to discuss the results with results of as many authors as possible. However these author's results should be latest one. If the results obtained are of fundamental nature, it should be highlighted by presenting implications and treading for a new path of research. If the results are of practical and economic utility it should be clearly stated that how much economic returns will be obtained by using this research finding.

If the research work is based on sample survey data then the generalization has to be done carefully based on the method of sampling adopted. If the method of sampling is based on probability then generalization of the sample to the universe can be attempted. If the method of sampling is purposive then generalization of sample results should not be attempted. When generalization is attempted then care should be taken with respect to standard error involved in the estimate. Further the time of survey conducted should also be taken into consideration as the estimates may be outdated by the time they are published. Also the comparison with similar surveys conducted by different agencies should be considered. The authenticity of agencies, the size of the sample and method of sample selection should be considered before comparison.

In the sample surveys, the data collected is at the level of nominal or ordinal level of measurement the schedule or questionnaire used for collecting the information has to be examined carefully by experts before generalization to universe. The questionnaire or schedule copy should be enclosed at the end in the project report or thesis. In opinion surveys the size of sample plays important role. As size of the sample and proportion of sampled population from different strata of people will be key parameters for forecasting the opinion of population.

In laboratory and agricultural field experiments, the type of statistical experimental design will be of considerable importance. If the design used is appropriate it will bring out important comparisons among treatments and also extract important information from the data which otherwise unutilized. The proper experimental design will lead to proper discussion of the results. For a research work leading to Ph.D. degree, the same design is repeated in the field for more than one season or same season for two years to make the results more robust. In laboratory experiments the sample size should be more as for as feasible and the number of replications should be more as for as possible. In plant breeding experiments, the number of plants to be selected should be minimum 5 and in agronomy experiments the net plot size should be considered for yield data. For correlation studies, the pair wise sample should be at least 10 so that proper interpretation can be drawn. In multiple regression studies, the number of observations should be considerably larger than number of independent variables involved in the analysis. For example, if the number of independent variables is 10 then the number of observations can be 22 or more so that error degrees of freedom is more than regression degrees of freedom in the analysis of variance table for testing overall regression.

In plant physiology experiments, the number of plants, number of leaves to be selected from each plant could be 5 to 10 depending upon the time available for analysis of data. In Entomology experiments conducted in laboratory, the number of insects to be experimented could be 5 to 10. In field experiments of Entomology, the number of plants to be selected based on the number of insects available on each plant. In social surveys the size of the sample should be as large as possible subject to availability of time and money and nature of the universe or sampling frame. In discussion of the results, the limitations of survey such as sample selection. Sample size, sampling frame, type of instrument used for collecting information should be mentioned. Generalization of results as for as possible should be avoided unless very necessary for meeting the objectives for the project.

18.3 Formats of Project Report

The formats of presentation of report are different for different research projects. For example, the format for research project is different from format of presentation of thesis for obtaining degree like Ph.D. The format for presentation of thesis for the award of M.Phil, Ph.D. degrees are approved by Faculty Boards, Academic councils etc., in respective universities. Though the procedure of presentation may be more or less is same in several universities still they maintain some individuality by slightly modifying the format here and there.

18.3.1 Format for Ph.D Thesis

The format for presentation of Ph.D. thesis will be in different chapters such as

(i) Introduction

(ii) Materials and Methods

(iii) Results and discussion

(iv) Summary and conclusions and

(v) Bibliography or literature cited

18.3.1.1 Introduction

In the chapter of introduction, the background of the research work and how it has lead to the initiation of research work, motivation of starting research work and aim and objectives of research work are presented.

The objectives of the research work should be written in simple language and the number of objectives should be as small as possible and pointed.

If the number of objectives are more then the data to be collected will be more and the analysis will be more and which sometimes lead to conflicting conclusions. Further, sometimes the data or fundamental research may not be accomplished to meet the objectives. Of course in some universities there is a flexibility to modify the objectives later on but it is not so in the case of some other universities. The objectives are to be framed depending upon the availability of land, equipment, material, personnel, money, time, literature etc.

18.3.1.2 Materials and Methods

In this chapter the material required for conducting the investigation is presented. For example, if it is a field experiment what type of treatments are to be tested and what type of land is available, what type of equipment or kits are available for conducting the experiment, what type and how much quantity of seed material is available, the experimental design to be used, season etc., are used to be considered. The detailed information has to be written in this chapter.

In sample survey the description of the population or universe, the sampling frame, the preparation and description of schedule or questionnaire, the contents of schedule, the parameters to be considered for survey, the area to be sampled, the population to be sampled, the sample design to be used etc., will be presented in this chapter. Further how to proceed to conduct the survey also is described in this chapter.

In the laboratory experiment, the details of preparation of chemicals, the treatments to be tested, the statistical design, if any, to be adopted, the replications to be taken etc., are presented elaborately. If it is an animal experiment, the number of animals to be experimented for each replication, the statistical design to be adopted, the treatments to be tested, the control treatment to be added for comparison with experimental treatments, the other statistical techniques to be used are explained in this chapter.

18.3.1.3 Results and Discussion

This chapter is very important for any thesis since the results of research investigation is presented and also interpreted and also discussed in detail with respect to new knowledge created and compared with existing knowledge in the area concerned and also connects up with the contemporary author's research findings. Usually the quality of research work is assessed by going through this chapter. If the findings are new and important either basic or applied research point of view then the thesis is recommended for its acceptance. The presentation of findings should be in logical order as per the importance of parameters considered in the problem of research. The important tables only are presented in the body of this chapter and other relevant tables are given in Appendices. The statistical analysis results are presented, interpreted and discussed by giving implications are presented in this chapter. The extraction of important conclusions drawn from statistical analysis will add to the quality of thesis. Before finalizing this chapter it is always advisable to consult statistician for drawing appropriate conclusions from statistical analysis. If the research work is of fundamental nature or completely new area of research, the discussion will be only on new findings without comparing with other author's work. There can be more chapters on new findings instead of single chapter on results and discussion.

18.3.1.4 Summary and Conclusions

This chapter of thesis gives the summary of research work conducted in nutshell and the conclusions drawn based on the results obtained in relation to objectives set forth at the beginning of research investigation. The summary includes briefly :

(i) the introduction

(ii) the material and methods

(iii) the results and discussion and

(iv) broad conclusions.

However the conclusions are listed separately with serial number taken into consideration of importance of parameters. The whole chapter usually will not exceed 6 to 7 pages. The conclusions should be written according to the point avoiding lengthy explanation.

18.3.1.5 Bibliography or Literature Cited

The list of articles, research papers, books referred in this thesis are presented in a systematic manner at the end of the thesis. This list is called 'literature cited'. Sometimes some articles, research papers, books which are not referred are also included then it is known as 'bibliography'. Usually literature cited is presented in this thesis. The format or procedure of presentation of literature cited is prescribed by the 'Academic Councils' of the respective universities which are awarding Ph.D. degrees. The general procedure can be written as authors in alphabetical order, year of publication as per ascending order, title of the article or research paper, title of the journal, volume number and page numbers. For example,

(i) Allard RW and Brad shaw 1964 Implications of genotype environmental interactions in applied plant breeding Crop science 4 : 503-508.

(ii) Baker RJ 1969 Genotype – environment interactions in yield of wheat. Canadian journal of plant science 49 : 743-751.

(iii) Choudhary SK and Haque MN 1977 Stability performance of some greengram varieties. Indian Journal of Agricultural Sciences, 47 : 303-304.

(iv) Chunilal Basu MS and Ranvir Singh 1998 Stability analysis for pod and kernel yield in Spanish bunch groundnut. Indian Journal of Genetics and Plant Breeding. 58 : 125-126.

It can be seen that the list of authors are arranged in alphabetical order and when several authors are to be quoted in the same year then they are listed according to alphabetical order. Further, years of publishing of articles or research papers are arranged according to ascending order starting from very old to letest. Usually the books are listed in bold letters distinguishing from research articles.

Appendix

Table I Table of normal deviates *z* corresponding to proportions p of a dichotomized unit normal distribution

p	0	1	2	3	4	5	6	7	8	9
.99	2.326	2.366	2.409	2.457	2.512	2.576	2.652	2.748	2.878	3.090
.98	2.054	2.075	2.097	2.120	2.144	2.170	2.197	2.226	2.257	2.290
.97	1.881	1.896	1.911	1.927	1.943	1.960	1.977	1.995	2.014	2.034
.96	1.751	1.762	1.774	1.787	1.799	1.812	1.825	1.838	1.852	1.866
.95	1.645	1.655	1.665	1.675	1.685	1.695	1.706	1.717	1.728	1.739
.94	1.555	1.563	1.572	1.580	1.589	1.598	1.607	1.616	1.626	1.635
.93	1.476	1.483	1.491	1.499	1.506	1.514	1.522	1.530	1.538	1.546
.92	1.405	1.412	1.419	1.426	1.433	1.440	1.447	1.454	1.461	1.468
.91	1.341	1.347	1.353	1.359	1.366	1.372	1.379	1.385	1.392	1.398
.90	1.282	1.287	1.293	1.299	1.305	1.311	1.317	1.323	1.329	1.335
.89	1.227	1.232	1.237	1.243	1.248	1.254	1.259	1.265	1.270	1.276
.88	1.175	1.180	1.185	1.190	1.195	1.200	1.206	1.211	1.216	1.221
.87	1.126	1.131	1.136	1.141	1.146	1.150	1.155	1.160	1.165	1.170
.86	1.080	1.085	1.089	1.094	1.098	1.103	1.108	1.112	1.117	1.122
.85	1.036	1.041	1.045	1.049	1.054	1.058	1.063	1.067	1.071	1.076
.84	.994	.999	1.003	1.007	1.011	1.015	1.019	1.024	1.028	1.032
.83	.954	.958	.962	.966	.970	.974	.978	.982	.986	.990
.82	.915	.919	.923	.927	.931	.935	.938	.942	.946	.950
.81	.878	.882	.885	.889	.893	.896	.900	.904	.908	.912
.80	.842	.845	.849	.852	.856	.860	.863	.867	.871	.874
.79	.806	.810	.813	.817	.820	.824	.827	.831	.834	.838
.78	.772	.776	.779	.782	.786	.789	.793	.796	.800	.803
.77	.739	.742	.745	.749	.752	.755	.759	.762	.765	.769
.76	.706	.710	.713	.716	.719	.722	.726	.729	.732	.736
.75	.674	.678	.681	.684	.687	.690	.693	.697	.700	.703
.74	.643	.646	.650	.653	.656	.659	.662	.665	.668	.671
.73	.613	.616	.619	.622	.625	.628	.631	.634	.637	.640
.72	.583	.586	.589	.592	.595	.598	.601	.604	.607	.610
.71	.553	.556	.559	.562	.565	.568	.571	.574	.577	.580
.70	.524	.527	.530	.533	.536	.539	.542	.545	.548	.550
.69	.496	.499	.502	.504	.507	.510	.513	.516	.519	.522
.68	.468	.470	.473	.476	.479	.482	.485	.487	.490	.493
.67	.440	.443	.445	.448	.451	.454	.457	.459	.462	.465
.66	.412	.415	.418	.421	.423	.426	.429	.432	.434	.437
.65	.385	.388	.391	.393	.396	.399	.402	.404	.407	.410
.64	.358	.361	.364	.366	.369	.372	.375	.377	.380	.383
.63	.332	.335	.337	.340	.342	.345	.348	.350	.353	.356
.62	.305	.308	.311	.313	.316	.319	.321	.324	.327	.329
.61	.279	.282	.285	.287	.290	.292	.295	.298	.300	.303
.60	.253	.256	.259	.261	.264	.266	.269	.272	.274	.277
.59	.228	.230	.233	.235	.238	.240	.243	.246	.248	.251
.58	.202	.204	.207	.210	.212	.215	.217	.220	.222	.225
.57	.176	.179	.181	.184	.187	.189	.192	.194	.197	.199
.56	.151	.154	.156	.159	.161	.164	.166	.169	.171	.174
.55	.126	.128	.131	.133	.136	.138	.141	.143	.146	.148
.54	.100	.103	.105	.108	.111	.113	.116	.118	.121	.123
.53	.075	.078	.080	.083	.085	.088	.090	.093	.095	.098
.52	.050	.053	.055	.058	.060	.063	.065	.068	.070	.073
.51	.025	.028	.030	.033	.035	.038	.040	.043	.045	.048
.50	.000	.003	.005	.008	.010	.013	.015	.018	.020	.023

Table I *Contd...*

P	0	1	2	3	4	5	6	7	8	9
.49	-.025	-.023	-.020	-.018	-.015	-.013	-.010	-.008	-.005	-.003
.48	-.050	-.048	-.045	-.043	-.040	-.038	-.035	-.033	-.030	-.028
.47	-.075	-.073	-.070	-.068	-.065	-.063	-.060	-.058	-.055	-.053
.46	-.100	-.098	-.095	-.093	-.090	-.088	-.085	-.083	-.080	-.078
.45	-.126	-.123	-.121	-.118	-.116	-.113	-.111	-.108	-.105	-.103
.44	-.151	-.148	-.146	-.143	-.141	-.138	-.136	-.133	-.131	-.128
.43	-.176	-.174	-.171	-.169	-.166	-.164	-.161	-.159	-.156	-.154
.42	-.202	-.199	-.197	-.194	-.192	-.189	-.187	-.184	-.181	-.179
.41	-.228	-.225	-.222	-.220	-.217	-.215	-.212	-.210	-.207	-.204
.40	-.253	-.251	-.248	-.246	-.243	-.240	-.238	-.235	-.233	-.230
.39	-.279	-.277	-.274	-.272	-.269	-.266	-.264	-.261	-.259	-.256
.38	-.305	-.303	-.300	-.298	-.295	-.292	-.290	-.287	-.285	-.282
.37	-.332	-.329	-.327	-324	-.321	-.319	-.316	-.313	-.311	-.308
.36	-.358	-.356	-.353	-.350	-.348	-.345	-.342	-.340	-.337	-.335
.35	-.385	-.383	-.380	-.377	-.375	-.372	-.369	-.366	-.364	-.361
.34	-.412	-.410	-.407	-.404	-.402	-.399	-.396	-.393	-.391	-.388
.33	-.440	-.437	-.434	-.432	-.429	-.426	-.423	-.421	-.418	-.415
.32	-.468	-.465	-.462	-.459	-.457	-.454	-.451	-.448	-.445	-.443
.31	-.496	-.493	-.490	-.487	-.485	-.482	-.479	-.476	-.473	-.470
.30	-.524	-.522	-.519	-.516	-.513	-.510	-.507	-.504	-.502	-.499
.29	-.553	-.550	-.548	-.545	-.542	-.539	-.536	-.533	-.530	-.527
.28	-.583	-.580	-.577	-.574	-.571	-.568	-.565	-.562	-.559	-.556
.27	-.613	-.610	-.607	-.604	-.601	-.598	-.595	-.592	-.589	-.586
.26	-.643	-.640	-.637	-.634	-.631	-.628	-.625	-.622	-.619	-.616
.25	-.674	-.671	-.668	-.665	-.662	-.659	-.656	-.653	-.650	-.646
.24	-.706	-.703	-.700	-.697	-.693	-.690	-.687	-.684	-.681	-.678
.23	-.739	-.736	-.732	-.729	-.726	-.722	-.719	-.716	-.713	-.710
.22	-.772	-.769	-.765	-.762	-.759	-.755	-.752	-.749	-.745	-.742
.21	-.806	-.803	-.800	-.796	-.793	-.789	-.786	-.782	-.779	-.776
.20	-.842	-.838	-.834	-.831	-.827	-.824	-.820	-.817	-.813	-.810
.19	-.878	-.874	-.871	-.867	-.863	-.860	-.856	-.852	-.849	-.845
.18	-.915	-.912	-.908	-.904	-.900	-.896	-.893	-.889	-.885	-.882
.17	-.954	-.950	-.946	-.942	-.938	-.935	-.931	-.927	-.923	-.919
.16	-.994	-.990	-.986	-.982	-.978	-.974	-.970	-.966	-.962	-.958
.15	-1.036	-1.032	-1.028	-1.024	-1.019	-1.015	-1.011	-1.007	-1.003	-.999
.14	-1.080	-1.076	-1.071	-1.067	-1.063	-1.058	-1.054	-1.049	-1.045	-1.041
.13	-1.126	-1.122	-1.117	-1.112	-1.108	-1.103	-1.098	-1.094	-1.089	-1.085
.12	-1.175	-1.170	-1.165	-1.160	-1.155	-1.150	-1.146	-1.141	-1.136	-1.131
.11	-1.227	-1.221	-1.216	-1.211	-1.206	-1.200	-1.195	-1.190	-1.185	-1.180
.10	-1.282	-1.276	-1.270	-1.265	-1.259	-1.254	-1.248	-1.243	-1.237	-1.232
.09	-1.341	-1.335	-1.329	-1.323	-1.317	-1.311	-1.305	-1.299	-1.293	-1.287
.08	-1.405	-1.398	-1.392	-1.385	-1.379	-1.372	-1.366	-1.359	-1.353	-1.347
.07	-1.476	-1.468	-1.461	-1.454	-1.447	-1.440	-1.433	-1.426	-1.419	-1.412
.06	-1.555	-1.546	-1.538	-1.530	-1.522	-1.514	-1.506	-1.499	-1.491	-1.483
.05	-1.645	-1.635	-1.626	-1.616	-1.607	-1.598	-1.589	-1.580	-1.572	-1.563
.04	-1.751	-1.739	-1.728	-1.717	-1.706	-1.695	-1.685	-1.675	-1.665	-1.655
.03	-1.881	-1.866	-1.852	-1.838	-1.825	-1.812	-1.799	-1.787	-1.774	-1.762
.02	-2.054	-2.034	-2.014	-1.995	-1.977	-1.960	-1.943	-1.927	-1.911	-1.896
.01	-2.326	-2.290	-2.257	-2.226	-2.197	-2.170	-2.144	-2.120	-2.097	-2.075
.00		-3.090	-2.878	-2.748	-2.652	-2.576	-2.512	-2.457	-2.409	-2.366

Table II Table of the angular transformation of percentages to degrees*

p	0	1	2	3	4	5	6	7	8	9
0.0	0	0.57	0.81	0.99	1.15	1.28	1.40	1.52	1.62	1.72
0.1	1.81	1.90	1.99	2.07	2.14	2.22	2.29	2.36	2.43	2.50
0.2	2.56	2.63	2.69	2.75	2.81	2.87	2.92	2.98	3.03	3.09
0.3	3.14	3.19	3.24	3.29	3.34	3.39	3.44	3.49	3.53	3.58
0.4	3.63	3.67	3.72	3.76	3.80	3.85	3.89	3.93	3.97	4.01
0.5	4.05	4.09	4.13	4.17	4.21	4.25	4.29	4.33	4.37	4.40
0.6	4.44	4.48	4.52	4.55	4.59	4.62	4.66	4.69	4.73	4.76
0.7	4.80	4.83	4.87	4.90	4.93	4.97	5.00	5.03	5.07	5.10
0.8	5.13	5.16	5.20	5.23	5.26	5.29	5.32	5.35	5.38	5.41
0.9	5.44	5.47	5.50	5.53	5.56	5.59	5.62	5.65	5.68	5.71
1	5.74	6.02	6.29	6.55	6.80	7.04	7.27	7.49	7.71	7.92
2	8.13	8.33	8.53	8.72	8.91	9.10	9.28	9.46	9.63	9.81
3	9.98	10.14	10.31	10.47	10.63	10.78	10.94	11.09	11.24	11.39
4	11.54	11.68	11.83	11.97	12.11	12.25	12.39	12.52	12.66	12.79
5	12.92	13.05	13.18	13.31	13.44	13.56	13.69	13.81	13.94	14.06
6	14.18	14.30	14.42	14.54	14.65	14.77	14.89	15.00	15.12	15.23
7	15.34	15.45	15.56	15.68	15.79	15.89	16.00	16.11	16.22	16.32
8	16.43	16.54	16.64	16.74	16.85	16.95	17.05	17.16	17.26	17.36
9	17.46	17.56	17.66	17.76	17.85	17.95	18.05	18.15	18.24	18.34
10	18.44	18.53	18.63	18.72	18.81	18.91	19.00	19.09	19.19	19.28
11	19.37	19.46	19.55	19.64	19.73	19.82	19.91	20.00	20.09	20.18
12	20.27	20.36	20.44	20.53	20.62	20.70	20.79	20.88	20.96	21.05
13	21.13	21.22	21.30	21.39	21.47	21.56	21.64	21.72	21.81	21.89
14	21.97	22.06	22.14	22.22	22.30	22.38	22.46	22.55	22.63	22.71
15	22.79	22.87	22.95	23.03	23.11	23.19	23.26	23.34	23.42	23.50
16	23.58	23.66	23.73	23.81	23.89	23.97	24.04	24.12	24.20	24.27
17	24.35	24.43	24.50	24.58	24.65	24.73	24.80	24.88	24.95	25.03
18	25.10	25.18	25.25	25.33	25.40	25.48	25.55	25.62	25.70	25.77
19	25.84	25.92	25.99	26.06	26.13	26.21	26.28	26.35	26.42	26.49
20	26.56	26.64	26.71	26.78	26.85	26.92	26.99	27.06	27.13	27.20
21	27.28	27.35	27.42	27.49	27.56	27.63	27.69	27.76	27.83	27.90
22	27.97	28.04	28.11	28.18	28.25	28.32	28.38	28.45	28.52	28.59
23	28.66	28.73	28.79	28.86	28.93	29.00	29.06	29.13	29.20	29.27
24	29.33	29.40	29.47	29.53	29.60	29.67	29.73	29.80	29.87	29.93
25	30.00	30.07	30.13	30.20	30.26	30.33	30.40	30.46	30.53	30.59
26	30.66	30.72	30.79	30.85	30.92	30.98	31.05	31.11	31.18	31.24
27	31.31	31.37	31.44	31.50	31.56	31.63	31.69	31.76	31.82	31.88
28	31.95	32.01	32.08	32.14	32.20	32.27	32.33	32.39	32.46	32.52
29	32.58	32.65	32.71	32.77	32.83	32.90	32.96	33.02	33.09	33.15

*Table II is reprinted from Table 11.12.1 of Snedecor: *Statistical Methods*, Iowa State College Press, Ames, Iowa, by permission of the author and his publisher, and by permission of C. I. Bliss, who computed the tabled entries.

Table II *Contd...*

p	0	1	2	3	4	5	6	7	8	9
30	33.21	33.27	33.34	33.40	33.46	33.52	33.58	33.65	33.71	33.77
31	33.83	33.89	33.96	34.02	34.08	34.14	34.20	34.27	34.33	34.39
32	34.45	34.51	34.57	34.63	34.70	34.76	34.82	34.88	34.94	35.00
33	35.06	35.12	35.18	35.24	35.30	35.37	35.43	35.49	35.55	35.61
34	35.67	35.73	35.79	35.85	35.91	35.97	36.03	36.09	36.15	36.21
35	36.27	36.33	36.39	36.45	36.51	36.57	36.63	36.69	36.75	36.81
36	36.87	36.93	36.99	37.05	37.11	37.17	37.23	37.29	37.35	37.41
37	37.47	37.52	37.58	37.64	37.70	37.76	37.82	37.88	37.94	38.00
38	38.06	38.12	38.17	38.23	38.29	38.35	38.41	38.47	38.53	38.59
39	38.65	38.70	38.76	38.82	38.88	38.94	39.00	39.06	39.11	39.17
40	39.23	39.29	39.35	39.41	39.47	39.52	39.58	39.64	39.70	39.76
41	39.82	39.87	39.93	39.99	40.05	40.11	40.16	40.22	40.28	40.34
42	40.40	40.46	40.51	40.57	40.63	40.69	40.74	40.80	40.86	40.92
43	40.98	41.03	41.09	41.15	41.21	41.27	41.32	41.38	41.44	41.50
44	41.55	41.61	41.67	41.73	41.78	41.84	41.90	41.96	42.02	42.07
45	42.13	42.19	42.25	42.30	42.36	42.42	42.48	42.53	42.59	42.65
46	42.71	42.76	42.82	42.88	42.94	42.99	43.05	43.11	43.17	43.22
47	43.28	43.34	43.39	43.45	43.51	43.57	43.62	43.68	43.74	43.80
48	43.85	43.91	43.97	44.03	44.08	44.14	44.20	44.25	44.31	44.37
49	44.43	44.48	44.54	44.60	44.66	44.71	44.77	44.83	44.89	44.94
50	45.00	45.06	45.11	45.17	45.23	45.29	45.34	45.40	45.46	45.52
51	45.57	45.63	45.69	45.75	45.80	45.86	45.92	45.97	46.03	46.09
52	46.15	46.20	46.26	46.32	46.38	46.43	46.49	46.55	46.61	46.66
53	46.72	46.78	46.83	46.89	46.95	47.01	47.06	47.12	47.18	47.24
54	47.29	47.35	47.41	47.47	47.52	47.58	47.64	47.70	47.75	47.81
55	47.87	47.93	47.98	48.04	48.10	48.16	48.22	48.27	48.33	48.39
56	48.45	48.50	48.56	48.62	48.68	48.73	48.79	48.85	48.91	48.97
57	49.02	49.08	49.14	49.20	49.26	49.31	49.37	49.43	49.49	49.54
58	49.60	49.66	49.72	49.78	49.84	49.89	49.95	50.01	50.07	50.13
59	50.18	50.24	50.30	50.36	50.42	50.48	50.53	50.59	50.65	50.71
60	50.77	50.83	50.89	50.94	51.00	51.06	51.12	51.18	51.24	51.30
61	51.35	51.41	51.47	51.53	51.59	51.65	51.71	51.77	51.83	51.88
62	51.94	52.00	52.06	52.12	52.18	52.24	52.30	52.36	52.42	52.48
63	52.53	52.59	52.65	52.71	52.77	52.83	52.89	52.95	53.01	53.07
64	53.13	53.19	53.25	53.31	53.37	53.43	53.49	53.55	53.61	53.67
65	53.73	53.79	53.85	53.91	53.97	54.03	54.09	54.15	54.21	54.27
66	54.33	54.39	54.45	54.51	54.57	54.63	54.70	54.76	54.82	54.88
67	54.94	55.00	55.06	55.12	55.18	55.24	55.30	55.37	55.43	55.49
68	55.55	55.61	55.67	55.73	55.80	55.86	55.92	55.98	56.04	56.11
69	56.17	56.23	56.29	56.35	56.42	56.48	56.54	56.60	56.66	56.73

Table II *Contd...*

p	0	1	2	3	4	5	6	7	8	9
70	56.79	56.85	56.91	56.98	57.04	57.10	57.17	57.23	57.29	57.35
71	57.42	57.48	57.54	57.61	57.67	57.73	57.80	57.86	57.92	57.99
72	58.05	58.12	58.18	58.24	58.31	58.37	58.44	58.50	58.56	58.63
73	58.69	58.76	58.82	58.89	58.95	59.02	59.08	59.15	59.21	59.28
74	59.34	59.41	59.47	59.54	59.60	59.67	59.74	59.80	59.87	59.93
75	60.00	60.07	60.13	60.20	60.27	60.33	60.40	60.47	60.53	60.60
76	60.67	60.73	60.80	60.87	60.94	61.00	61.07	61.14	61.21	61.27
77	61.34	61.41	61.48	61.55	61.62	61.68	61.75	61.82	61.89	61.96
78	62.03	62.10	62.17	62.24	62.31	62.37	63.44	62.51	62.58	62.65
79	62.72	62.80	62.87	62.94	63.01	63.08	63.15	63.22	63.29	63.36
80	63.44	63.51	63.58	63.65	63.72	63.79	63.87	63.94	64.01	64.08
81	64.16	64.23	64.30	64.38	64.45	64.52	64.60	64.67	64.75	64.82
82	64.90	64.97	65.05	65.12	65.20	65.27	65.35	65.42	65.50	65.57
83	65.65	65.73	65.80	65.88	65.96	66.03	66.11	66.19	66.27	66.34
84	66.42	66.50	66.58	66.66	66.74	66.81	66.89	66.97	67.05	67.13
85	67.21	67.29	67.37	67.45	67.54	67.62	67.70	67.78	67.86	67.94
86	68.03	68.11	68.19	68.28	68.36	68.44	68.53	68.61	68.70	68.78
87	68.87	68.95	69.04	69.12	69.21	69.30	69.38	69.47	69.56	69.64
88	69.73	69.82	69.91	70.00	70.09	70.18	70.27	70.36	70.45	70.54
89	70.63	70.72	70.81	70.91	71.00	71.09	71.19	71.28	71.37	71.47
90	71.56	71.66	71.76	71.85	71.95	72.05	72.15	72.24	72.34	72.44
91	72.54	72.64	72.74	72.84	72.95	73.05	73.15	73.26	73.36	73.46
92	73.57	73.68	73.78	73.89	74.00	74.11	74.21	74.32	74.44	74.55
93	74.66	74.77	74.88	75.00	75.11	75.23	75.35	75.46	75.58	75.70
94	75.82	75.94	76.06	76.19	76.31	76.44	76.56	76.69	76.82	76.95
95	77.08	77.21	77.34	77.48	77.61	77.75	77.89	78.03	78.17	78.32
96	78.46	78.61	78.76	78.91	79.06	79.22	79.37	79.53	79.69	79.86
97	80.02	80.19	80.37	80.54	80.72	80.90	81.09	81.28	81.47	81.67
98	81.87	82.08	82.29	82.51	82.73	82.96	83.20	83.45	83.71	83.98
99.0	84.26	84.29	84.32	84.35	84.38	84.41	84.44	84.47	84.50	84.53
99.1	84.56	84.59	84.62	84.65	84.68	84.71	84.74	84.77	84.80	84.84
99.2	84.87	84.90	84.93	84.97	85.00	85.03	85.07	85.10	85.13	85.17
99.3	85.20	85.24	85.27	85.31	85.34	85.38	85.41	85.45	85.48	85.52
99.4	85.56	85.60	85.63	85.67	85.71	85.75	85.79	85.83	85.87	85.91
99.5	85.95	85.99	86.03	86.07	86.11	86.15	86.20	86.24	86.28	86.33
99.6	86.37	86.42	86.47	86.51	86.56	86.61	86.66	86.71	86.76	86.81
99.7	86.86	86.91	86.97	87.02	87.08	87.13	87.19	87.25	87.31	87.37
99.8	87.44	87.50	87.57	87.64	87.71	87.78	87.86	87.93	88.01	88.10
99.9	88.19	88.28	88.38	88.48	88.60	88.72	88.85	89.01	89.19	89.43
100.0	90.00	——	——	——	——	——	——	——	——	——

Table III Table of x^2*

Degrees of Freedom	P = .99	.98	.95	.90	.80	.70	.50	.30	.20	.10	.05	.02	.01
1	.000157	.000628	.00393	.0158	.0642	.148	.455	1.074	1.642	2.706	3.841	5.412	6.635
2	.0201	.0404	.103	.211	.446	.713	1.386	2.408	3.219	4.605	5.991	7.824	9.210
3	.115	.185	.352	.584	1.005	1.424	2.366	3.665	4.642	6.251	7.815	9.837	11.341
4	.297	.429	.711	1.064	1.649	2.195	3.357	4.878	5.989	7.779	9.488	11.668	13.277
5	.554	.752	1.145	1.610	2.343	3.000	4.351	6.064	7.289	9.236	11.070	13.388	15.086
6	.872	1.134	1.635	2.204	3.070	3.828	5.348	7.231	8.558	10.645	12.592	15.033	16.812
7	1.239	1.564	2.167	2.833	3.822	4.671	6.346	8.383	9.803	12.017	14.067	16.622	18.475
8	1.646	2.032	2.733	3.490	4.594	5.527	7.344	9.524	11.030	13.362	15.507	18.168	20.090
9	2.088	2.532	3.325	4.168	5.380	6.393	8.343	10.656	12.242	14.684	16.919	19.679	21.666
10	2.558	3.059	3.940	4.865	6.179	7.267	9.342	11.781	13.442	15.987	18.307	21.161	23.209
11	3.053	3.609	4.575	5.578	6.989	8.148	10.341	12.899	14.631	17.275	19.675	22.618	24.725
12	3.571	4.178	5.226	6.304	7.807	9.034	11.340	14.011	15.812	18.549	21.026	24.054	26.217
13	4.107	4.765	5.892	7.042	8.634	9.926	12.340	15.119	16.985	19.812	22.362	25.472	27.688
14	4.660	5.368	6.571	7.790	9.467	10.821	13.339	16.222	18.151	21.064	23.685	26.873	29.141
15	5.229	5.985	7.261	8.547	10.307	11.721	14.339	17.322	19.311	22.307	24.996	28.259	30.578
16	5.812	6.614	7.962	9.312	11.152	12.624	15.338	18.418	20.465	23.542	26.296	29.633	32.000
17	6.408	7.255	8.672	10.085	12.002	13.531	16.338	19.511	21.615	24.769	27.587	30.995	33.409
18	7.015	7.906	9.390	10.865	12.857	14.440	17.338	20.601	22.760	25.989	28.869	32.346	34.805
19	7.633	8.567	10.117	11.651	13.716	15.352	18.338	21.689	23.900	27.204	30.144	33.687	36.191
20	8.260	9.237	10.851	12.443	14.578	16.266	19.337	22.775	25.038	28.412	31.410	35.020	37.566
21	8.897	9.915	11.591	13.240	15.445	17.182	20.337	23.858	26.171	29.615	32.671	36.343	38.932
22	9.542	10.600	12.338	14.041	16.314	18.101	21.337	24.939	27.301	30.813	33.924	37.659	40.289
23	10.196	11.293	13.091	14.848	17.187	19.021	22.337	26.018	28.429	32.007	35.172	38.968	41.638
24	10.856	11.992	13.848	15.659	18.062	19.943	23.337	27.096	29.553	33.196	36.415	40.270	42.980
25	11.524	12.697	14.611	16.473	18.940	20.867	24.337	28.172	30.675	34.382	37.652	41.566	44.314
26	12.198	13.409	15.379	17.292	19.820	21.792	25.336	29.246	31.795	35.563	38.885	42.856	45.642
27	12.879	14.125	16.151	18.114	20.703	22.719	26.336	30.319	32.912	36.741	40.113	44.140	46.963
28	13.565	14.847	16.928	18.939	21.588	23.647	27.336	31.391	34.027	37.916	41.337	45.419	48.278
28	14.256	15.574	17.708	19.768	22.475	24.577	28.336	32.461	35.139	39.087	42.557	46.693	49.588
30	14.953	16.306	18.493	20.599	23.364	25.508	29.336	33.530	36.250	40.256	43.773	47.962	50.892

*Table III is reprinted from Table III of Fisher: *Statistical Methods for Research Workers*. Oliver & Boyd Ltd., Edinburgh, by permission of the author and his publishers.

For larger values of *df*, the expression $\sqrt{2x^2} - \sqrt{2(df) - 1}$ may be used as a normal deviate with unit standard error.

Table IV The Normal Probability Integral

x		0	1	2	3	4	5	6	7	8	9
0·0	0·	50000	49601	49202	48803	48405	48006	47608	47210	46812	46414
0·1		46017	45620	45224	44828	44433	44038	43644	43251	42858	42465
0·2		42074	41683	41294	40905	40517	40129	39743	39358	38974	38591
0·3		38209	37828	37448	37070	36693	36317	35942	35569	35197	34827
0·4		34458	34090	33724	33360	32997	32636	32276	31918	31561	31207
0·5		30854	30503	30153	29806	29460	29116	28774	28434	28096	27760
0·6		27425	27093	26763	26435	26109	25785	25463	25143	24825	24510
0·7		24196	23885	23576	23270	22965	22663	22363	22065	21770	21476
0·8		21186	20897	20611	20327	20045	19766	19489	19215	18943	18673
0·9		18406	18141	17879	17619	17361	17106	16853	16602	16354	16109
1·0		15866	15625	15386	15151	14917	14686	14457	14231	14007	13786
1·1		13567	13350	13136	12924	12714	12507	12302	12100	11900	11702
1·2		11507	11314	11123	10935	10749	10565	10383	10204	10027	98525
1·3	0·0	96800	95098	93418	91759	90123	88508	86915	85343	83793	82264
1·4		80757	79270	77804	76359	74934	73529	72145	70781	69437	68112
1·5		66807	65522	64255	63008	61780	60571	59380	58208	57053	55917
1·6		54799	53699	52616	51551	50503	49471	48457	47460	46479	45514
1·7		44565	43633	42716	41815	40930	40059	39204	38364	37538	36727
1·8		35930	35148	34380	33625	32884	32157	31443	30742	30054	29379
1·9		28717	28067	27429	26803	26190	25588	24998	24419	23852	23295
2·0		22750	22216	21692	21178	20675	20182	19699	19226	18763	18309
2·1		17864	17429	17003	16586	16177	15778	15386	15003	14629	14262
2·2		13903	13553	13209	12874	12545	12224	11911	11604	11304	11011
2·3		10724	10444	10170	99031	96419	93867	91375	88940	86563	84242
2·4	$0{\cdot}0^{2}$	81975	79763	77603	75494	73436	71428	69469	67557	65691	63872
·5		62097	50366	58677	57031	55426	53861	52336	50849	49400	47988
·6		46612	45271	43965	42692	41453	40246	39070	37926	36811	35726
·7		34670	33642	32641	31667	30720	29798	28901	28028	27179	26354
·8		25551	24771	24012	23274	22557	21860	21182	20524	19884	19262
·9		18658	18071	17502	16948	16411	15889	15382	14890	14412	13949
·0		13499	13062	12639	12228	11829	11442	11067	10703	10350	10008
·1	$0{\cdot}0^{3}$	96760	93544	90426	87403	84474	81635	78885	76219	73638	71136
·2		68714	66367	64095	61895	59765	57703	55706	53774	51904	50094
·3		48342	46648	45009	43423	41889	40406	38971	37584	36243	34946
·4		33693	32481	31311	30179	29086	28029	27009	26023	25071	24151

Table IV is adopted from Table II, of Fisher and Yates; Statistical Tables for Biological, Agricultural and Medical Research. Published by Longman Group Ltd., (Previously Published by Oliver and Boyd. Edinburgh). and by Permission of the author and Publishers.

Table V Distribution of Probability

d.f.	.1	.05	.02	.01	.001
1	6.314	12.706	31.821	63.657	636.619
2	2.920	4.303	6.965	9.925	31.598
3	2.353	3.182	4.541	5.841	12.924
4	2.132	2.776	3.747	4.604	8.610
5	2.015	2 571	3.365	4.032	6.869
6	1.943	2.447	3.143	3.707	5.959
7	1.895	2.365	2.998	3.499	5.408
8	1.860	2.306	2.896	3.355	5.041
9	1.833	2.262	2.821	3.250	4.781
10	1.812	2.228	2.764	3.169	4.587
11	1.796	2.201	2.718	3.106	4.437
12	1.782	2.179	2.681	3.055	4.318
13	1.771	2.160	2.650	3.012	4.221
14	1.761	2.145	2.624	2.977	4.140
15	1.753	2.131	2.602	2.947	4.073
16	1.746	2.120	2.583	2.92	4.015
17	1.740	2.110	2.567	2.898	3.965
18	1.734	2.101	2.552	2.878	3.922
19	1.729	2.093	2.539	2.861	3.883
20	1.725	2.086	2.528	2.845	3.850
21	1.721	2.080	2.518	2.83	3.819
22	1.717	2.074	2.58	2.819	3.792
23	1.714	2.069	2.500	2.807	3.767
24	1.711	2.064	2.492	2.797	3.745
25	1.708	2.060	2.485	2.787	3.725
26	1.706	2.056	2.479	2.779	3.707
27	1.703	2.052	2.473	2.771	3.690
28	1.701	2.048	2.467	2.763	3.674
29	1.699	2.045	2.462	2.75	3.659
30	1.697	2.042	2.457	2.750	3.646
40	2.021	2.423	2.704	3.551	3.551
50	1.671	2.000	2.390	2.660	3.460
60	1.658	1.980	2.358	2.17	3.373
∝	1.645	1.960	2.326	2.576	3.291

Table V is taken from table Table III of Fisher and Yates : Statistical Tables for Biological, Agricultural and Medial Research, Published by Longman Group Ltd., London. (Previously published by Oliver and Boyd. Edin burgh). and by Permission of the Authors and Publishers.

Table VI (a) F-distribution

5 per cent points

df_2 \ df_1	1	2	3	4	5	6	7	8	9	10	12	15	20	24	30	40	60	120	∞
5	6.61	5.79	5.41	5.19	5.05	4.95	4.88	4.82	4.77	4.74	4.68	4.62	4.56	4.53	4.50	4.46	4.43	4.40	4.36
6	5.99	5.14	4.76	4.53	4.39	4.28	4.21	4.15	4.10	4.06	4.00	3.94	3.87	3.84	3.81	3.77	3.74	3.70	3.67
7	5.59	4.74	4.35	4.12	3.97	3.87	3.79	3.73	3.68	3.64	3.57	3.51	3.44	3.41	3.38	3.34	3.30	3.27	3.23
8	5.32	4.46	4.07	3.84	3.69	3.58	3.50	3.44	3.39	3.35	3.28	3.22	3.15	3.12	3.08	3.04	3.01	2.97	2.93
9	5.12	4.26	3.86	3.63	3.48	3.37	3.29	3.23	3.18	3.14	3.07	3.01	2.94	2.90	2.86	2.83	2.79	2.75	2.71
10	4.96	4.10	3.71	3.48	3.33	3.22	3.14	3.07	3.02	2.98	2.91	2.84	2.77	2.74	2.70	2.66	2.62	2.58	2.54
11	4.84	3.98	3.59	3.36	3.20	3.09	3.01	2.95	2.90	2.85	2.79	2.72	2.65	2.61	2.57	2.53	2.49	2.45	2.40
12	4.75	3.89	3.49	3.26	3.11	3.00	2.91	2.85	2.80	2.75	2.69	2.62	2.54	2.51	2.47	2.43	2.38	2.34	2.30
13	4.67	3.81	3.41	3.18	3.03	2.92	2.83	2.77	2.71	2.67	2.60	2.53	2.46	2.42	2.38	2.34	2.30	2.25	2.21
14	4.60	3.74	3.34	3.11	2.96	2.85	2.76	2.70	2.65	2.60	2.53	2.46	2.39	2.35	2.31	2.27	2.22	2.18	2.13
15	4.54	3.68	3.29	3.06	2.90	2.79	2.73	2.64	2.59	2.54	2.48	2.40	2.33	2.29	2.25	2.20	2.16	2.11	2.07
16	4.49	3.63	3.24	3.01	2.85	2.74	2.66	2.59	2.54	2.49	2.42	2.35	2.28	2.24	2.19	2.15	2.11	2.06	2.01
17	4.45	3.59	3.20	2.96	2.81	2.70	2.61	2.55	2.49	2.45	2.38	2.31	2.23	2.19	2.15	2.10	2.06	2.01	1.96
18	4.41	3.55	3.16	2.93	2.77	2.66	2.58	2.51	2.46	2.41	2.34	2.27	2.19	2.15	2.11	2.06	2.02	1.97	[illegible]
19	4.38	3.52	3.13	2.90	2.74	2.63	2.54	2.48	2.42	2.38	2.31	2.23	2.16	2.11	2.07	2.03	1.98	1.93	[illegible]
20	4.35	4.49	3.10	2.87	2.71	2.60	2.51	2.45	2.39	2.35	2.28	2.20	2.12	2.08	2.04	1.99	1.95	1.90	1.84
21	4.32	3.47	3.07	2.84	2.68	2.57	2.49	2.42	2.37	2.32	2.25	2.18	2.10	2.05	2.01	1.96	1.92	1.87	1.81
22	4.30	3.44	3.05	2.82	2.66	2.55	2.46	2.40	2.34	2.30	2.23	2.15	2.07	2.03	2.98	1.94	1.89	1.84	1.78
23	4.28	3.42	3.03	2.80	2.64	2.53	2.44	2.37	2.32	2.27	2.20	2.13	2.05	2.00	1.96	1.91	1.86	1.81	1.76
24	4.26	3.40	3.01	2.78	2.62	2.51	2.42	2.36	2.30	2.25	2.18	2.11	2.03	1.98	1.94	1.89	1.84	1.79	1.73
25	4.24	3.39	2.99	2.76	2.60	2.49	2.40	2.34	2.28	2.24	2.16	2.09	2.01	1.96	1.92	1.87	1.82	1.77	1.71
26	4.23	3.37	2.98	2.74	2.59	2.47	2.39	2.32	2.27	2.22	2.15	2.07	1.99	1.95	1.90	1.85	1.80	1.75	1.69
27	4.21	3.35	3.96	2.73	2.57	2.46	2.37	2.31	2.25	2.20	2.13	2.06	1.97	1.93	1.88	1.84	1.79	1.73	1.67
28	4.20	3.34	2.95	2.71	2.56	2.45	2.36	2.29	2.24	2.19	2.12	2.04	1.96	1.91	1.87	1.82	1.77	1.71	1.65
29	4.18	3.33	2.93	2.70	2.55	2.43	2.35	2.28	2.22	2.18	2.10	2.03	1.94	1.90	1.85	1.81	1.75	1.70	1.64
30	4.17	3.32	2.92	2.69	2.53	2.42	2.33	2.27	2.21	2.16	2.09	2.01	1.93	1.89	1.84	1.79	1.74	1.68	1.62
40	4.08	3.23	2.84	2.61	2.45	2.34	2.25	2.18	2.12	2.08	2.00	1.92	1.84	1.79	1.74	1.69	1.64	1.58	1.51
60	4.00	3.15	2.76	2.53	2.37	2.25	2.17	2.10	2.04	1.99	1.92	1.84	1.75	1.70	1.65	1.59	1.53	1.47	1.39
120	3.92	3.07	2.68	2.45	2.29	2.18	2.09	2.02	1.96	1.91	1.83	1.75	1.66	1.61	1.55	1.50	1.43	1.35	1.25
∞	3.84	3.00	2.60	2.37	2.21	2.10	2.01	1.94	1.88	1.83	1.75	1.67	1.57	1.52	1.46	1.39	1.32	1.22	1.00

Adopted from Table 18, Biometrika Tables for Statisticians, Vol. 1, 3rd edition (1966) with the kind permission of Publishers of Biometrika.

Table VI (b) F-distribution

5 per cent points

df_2 \ df_1	1	2	3	4	5	6	7	8	9	10	12	15	20	24	30	40	60	120	∞
5	6.61	5.79	5.41	5.19	5.05	4.95	4.88	4.82	4.77	4.74	4.68	4.62	4.56	4.53	4.50	4.46	4.43	4.40	4.36
6	5.99	5.14	4.76	4.53	4.39	4.28	4.21	4.15	4.10	4.06	4.00	3.94	3.87	3.84	3.81	3.77	3.74	3.70	3.67
7	5.59	4.74	4.35	4.12	3.97	3.87	3.79	3.73	3.68	3.64	3.57	3.51	3.44	3.41	3.38	3.34	3.30	3.27	3.23
8	5.32	4.46	4.07	3.84	3.69	3.58	3.50	3.44	3.39	3.35	3.28	3.22	3.15	3.12	3.08	3.04	3.01	2.97	2.93
9	5.12	4.26	3.86	3.63	3.48	3.37	3.29	3.23	3.18	3.14	3.07	3.01	2.94	2.90	2.86	2.83	2.79	2.75	2.71
10	4.96	4.10	3.71	3.48	3.33	3.22	3.14	3.07	3.02	2.98	2.91	2.84	2.77	2.74	2.70	2.66	2.62	2.58	2.54
11	4.84	3.98	3.59	3.36	3.20	3.09	3.01	2.95	2.90	2.85	2.79	2.72	2.65	2.61	2.57	2.53	2.49	2.45	2.40
12	4.75	3.89	3.49	3.26	3.11	3.00	2.91	2.85	2.80	2.75	2.69	2.62	2.54	2.51	2.47	2.43	2.38	2.34	2.30
13	4.67	3.81	3.41	3.18	3.03	2.92	2.83	2.77	2.71	2.67	2.60	2.53	2.46	2.42	2.38	2.34	2.30	2.25	2.21
14	4.60	3.74	3.34	3.11	2.96	2.85	2.76	2.70	2.65	2.60	2.53	2.46	2.39	2.35	2.31	2.27	2.22	2.18	2.13
15	4.54	3.68	3.29	3.06	2.90	2.79	2.73	2.64	2.59	2.54	2.48	2.40	2.33	2.29	2.25	2.20	2.16	2.11	2.07
16	4.49	3.63	3.24	3.01	2.85	2.74	2.66	2.59	2.54	2.49	2.42	2.35	2.28	2.24	2.19	2.15	2.11	2.06	2.01
17	4.45	3.59	3.20	2.96	2.81	2.70	2.61	2.55	2.49	2.45	2.38	2.31	2.23	2.19	2.15	2.10	2.06	2.01	1.96
18	4.41	3.55	3.16	2.93	2.77	2.66	2.58	2.51	2.46	2.41	2.34	2.27	2.19	2.15	2.11	2.06	2.02	1.97	[illegible]
19	4.38	3.52	3.13	2.90	2.74	2.63	2.54	2.48	2.42	2.38	2.31	2.23	2.16	2.11	2.07	2.03	1.98	1.93	[illegible]
20	4.35	4.49	3.10	2.87	2.71	2.60	2.51	2.45	2.39	2.35	2.28	2.20	2.12	2.08	2.04	1.99	1.95	1.90	1.84
21	4.32	3.47	3.07	2.84	2.68	2.57	2.49	2.42	2.37	2.32	2.25	2.18	2.10	2.05	2.01	1.96	1.92	1.87	1.81
22	4.30	3.44	3.05	2.82	2.66	2.55	2.46	2.40	2.34	2.30	2.23	2.15	2.07	2.03	2.98	1.94	1.89	1.84	1.78
23	4.28	3.42	3.03	2.80	2.64	2.53	2.44	2.37	2.32	2.27	2.20	2.13	2.05	2.00	1.96	1.91	1.86	1.81	1.76
24	4.26	3.40	3.01	2.78	2.62	2.51	2.42	2.36	2.30	2.25	2.18	2.11	2.03	1.98	1.94	1.89	1.84	1.79	1.73
25	4.24	3.39	2.99	2.76	2.60	2.49	2.40	2.34	2.28	2.24	2.16	2.09	2.01	1.96	1.92	1.87	1.82	1.77	1.71
26	4.23	3.37	2.98	2.74	2.59	2.47	2.39	2.32	2.27	2.22	2.15	2.07	1.99	1.95	1.90	1.85	1.80	1.75	1.69
27	4.21	3.35	2.96	2.73	2.57	2.46	2.37	2.31	2.25	2.20	2.13	2.06	1.97	1.93	1.88	1.84	1.79	1.73	1.67
28	4.20	3.34	2.95	2.71	2.56	2.45	2.36	2.29	2.24	2.19	2.12	2.04	1.96	1.91	1.87	1.82	1.77	1.71	1.65
29	4.18	3.33	2.93	2.70	2.55	2.43	2.35	2.28	2.22	2.18	2.10	2.03	1.94	1.90	1.85	1.81	1.75	1.70	1.64
30	4.17	3.32	2.92	2.69	2.53	2.42	2.33	2.27	2.21	2.16	2.09	2.01	1.93	1.89	1.84	1.79	1.74	1.68	1.62
40	4.08	3.23	2.84	2.61	2.45	2.34	2.25	2.18	2.12	2.08	2.00	1.92	1.84	1.79	1.74	1.69	1.64	1.58	1.51
60	4.00	3.15	2.76	2.53	2.37	2.25	2.17	2.10	2.04	1.99	1.92	1.84	1.75	1.70	1.65	1.59	1.53	1.47	1.39
120	3.92	3.07	2.68	2.45	2.29	2.18	2.09	2.02	1.96	1.91	1.83	1.75	1.66	1.61	1.55	1.50	1.43	1.35	1.25
∞	3.84	3.00	2.60	2.37	2.21	2.10	2.01	1.94	1.88	1.83	1.75	1.67	1.57	1.52	1.46	1.39	1.32	1.22	1.00

Adopted from Table 18, Biometrika Tables for Statisticians, Vol. 1, 3rd edition (1966) with the kind permission of Publishers of Biometrika.

THE CORRELATION COEFFICIENT

Table VII Values of the Correlation Coefficient for Different Levels of Significance

n	·1	·05	·02	·01	·001	n	·1	·05	·02	·01	·001
1	·98769	·99692	·999507	·999877	·9999988	16	·4000	·4683	·5425	·5897	·7084
2	·90000	·95000	·98000	·990000	·99900	17	·3887	·4555	·5285	·5751	·6932
3	·8054	·8783	·93433	·95873	·99116	18	·3783	·4438	·5155	·5614	·6787
4	·7293	·8114	·8822	·91720	·97406	19	·3687	·4329	·5034	·5487	·6652
5	·6694	·7545	·8329	·8745	·95074	20	·3598	·4227	·4921	·5368	·6524
6	·6215	·7067	·7887	·8343	·92493	25	·3233	·3809	·4451	·4869	·5974
7	·5822	·6664	·7498	·7977	·8982	30	·2960	·3494	·4093	·4487	·5541
8	·5494	·6319	·7155	·7646	·8721	35	·2746	·3246	·3810	·4182	·5189
9	·5214	·6021	·6851	·7348	·8471	40	·2573	·3044	·3578	·3932	·4896
10	·4973	·5760	·6581	·7079	·8233	45	·2428	·2875	·3384	·3721	·4648
11	·4762	·5529	·6339	·6835	·8010	50	·2306	·2732	·3218	·3541	·4433
12	·4575	·5324	·6120	·6614	·7800	60	·2108	·2500	·2948	·3248	·4078
13	·4409	·5139	·5923	·6411	·7603	70	·1954	·2319	·2737	·3017	·3799
14	·4259	·4973	·5742	·6226	·7420	80	·1829	·2172	·2565	·2830	·3568
15	·4124	·4821	·5577	·6055	·7246	90	·1726	·2050	·2422	·2673	·3375
						100	·1638	·1946	·2301	·2540	·3211

Table VIII is reproduced from Table VII. Of Fisher and Yates: Statistical Tables for Biological, Agricultural and Medical Research. Published by Longman Group Ltd., London. (Previously Published by Oliver and Boyd. Edinburgh), and by Permission of the Authors and Publishers.

Table VIII Table of Probabilities Associated with Values as Small as Observed Values of W in the Mann-Whitney Test*

$n_2 = 3$

W \ n_1	1	2	3
0	.250	.100	.050
1	.500	.200	.100
2	.750	.400	.200
3		.600	.350
4			.500
5			.650

$n_2 = 4$

W \ n_1	1	2	3	4
0	.200	.067	.028	.014
1	.400	.133	.057	.029
2	.600	.267	.114	.057
3		.400	.200	.100
4		.600	.314	.171
5			.429	.243
6			.571	.343
7				.443
8				.557

$n_2 = 5$

W \ n_1	1	2	3	4	5
0	.167	.047	.018	.008	.004
1	.333	.095	.036	.016	.008
2	.500	.190	.071	.032	.016
3	.667	.286	.125	.056	.028
4		.429	.196	.095	.048
5		.571	.286	.143	.075
6			.393	.206	.111
7			.500	.278	.155
8			.607	.365	.210
9				.452	.274
10				.548	.345
11					.421
12					.500
13					.579

$n_2 = 6$

W \ n_1	1	2	3	4	5	6
0	.143	.036	.012	.005	.002	.001
1	.286	.071	.024	.010	.004	.002
2	.428	.143	.048	.019	.009	.004
3	.571	.214	.083	.033	.015	.008
4		.321	.131	.057	.026	.013
5		.429	.190	.086	.041	.021
6		.571	.274	.129	.063	.032
7			.357	.176	.089	.047
8			.452	.238	.123	.066
9			.548	.305	.165	.090
10				.381	.214	.120
11				.457	.268	.155
12				.545	.331	.197
13					.396	.242
14					.465	.294
15					.535	.350
16						.409
17						.469
18						.531

* Reproduced from Mann, H. B., and Whitney, D. R. 1947. On a test of whether one of two random variables is stochastically larger than the other. *Ann. Math. Statist.*, **18**, 52–54, with the kind permission of the authors and the publisher.

Table IX Table of Probabilities Associated with Values as Small as Observed Values of W in the Mann-Whitney Test*

$n_2 = 7$

n_1	1	2	3	4	5	6	7
0	.125	.028	.008	.003	.001	.001	.000
1	.250	.056	.017	.006	.003	.001	.001
2	.375	.111	.033	.012	.005	.002	.001
3	.500	.167	.058	.021	.009	.004	.002
4	.625	.250	.092	.036	.015	.007	.003
5		.333	.133	.055	.024	.011	.006
6		.444	.192	.082	.037	.017	.009
7		.556	.258	.115	.053	.026	.013
8			.333	.158	.074	.037	.019
9			.417	.206	.101	051	.027
10			.500	.264	.134	069	.036
11			.583	.324	.172	.090	.049
12				.394	.216	.117	.064
13				.464	.265	.147	.082
14				.538	.319	.183	.104
15					.378	.223	.130
16					.438	.267	.159
17					.500	.314	.191
18					.562	.365	.228
19						.418	.267
20						.473	.310
21						.527	.355
22							.402
23							.451
24							.500
25							.549

* Reproduced from Mann, H. B., and Whitney, D. R. 1947. On a test of whether one of two random variables is stochastically larger than the other. *Ann. Math. Statist.*, **18**, 52–54, with the kind permission of the authors and the publisher.

Table X Table of Probabilities Associated with Values as Small as Observed Values of W in the Mann-Whitney Test*

$n_2 = 8$

W \ n_1	1	2	3	4	5	6	7	8	t	Normal
0	.111	.022	.006	.002	.001	.000	.000	.000	3.308	.001
1	.222	.044	.012	.004	.002	.001	.000	.000	3.203	.001
2	.333	.089	.024	.008	.003	.001	.001	.000	3.098	.001
3	.444	.133	.042	.014	.005	.002	.001	.001	2.993	.001
4	.556	.200	.067	.024	.009	.004	.002	.001	2.888	.002
5		.267	.097	.036	.015	.006	.003	.001	2.783	.003
6		.356	.139	.055	.023	.010	.005	.002	2.678	.004
7		.444	.188	.077	.033	.015	.007	.003	2.573	.005
8		.556	.248	.107	.047	.021	.010	.005	2.468	.007
9			.315	.141	.064	.030	.014	.007	2.363	.009
10			.387	.184	.085	.041	.020	.010	2.258	.012
11			.461	.230	.111	.054	.027	.014	2.153	.016
12			.539	.285	.142	.071	.036	.019	2.048	.020
13				.341	.177	.091	.047	.025	1.943	.026
14				.404	.217	.114	.060	.032	1.838	.033
15				.467	.262	.141	.076	.041	1.733	.041
16				.533	.311	.172	.095	.052	1.628	.052
17					.362	.207	.116	.065	1.523	.064
18					.416	.245	.140	.080	1.418	.078
19					.472	.286	.168	.097	1.313	.094
20					.528	.331	.198	.117	1.208	.113
21						.377	.232	.139	1.102	.135
22						.426	.268	.164	.998	.159
23						.475	.306	.191	.893	.185
24						.525	.347	.221	.788	.215
25							.389	.253	.683	.247
26							.433	.287	.578	.282
27							.478	.323	.473	.318
28							.522	.360	.368	.356
29								.399	.263	.396
30								.439	.158	.437
31								.480	.052	.481
								520		

On a test of whether
other. *Ann. Math.*
the publisher.

Bibliography

1. Cochran, W.G. (1953): Sampling Techniques. John Wiley and Sons. Lnc., New York.
2. Cochran, W.G. and Cox, G.M. (1957): Experimental Designs. John Wiley and Sons, lnc., New York.
3. Donald F. Morrison (1990): Multivariate Statistical Methods. Mc Graw-Hill Publishing Co. New York.
4. Edwards, A.L. (1969): Techniques of Attitude Scale Construction, Vakils, Feffer and Simons Pvt. Ltd., Bombay.
5. Fisher, R.A. and Yates, F (1948): statistical Tables for Agricultural, Biological and Medical Research, Oliver and Boyd, Edinburgh, 3rd Edition.
6. Goulden, C.H. (1939): Methods of Statistical Analysis, John Wiley and Sons lnc., New York.
7. Kruskal, W.G. (1957): Historical Notes on the Wilcoxon unpaired two sample test. Jour. Ames. Stat. Assn., S2: 356-60.
8. Likert, R (1932): A technique for the measurement of attitudes. Arch. Psychol: No. 140.
9. Loomba, N.P., (1964): Linear Programming – An Introductory Analysis, Tata Mc Graw – Hill Publishing Co., Ltd., Bombay.
10. Mann, H.B. and Whitney, D.R. (1947): On a test whether one of two random variables is stochastically larger than the other. Ann. Math. Stat., 18:50.
11. Ostle, B (1966): Statistics in Research Oxford and I.B.H. Publishing Co., New Delhi.
12. Rao, G. Nageswara (1973): Some Contributions to Construction and Analysis of non-orthogonal designs, unpublished Ph.D. Thesis submitted to Punjab Agricultural University, Ludhiana, Punjab.

13. Rao, G. Nageswara (2007): Statistics for Agricultural Sciences, B.S. Publications, Hyderabad, 2nd Edition.

14. Rao, G. Nageswara and Tiwari, N.K. (2008): Biostatistics and Computer Applications. B.S. Publications, Hyderabad.

15. Reddy. S.B.S. (1992): M.Sc (Ag.) Statistics Thesis submitted to A.P. Agricultural University, Hyderabad.

16. Siegel, Sydney (1956): Non-Parametric Statistics for the Behavioral Sciences, Mc Graw Hill Book Co. lnc., New York.

17. Snedecor, G.W. and Cochran, W.G. (1968): Statistical Methods. Oxford and I.B.H. Publishing Co., New Delhi.

18. Sukhatme, P.V. (1953): Sampling theory of Surveys with Applications, Indian Society of Agricultural Statistics, New Delhi.

19. Thiagarajan, Balaji (1989): M.Sc. (Ag) Statistics Thesis submitted to A.P. Agricultural University, Hyderabad.

20. Thurstone (1932): Stimulus dispersions in the method of constant stimuli. Jour. Exp. Psychol. 15: 284-297.

21. Thurstone, L.L., and Chave, E.J. (1929): The measurement of attitude, Chicago: Univ. Chicago Press.

22. Umarji, R.R. (1962): Probability and Mathematical Statistics. Asia Publishing House, Bombay.

Index

E

F

G

H

I

J

K

L

M

N

O

P

Q

R

S

T

V

W

Y

Z

www.ingramcontent.com/pod-product-compliance
Lightning Source LLC
Chambersburg PA
CBHW071240230926
51849CB00001B/168
9789385433337